St. Pauli

St. Pauli

Another Football is Possible

Carles Viñas and Natxo Parra

Foreword by Deniz Naki

Translated from the Catalan by Luke Stobart

First published in Spanish as *FC Sankt Pauli* by Capitán Swing, 2017
Published in Catalan as *Sankt Pauli: un altre futbol és possible* by Tigre de paper, 2017
English language edition first published 2020 by Pluto Press
345 Archway Road, London N6 5AA

www.plutobooks.com

This translation is published by arrangement with Oh!Books Agencia Literaria
The translation of this work has been supported by the Institut Ramon Llull

Catalan Language and Culture

British Library Cataloguing in Publication Data
A catalogue record for this book is available from the British Library

ISBN   978 0 7453 4090 6   Paperback
ISBN   978 1 7868 0671 0   PDF eBook
ISBN   978 1 7868 0673 4   Kindle eBook
ISBN   978 1 7868 0672 7   EPUB eBook

This book is printed on paper suitable for recycling and made from fully managed and sustained forest sources. Logging, pulping and manufacturing processes are expected to conform to the environmental standards of the country of origin.

Typeset by Stanford DTP Services, Northampton, England
Simultaneously printed in the United Kingdom and United States of America

To Laia and Ona; Quim, Arriel, Roc and Aina; Guillem, Àsia and Frid; Roc and Olívia; Otger, Aniol and Arlet; Laia, Berta, Ona and Bru; Aina and Valeria.

May one day you see our ideal made real: that another football (and society) is possible.

Contents

Acknowledgements   ix
Foreword by Deniz Naki   xi
Abbreviations   xiii
Preface   xvii

PART I   INFORMAL BEGINNINGS

1. The Birth of German Football   3
2. Football Reaches Hamburg, *Sankt Pauli* is Founded   9
3. The Club's Early Years   26

PART II   WAR AND PEACE:
FROM THE THIRD REICH TO THE *BUNDESLIGA*

4. *Sankt Pauli* under the Swastika   35
5. Postwar Successes and the Magnificent Eleven   47
6. The New Millerntor Stadium   52
7. Creation of the German League   55

PART III   CULT PIRATES OF THE LEAGUE

8. From the Regional Leagues to the Second Division   63
9. Transition from Neighbourhood to *Kult* Club   68
10. Fußball Gegen Nazis   110

PART IV   STANDS WITH A CONSCIENCE

11. A Unique Mix of Football and Social Projects   125
12. The Rebel's Choice of St. Pauli-Celtic   137
13. From Hell to Centenary   142
14. Social Romantics Try to Reclaim the Club   156
15. Stadium *Ultras'* Antifascism in 2002   178

PART V   ST. PAULI: PASSION WITHOUT BORDERS

16. Global Expansion and the Fan Clubs in England,
    Scotland and Ireland   191
17. The Unfinished Business of Women's Football   196
18. Music, Democracy and Solidarity in the District and
    Stadium   204
19. St. Pauli is the Only Option   220

Epilogue: Against Modern Football   229

Bibliography   242
Index   248

Acknowledgements

This book would have been impossible without the generous cooperation of many FC St. Pauli fans, experts, and even players. Without that, the book would have had notable shortcomings. In this regard, we are especially grateful to Guida Maymó and Deniz Naki for their willingness to help the project from the beginning; as well as for their goals on the pitch, work and commitment. These all have been a continuing source of inspiration.

We also have been fortunate to have benefited from the collaboration of Romina Garcia Hinsch, like Maymó, a member of the St. Pauli women's football squad. Both players have provided testimonies that have enabled us to know deeply and first hand the club's secrets and the experiences in the club of its main figures. FC St. Pauli itself has facilitated all that we needed to do our investigation, always very kindly heeding our requests. We therefore wish to acknowledge the courteous treatment we were given by Sven Brux, Sönke Goldbeck, Hendrik Luettmer, and FC St. Pauli Frauen. A gratitude that we would like to extend to Heiko Schlesselmann, whom we met years ago when he was organising club-related anti-racist projects; and also to Hagar Groeteke, ex-footballer and today coach of FC Lampedusa St. Pauli, who provided us with new information regarding the creation of the club's women's team.

Nor do we want to leave out those fans – the Pirates' very soul – that we have interviewed or who have provided information. These include Volker Gajewski (thanks also for your hospitality each time we visited), Karl Heinz 'Pio' Piotrowski, and the indefatigable Hernán 'Pirate of the South' García. Likewise, a mention must be given to the great Stefan Groenveld, the photographer that has captured best St. Pauli's aesthetic essence.

Lastly we would like to thank Ercan Ayboga for arranging the participation of Deniz Naki from distant Amed (Kurdistan); Bítel, for his invaluable collaboration as translator; Toni Padilla and Frederic Porta, our first stealthy readers; and Aitor Lagunas, Roger Xuriach, and all of the fine people at Panenka magazine for putting their trust in us.

Our final regards go to Esteve Martorell and Francesc Poblet, who made up the managing core of the project and have always followed its development with interest. And other very special greetings go to the fan clubs in England, Scotland, Ireland and Catalonia, groups who, by their passion, commitment and solidarity, dignify love of football.

Foreword

Often I have been asked what is it that drives me to run after a ball for 90 minutes and what I hope to achieve by doing so. Having been born the son of some simple Kurdish economic migrants in the heart of Germany made me aware from very early on about what class society means. From an early age I wanted to be 'something'. I could only dream of obtaining the fruits of wealth through the seed of football – a truly simple pastime.

Over time, I became a focus of people's attention. I am more aware now than ever that true wealth does not lie in football or the benefits or gifts provided by professional status, nor are they anything material. I have lived and learned, particularly in the period that I played at St. Pauli, that fraternity and solidarity among teammates but also with rivals can be an incredible strength. I saw that when we stand our ground backing each other up, nothing could beat us.

This team – the pride of true Hamburgers[1] – taught me that borders only exist in our minds. It taught me what it means for people to support each other and to play for our teammates, coach, fans, and particularly the ticket sellers in the stadium. It taught me to be able to provide a positive experience for each of them. I no longer played just for me but for everyone. And everyone – from car-park attendants to team captain – makes the same contribution to achieving success.

Since my time at St. Pauli, I have continued to extend my motivation beyond the playing field. I try to use my platform in the media so that kids watching have a positive role model to identify with, and to draw people's attention to crimes against humanity that are taking place. My aim is to bring a smile back to the faces of those

---

1. [Translator's note]: inhabitants of Hamburg

suffering. Since playing for Amedspor,[2] I have been keener than ever to fight for these aims. I went with great enthusiasm to Amed, a city with a long history and walls as marvellous as its inhabitants. Both its walls and people have stood firm since eternity and form symbols of the fraternity between the different cultures that co-exist there. Yet in Amed children are dying and adults are butchered and imprisoned. And all of this is painful, really painful.

I wish to oppose and resist any form of oppression. With all of the resources I have at my disposal. Despite the repression suffered, I shall continue rebelling and not give in. The last thing they can take from me is my soul and my longing for freedom. St. Pauli taught me that the better I play with the team on the field, the more I can achieve. In Amed, I came across a lot of solidarity among its warm and affectionate people. I met proud people who resist out of dignity. I have learned a great deal from Amedspor, maybe the Kurdish St. Pauli, and will continue to do so.

Deniz Naki

---

2.   [Translator's note]: a team associated with the Kurdish people

Abbreviations

AFA/NO   Anti-Fascist Action/National Organisation

AfD   *Alternative für Deutschland* (Alternative for Germany)

AFM   *Abteilung Fördernde Mitglieder* (Active Support Members' Department)

AGIM   *Arbeitsgemeinschaft Interessierter Mitglieder* (Interested Members' Group)

ANS/NA   *Aktionsfront Nationaler Sozialisten/Nationale Aktivisten* (Action Front of National Socialists/National Activists)

APO   *Außerparlamentarische Opposition* (Extra-Parliamentary Opposition)

ATSB   *Arbeiter-Turn- und Sportbund* (Workers' Gymnastics and Sport Association)

BAFF   *Bündnis Aktiver Fußball-Fans* (Active Football Supporters' Association)

CDU   *Christlich Demokratische Union Deutschlands* (Christian Democratic Union of Germany)

DA   *Deutsche Alternative* (German Alternative)

DFB   *Deutscher Fußball-Bund* (German Football Association)

DFL   *Deutsche Fußball Liga* (German Football League)

DVU   *Deutsche Volksunion* (German People's Union)

FAP   *Freiheitliche Deutsche Arbeiterpartei* (Free German Workers' Party)

FARE   Football Against Racism in Europe

FCSP   *Fußball Club Sankt Pauli* (St. Pauli Football Club)

FPÖ   *Freiheitliche Partei Österreichs* (Freedom Party of Austria)

FRG   Federal Republic of Germany (West Germany)

GDR   German Democratic Republic (East Germany)

HoGeSa   *Hooligans gegen Salafisten* (Hooligans against Salafists)

HSV	*Hamburger Sport-Verein* (SV Hamburg, football club)
KPD	*Kommunistische Partei Deutschlands* (Communist Party of Germany)
MR!	*Millerntor Roar!*
NATO	North Atlantic Treaty Organization
NFV	*Norddeutscher Fußball-Verband* (Northern German Football Association)
NKSS	*Nationales Konzept Sport und Sicherheit* (National Concept for Security and Sport)
NPD	*Nationaldemokratische Partei Deutschlands* (National Democratic Party of Germany)
NSDAP	*Nationalsozialistische Deutsche Arbeiterpartei* (National Socialist German Workers' Party)
Pegida	*Patriotische Europäer gegen die Islamisierung des Abendlandes* (Patriotic Europeans against the Islamisation of the West)
RAF	*Rote Armee Fraktion* (Red Army Fraction)
REP	*Die Republikaner* (The Republicans)
SA	*Sturmabteilung* (Stormtroopers, Brownshirts)
SAGA	*Siedlungs-Aktiengesellschaft Altona* (construction company)
SAPD	*Sozialistische Arbeiterpartei Deutschlands* (Socialist Workers' Party of Germany)
SED	*Sozialistische Einheitspartei Deutschlands* (Socialist Unity Party of Germany)
SPD	*Sozialdemokratische Partei Deutschlands* (Social Democratic Party of Germany)
SS	*Schutzstaffel* (Protection Squadron, Nazi paramilitary organisation)
TAL	*Tiocfaidh Ár Lá* (Our Day will Come)
USP	*Ultrà Sankt Pauli 2002* (association of St Pauli fan crews)

Here democracy is an active experience, with all of the consequences that entails. Whoever has not understood that, has not
understood St. Pauli.

Edward Lienen

Preface

The iconic image of a black T-shirt with printed skull and cross-bones is no longer unusual. Instead it has become part of our everyday surroundings, our common landscape, and our cities, towns and neighbourhoods. In the street or on the underground, at a concert or in any bar, it is less and less surprising to see young (and not so young) people wearing the Jolly Roger. Whatever differences there may be, the *Sankt Pauli* skull and crossbones seems to be following the footsteps of earlier icons such as the famous Ramones logo that became co-opted by large fashion chains.

Wearing the Jolly Roger above the words 'ST. PAULI' may have commercial implications (which of course we shall analyse). Yet it is really about taking a stance: one of political and social rebelliousness. We should forewarn that the history of *Sankt Pauli* is not an idyllic one. As with all great experiences it has fought tirelessly against its own contradictions and defects, in a world dominated by power and not love. It might not be the earthly paradise desired by those of us who love football but have an alternative vision for the sport based on the principle of radical solidarity. Yet undeniably St. Pauli is a magnificent starting point.

In order to understand the St. Pauli phenomenon, defend it and imagine it, you need to know the history of the club and the neighbourhood and city hosting it. Football clubs are not static entities; they evolve, and St. Pauli is no exception to that. Its history is one of vitality, commitment and rootedness. And it is one that fluctuates from providing football for the well-to-do to being a sport for the working classes; from being a select activity to a community one.

The book begins with the emergence of football in Germany – in Hamburg in particular, focusing on *Sankt Pauli*'s creation and first years of life. Then we look at the effect on the club of the rise of Nazism and the Second World War. This dark era must not be glossed over. Indeed, only by examining it is it possible to understand the club's subsequent evolution: *Sankt Pauli*'s journey to becoming a cult club. This is the basis of its international image as a rebellious and alternative club that prides itself on its antifascism, antiracism and opposition to homophobia, sexism and all forms of discrimination, as is now stated in the club's statutes.

We thought it appropriate to take the history of St. Pauli up to the present day. While chronicling it, we emphasise the club's structure and its link with other spheres (whether its local vicinity, music scenes or movements to defend minorities), as well as the present-day challenges it is tackling. In all, we explain how a club's supporters have empowered themselves and been able to influence the decision making of a professional football club.

This book provides a political and social contextualisation to St. Pauli. Only through this can we comprehend its meaning today and how it has won the heart of many and the sympathy of millions: a club that has no problem with adopting political stances or openly proclaiming itself antifascist. The book is our humble contribution to those who love football as a social activity – of solidarity and communalism – but who reject the business that capitalism has turned this sport into. In fact, paraphrasing Eduardo Galeano[3] while receiving the Manuel Vázquez Montalbán International Journalism Award, we wrote these pages because 'we think the best way to be on the left wing is defending the freedom of those brave enough to play for the pleasure of doing so in a world that tells you to play with the duty of winning'.

---

3. [Translator's note]: Uruguayan writer and journalist, author of the acclaimed *Open Veins of Latin America* and *Soccer in Sun and Shadow*.

PART I

Informal Beginnings

1

The Birth of German Football

To discover the origins of German football we must revisit the second half of the nineteenth century. It was a turbulent era. At the start of 1848, Europe witnessed a series of uprisings of a notably bourgeois and liberal hue that aimed to overthrow the *ancien régime*. Austrian and Prussian liberals followed the example of Italian and French revolutionaries – the first to rebel against the royal houses of Habsburg and Orleans – and rose against absolutist rule. Thus, in March that year, the March Revolution (*Märzrevolution*) began in German Confederation territories. Revolutionaries' demands included drafting constitutions, introducing free speech and a free press, unifying the German homeland and holding elections to a constituent assembly. Together these measures threatened the power of the existing rulers, who predictably rejected them. Some concessions were wrung from King Frederick William IV, a member of the Hohenzollern dynasty, such as the creation of a constitution of rights for property owners (but not others). Yet in truth the revolution failed. The monarch responded to the rebels' demands by mobilising the army to repress them. The counter-revolution's subsequent triumph meant the reintroduction of absolutism and the failure of the attempt to unify and modernise the country.

In such a context, and as happened in other European states, sporting activity was restricted to the well-to-do. In northern Europe, unlike in the Mediterranean area, sport was encouraged by Protestantism: a religious doctrine that defended the cult of effort and saw physical exercise as an expression of such. In Prussia 'physical culture'[1] became widespread from 1870. In 1806 its army

---

1. [Translator's note]: health and strength training.

– commanded by Frederick William III – had suffered a crushing defeat at the hands of the Napoleonic troops in the Battle of Jena-Auerstedt. This was followed by the Fall of Erfurt and Berlin and the Prussian royal family fleeing into exile. After this, gymnastics became a priority and obsession in order for the country to avoid future failures. To avoid more humiliating defeats it imposed the 'physical preparation of the German man for life and war'.[2] This explains why the gymnastics model adopted had a militaristic edge, based on discipline and order. Gymnastics spread across the country thanks to a wide network of sporting associations and educational institutions, which combined the sport with a glorification of the fatherland.[3] Over the next half-century, physical education classes (including gymnastics, swimming and hiking) were introduced in all schools.

In 1874, just three years after the territorial unification that produced the German Empire (which itself resulted from France's defeat in the Franco-Prussian War), the Dresden English Football Club was formed. This was the first football club in Germany. Sports clubs already existed, such as TSV 1860 Munich and SSV Ulm 1846, but these were multi-sport and did not include football until the end of the century. The pioneering role of Dresden English

2.   M. Petroni, *St. Pauli siamo noi: Pirati, punk e autonomi allo stadio e nelle strade di Amburgo* (Rome: DeriveApprodi, 2015), p. 81.
3.   One of gymnastics' main advocates was the educator Friedrich Ludwig Jahn. Known by his followers as *Turnvater* (the father of gymnastics), Jahn was the creator of the *Turnverein* (gymnastics clubs) movement in which athletics fused with politics. He believed that physical education was the cornerstone of national health and that its practise strengthened the German character and identity. Jahn opened his first gym in 1811, in Berlin. Eight years later, most gyms were closed because of the murder of journalist August von Kotzbue by the young student Karl Sand. This initiated what was known as *Turnsperre*, a dark period for the *turnverein* and Jahn himself – being imprisoned in Kolberg prison until 1825. After being freed, he was banned from giving gymnastics classes. After the 1840s, coinciding with the rise in political liberalism, the clubs were joined by craftsmen – many of whom were Jews, who helped radicalise them. It comes as no surprise, then, that some gymnasts participated in the 1848 revolutions, such as Gustav Struve in Baden, Otto Heubner in Dresden and August Schärttner in Hanau. Because of this involvement most of the clubs were closed down and their properties confiscated; their leaders were imprisoned or went into exile. It was not until the late 1860s – nearly a decade after German unification – that the *turnverein* could resume their sporting activity.

FC showed the British influence in the emergence of football in Germany – as in other countries. The club's promoters were British citizens that lived and worked in the city – the capital of Saxony – or its surroundings. The entity's name came from most of its 70-odd founding members being of British origin.

In April 1874, the Leipzig newspaper *Illustrierte Zeitung* published a report on a football match involving a Dresden team in which – according to its authors – 'they knocked a ball around by moving their feet forward.'[4] The newspaper was referring to matches that Dresden English FC was playing in a field near the Blüherpark. (This was land on which, in 1922, the Glückgas Stadion – later Dynamo Dresden's ground – would be built.) Indeed, between 1891 and 1894 Dresden English played seven matches with a spotless record: no defeats and the enviable statistics of 34 goals scored and 0 conceded. The club's first setback happened on 10 March 1894 when it was beaten 2–0 by Tor und Fußball Club Victoria 89. Four years later the team merged with another city club, Neue Dresdner FC, to form the Dresdner Sport-Club.

Over the next two decades the game spread to other cities and towns – particularly in north-eastern Germany. At first it had been considered an elitist sport. But by the last decade of the century football had become mainstream, with teams existing in places such as Berlin, Bremen, Hamburg, Hanover and Karlsruhe. The most prominent were Sport Club Germania (founded in 1887); Berliner Fußball-Club Germania 1888 – created that year in Berlin's Tempelhof district; Karlsruhe Fußball Verein (1891); Hertha Berliner Sport-Club (1892); Stuttgart Fußball Verein 1893, Munich 1893 and Verein für Bewegungsspiele Leipzig (1893);

---

4. The influence of the army on the growth of practising sport was significant. Not surprisingly, after the debacle the Prussian troops suffered at the hands of the Napoleonic forces in Jena, General Gerhard David von Scharnhorst chose to thoroughly reform the institution. As part of his attempt to modernise the country and improve military training, Scharnhorst introduced physical education at school, based on the teachings of educator and philosopher Johann Christoph Friedrich GutsMuths. Author of the book *Gymnastik für die Jugend* (Gymnastics for Youth), GutsMuths counterposed the idea of 'the perfect man' with the physical decline that he claimed humanity was undergoing.

Fußball Club Phönix Karlsruhe and Spandauer Sport Verein (1894); Fußball-und Cricket-Club Eintracht Braunschweig (1895); Deutscher Fußball Club Prag (1896); Freiburger Fußball Club (1897); Stuttgarter Kickers, Werder Breman, Turn-und Sportverein 1860 Munich and Viktoria 1889 Berlin (1899); and, in the first year of the new century, Fußball Club Holstein Kiel and Tasmania 1900 Berlin. In that period it was common to have more than one team in a city or town, as we can see from the list. Frankfurt housed the teams Football Club Germania (founded in 1894), Victoria Frankfurt (1899) and Kickers Frankfurt (1899).

A leading figure in the emergence of German club football was the educationalist Wilhelm Carl Johann Conrad Koch. A native of Brunswick,[5] 'Konrad Koch' became one of the country's most prominent promoters of the sport.[6]

After living temporarily in Britain to learn English, during which he discovered football, Koch returned to Germany with the aim of promoting the sport among his students and through it instilling ethical values such as discipline and cooperation. Thus, in 1874 he wrote the volume *Rules for a Football Match*, a treatise that regulated the sport for the first time in Germany. He also adapted

---

5.   Koch taught German, Latin and Greek at Brunswick's Martino-Katharineum school from 1868 to 1911 – the year of his death. Aware that outdoor leisure activities benefited students' development, he chose to organise, on top of the physical education they received, a 'school games', which included cricket, rugby and football. He was aided in this task by the institute's gymnastics teacher, August Hermann, who would become a member of the Central Committee on Public and Youth Games in Germany. Bizarrely the first soccer games played at Martino-Katharineum used a rugby ball, which players could only kick. In 1875 Koch created the first school football team which, thirteen years later, played its first match off the school premises against teams from Göttingen and Hanover. In 1890, the Konrad Koch Foundation led to the founding in Berlin of the German Football Federation and Cricket League. Koch was also one of the pioneers of *Raffball*, the forerunner of modern handball and basketball. His life even inspired the film *Der ganz große Traum von Konrad Koch* (Konrad Koch's Big Dream) that premiered in 2011. This was directed by Sebastian Glober and featured Barcelona-born actor Daniel Brühl in the educator's role.
6.   There is still today controversy over which was the first football match to be played in Germany. While some sources point to the one played by Dresden English FC, others cite as founding matches those held at Koch's Martino-Katharineum school.

footballing terminology to the German language in order to avoid accusations that football was 'too English' a sport.

It might seem surprising today but at the time Koch was thought to be mad because of his enthusiasm for football. He was even ridiculed by sporting peers such as Otto Jaeger and Karl Planck.[7] In a context characterised by a Prussian education model based on obedience and punishment, Jaeger and Planck attacked football as a crude 'English disease' (which they also scornfully labelled *Lümmelei* (loutishness)). The sport, they said, led to a decrease in moral standards among its partisans. Indeed they perceived football – despite being a team sport – as stressing a player's individuality, unlike gymnastics that valued discipline and harmony. For this reason, playing football was forbidden and pupils and teachers caught playing it were thrown out of their educational institutions. In Bavaria this ban remained in place until 1927.

In the late nineteenth century the first associations linking clubs were formed. These included the Bund Deutscher Fußballspieler and the Deutscher Fußball und Cricket-Bund. Yet it was not until 28 January 1900 that 86 teams – including some foreign clubs – met in Leipzig to form the *Deutscher Fußball-Bund* (DFB, the German Football Federation), the main regulating body for German football. Its main promoters included Walther Bensemann, who represented the clubs in Mannheim, E.J. Kirmse, president of the Leipzig Football Association, and Ferdinand Hueppe, president of Prague's Deutscher FC Prag.[8] Hueppe was chosen as the first DFB president.[9]

---

7. In 1898, Planck – gymnast and teacher – published an angry diatribe against Koch and football: 'We believe that this English sport is not just unpleasant but absurd, ugly and perverted' (quoted in U. Hesse–Lichtenberger, *Tor! The Story of German Football* (London: WSC Books, 2002), p. 26). Despite these criticisms, football was becoming more and more popular. Indeed, that year 5,000 spectators turned out for the match between Viktoria Berlin and Germania Hamburg.

8. At that time Prague, the Bohemian capital, was part of the Austro-Hungarian Empire. It included a significant German community that had its very own team: DFC Prag, founded in 1892.

9. As well as the DFB, other associations were set up and organised their own football championships. Among these was the *Arbeiter-Turn-und Sportbund* (Workers' Gymnastics and Sports Association, ATSB), which held different

ST. PAULI

Two years before the founding of the DFB, a first football championship was organised by *Verband Süddeutscher Fußball Vereine* (Association of Southern German Football Clubs). This brought together many of the clubs in this area of the country. It was not until 1903, however, that the first nationwide football tournament – won by VfB Leipzig – was held. Five years later, on 5 April 1908, a first international game involving Germany was played at Basle's Landhof Stadion. There the national squad took on Switzerland, who ended up beating the home team 5–3. Included in *die Mannschaft* (the Team's) historic line-up were the footballers Ernst Jordan, Walter Hempel, Karl Ludwig, Arthur Hiller, Hans Weymar, Gustav Hensel, Fritz Förderer, Eugen Kipp, Fritz Becker and the brothers Fritz and Willy Baumgärtner.

tournaments between 1919 and 1932. It even created a national squad that played 77 international matches. In 1928 the German Communist Party (KPD), thanks to an understanding between the ATSB and the Rotsport association (Red sport), organised its own football championship. In other sports similar initiatives took shape, such as the German Gymnastics Association and the Catholic Church's Sports Federation.

2

Football Reaches Hamburg, *Sankt Pauli* is Founded

Football also emerged in the Hanseatic city in the late nineteenth century. As well as the aforementioned Hamburger FC being created in 1888, three other teams (Sports-Club Germania, Cito and Excelsior) had been founded a year before. It was the turn of the century, in 1899, a few months after the death of Otto von Bismarck (the Iron Chancellor) and during the Second Boer War. A group of enthusiasts for the new sport created a team, on this occasion through the games and sports section of Hamburg-St. Pauli Turnverein. Hamburg-St. Pauli was a male-only institution founded by Franz Reese[1] in 1862 when doing gymnastics was booming on the right side of the city's river Elbe[2] (the area made up of the well-off areas of Karolinenviertel and Schanzenviertel). At that time St. Pauli had two clearly differentiated areas: the north (bourgeois and with a notably nationalistic character) and the south (close to the port and inhabited by workers).

---

1.   In August 1899, Reese chose to experiment with practising two sports until then unheard of at the club: football and volleyball. Petroni, *St. Pauli siamo noi*, p. 82.
2.   Hamburg-St. Pauli Turnverein was created on 1 April 1862 out of the merger between MTV Hamburg (founded 7 September 1852) and St. Pauli Turnverein (created 7 September 1860). Once created, the club's promoter's looked for and found land – near to Feldstraße – to set up in. Its headquarters – opened that same month – had some of the biggest sports halls in the period: 12,671 square metres located at the junction between Glacischaussee and Eimsbütteler (streets that today form Budapest Straße). It was one of the two gymnastics clubs in the area, along with Turnverein St. Pauli und vor dem Dammthore von 1860. The city's leading sports club had been built in 1816 (Hamburger Turnerschaft von 1816) but three years later its activity was suspended because the authorities suspected that the sportsmen's ideas were too liberal. This prohibition lasted until 1842. Today a few minutes away from the Millerntor stadium is Turnerstrasße – the street that included St. Pauli Turnverein von 1862's first head office.

Like other similar associations, Hamburg-St. Pauli Turnverein had two goals: promoting liberalism and spreading an intense nationalist sentiment. The first objective was in order to retrieve citizens' morale after the humiliating defeats inflicted by Napoleon's army in Jena and Auerstedt. This would be achieved by physically training the 'perfect German' for life and war. The French victory meant reforming the army, introducing the draft and introducing physical education in schools to optimise the performance of future conscripts. For this reason the institution developed a notably militaristic hallmark. The second aim was shown in its freedom of association, which allowed anybody that paid the corresponding membership fees to join the club. Both factors reflected the country's socio-political reality, which was still being determined by the 1848 March Revolution, an unsuccessful flare-up that sought – as we saw earlier – to abolish the nobility and introduce parliamentarianism and a free press.

The organisation took its name from the area – to the north of the Elbe river – that the city annexed in 1247. Until 1833 this was known as Hamburger Berg (Hamburg mountain)[3] as it was then the highest point in the area. Yet St. Pauli's mountain relief changed as a result of the Thirty Years War (1618–48). Then, the Hamburg Senate ordered the building of defensive bastions and the levelling of walls by taking sand and mud from the mountaintop to feed the city's brickworks. At that time St. Pauli was a kind of no man's land populated by 2,000 people, located half way between the town of

---

3. The city the mountain was named after was founded in 808 and initially called Treva. It took its name from its first building: a castle built to defend a baptistery built in 810 by order of Emperor Charlemagne. The fort was raised on top of the rocky patch of a marsh between the rivers Alster and Elbe, a key strategic point for resisting attacks by Slavic peoples. The castle was named Hammaburg ('*Hamma*' probably derives from 'woods' and '*burg*' from 'castle'). After 1189, the city gained the right to trade freely and its ships were exempted from paying customs duties, a prerogative awarded by King Frederick I of Hohenstaufen (1122–90, popularly known as 'Red Beard'). This allowed Hamburg to have free access to the sea, be economically independent and govern itself. That is, it was a de facto 'free' and autonomous city with its own diplomatic and military policies. This is reflected today in its official name *Freie und Hansestadt Hamburg* (Free and Hanseatic City of Hamburg). It kept these privileges when in 1871 it became a member of the German Reich.

Altona – then under Danish rule – and the port for the boats that sailed along the Elbe.[4]

Until the seventeenth century the area was little populated beyond members of religious orders and gangs of pirates that went there from the river. It was then an unprotected area, a fact that did not favour settlement by a large community. The few that went to live there were day labourers, fishermen, businessmen and craftsmen, who had fled the city because of its high cost of living. Alongside them emerged businesses that were deemed 'antisocial' because of the noise, pollution and strong smells they made: for instance, those in which artisans refined whale blubber to produce oil lamps. One of the trades that undoubtedly became the most renowned in the area was rope making, due to the large demand for rope on the boats that docked at the port. This was an activity that required fairly wide spaces because while one rope maker held up a wheel the hemp was rolled around, a second had to stretch and twist the hemp: an impossible job in narrow streets or reduced spaces. Rope making has been immortalised in the name of an archetypal St. Pauli road today: Reeperbahn, which can be translated as 'rope walk'.

The entrances to this suburb of craftspeople and foul jobs had three gates that allowed people and goods to circulate. One of these – Millerntor – has been documented as going back to 1246. Its name stems from its location, as it was the door between two others, a location that in old German was called *milderdor* or *mid-*

---

4. St. Pauli's geographical location explains why it became a place for leisure. It was here that the inhabitants of Altona, a conservative town that had preserved the puritanism of the Hanseatic spirit, relaxed. The area's first wooden theatres were built in the very centre of St. Pauli. These *Spielbuden* hosted the wildest shows. Also, unsurprisingly, the district had a red-light district where sailors coming offshore at the port would go for a drink and some company. The place gradually began to urbanise in 1864 when Altona was annexed to Prussia. This led to a curve in construction and demographic growth – as was shown by the 72,000 inhabitants counted in 1894. But it was not until the beginning of the nineteenth century that *Sankt Pauli* became a significant urban hub with its own workers' community. This happened under the wing of several newly established factories which located there due to lack of space inside the city walls. Alongside this growth, St. Pauli progressively became Hamburg's red-light district.

dele-thor.[5] Years later, the portal was removed and relocated as a result of the district's demographic expansion. Indeed for years it was where tolls were collected for the goods that entered the town, making it a kind of customs office of its time. The gateway was open from 1 January 1861, which allowed trading activity to further develop.[6] Eight centuries later the old gate gave FC St. Pauli's stadium its name.[7]

In the late seventeenth century the Hamburg Senate ordered that hospices and hospitals (*Pesthof*) be moved beyond the city's ramparts to the area that today is the St. Pauli district. That is when the so-called 'undesirables' came, the many diseased and destitute who joined the area's initial inhabitants. None were spared during the siege the Danish army subjected the area to at the end of that century. During the assault the church – built in 1682 and dedicated to Saint Paul – was totally destroyed. From then, as well as giving the neighbourhood its name, the church became an important symbol. It was rebuilt in the eighteenth century but suffered another disaster in 1814. This time it was by France's *Grand Armée* during the War of the Sixth Coalition (1812–14). It was Napoleon himself who ordered burning 'that suburb of ungovernable people' to avoid enemy soldiers from hiding in St. Pauli homes and premises. Finally, in 1833, the conurbation adopted the name of the church, which that very year was rebuilt on the spot of its

---

5. Curiously, the German word '*tor*' means 'goal'. N. Davidson, *Pirates, Punks and Politics. FC St. Pauli: Falling in Love with a Radical Football Club* (York: Sport Books, 2014), p. 25.

6. The gate's opening also encouraged the first theatres and dancehalls to be opened in the area. Also, there were the *kneipen* (taverns), then frequented by prostitutes. According to the socialist theoretician Kautsky, these were 'the proletariat's only bastion of political freedom'. N. Rondinelli, *Ribelli, Sociali e Romantici: FC St. Pauli tra calcio e resistenza* (Lecce: Bepress Edizioni, 2015), p. 24.

7. In 1963 the club built the ground, which seven years later was named the Wilhelm Koch Stadion in honour of St. Pauli's president over two periods (1931–45 and 1948–69). Yet after fans discovered he had been a Nazi Party member they put a motion to the club's General Assembly in 1997 to remove his name from the stadium. A year later, in October 1998, the resolution was narrowly passed. From the 1999–2000 season the venue was renamed Millerntor Stadion. In 2007, St. Pauli members agreed that its name would not be used for commercial purposes nor would it be sold to any company or sponsor.

original construction. Around that time, St. Pauli's 11,000 residents obtained civil rights and could enjoy advances such as the arrival of electricity and gas.

In the mid-nineteenth century the area went through enormous expansion and change. This was partly because of the 'Great Fire' that devastated central Hamburg on 5 May 1842, causing 51 fatalities and destroying 1,700 buildings.[8] It was also due to a growth in industrialisation linked to the activities of the port.[9] These two developments sparked a mass exodus to St. Pauli. It is calculated that as a consequence of the catastrophe and creation of new industries, around 20,000 people moved outside the city walls, seeking decent wages, to St. Pauli. The exodus produced urban crowding and sanitary deficiencies. This demographic growth, which transformed St. Pauli's social structure, encouraged the emergence in the area of brothels,[10] theatres, music halls and dancehalls.[11] The increase in inhabitants led the Hamburg Senate to agree to open

---

8. The fire happened on 5 May 1842, beginning in a cigarette factory at 42 Deichstraße. It spread fast due to drought and strong winds. Also affected were 100 wine cellars, two synagogues and around 60 schools and public buildings – among them the Bank of Hamburg and the city's Town Hall itself. The authorities even pulled down some buildings to create firewalls. Half of Hamburg's population – about 70,000 people – fled in panic, while 20,000 residents were left homeless. Economic losses have been estimated at 100 million marks.

9. The city's port grew in strength. An increase in transoceanic expeditions, its strategic position and the will of the Hanseatic League to make it a hub for trade in the Baltic Sea and North Sea turned it into 'Germany and Europe's most important port thanks to the growth of marine transport, which, with the spread of steamships, is introducing commodities and people into other continents'. Rondinelli, *Ribelli, Sociali e Romantici*, p. 28.

10. From 1809 a record of the area's prostitutes was kept. We subsequently know that, in 1834, the city had 18 brothels with 120 women sex workers, to which must be added those who did prostitution outside official censuses. Soon after, in 1841, there were 151 women in 20 brothels. In the first third of the nineteenth century the brothels were in today's Davidstraße. Prostitution was made a criminal offense in 1870 – when the German Reich was being constituted. Existing double standards, however, allowed prostitutes to be able to sit in the window fronts of Herbertstraße – a small alley away from the Reeperbahn. Two decades later there were 20 brothels in the alley. See V. Harris, *Selling Sex in the Reich: Prostitutes in German Society, 1914–1945* (New York: Oxford University Press, 2010).

11. In that period, while there were ten dancehalls in St. Pauli there were only 13 such establishments in the whole of Hamburg. These figures showed that St. Pauli had become the nightlife epicentre.

the Millerntorn gate at night, although, of course, anyone going through it after midnight had to pay (16 shillings).[12] Most of the newcomers settled in the port and Reeperbahn areas that became a centre for nightlife at the end of century. As a result of industrial growth a working-class community emerged,[13] turning St. Pauli into a left-wing stronghold.[14] Many of the neighbourhood's new residents were workers attracted to the chance of gaining a decent job and wage in trades such as carpentry, hemp rope making or warehousing. Indeed, these were the main occupations locally. The opening of shipyards such as HC Stülcken (in 1840), Blohm & Voss (1877) and Norderwerft (1906), thanks to the increase in trans-oceanic shipping, ended up giving the neighbourhood a marked proletarian tone.[15]

In the mid-nineteenth century there was a surge in local firms creating branches in different African and East Asian countries. As a result, in 1848 37 Hamburg trading companies had offices abroad. This commercial expansion obviously aided – along with the emergence of steamships – the development of local shipping.

12. Its definitive opening did not take place until 1860 when a crowd of male and female residents rallied before it to celebrate the New Year. Until then a drawbridge allowed or prevented access to St. Pauli, thus giving the Hamburg bourgeoisie the power to show or hide the city's shadiest and most mischievous suburb.
13. In 1845, different groups of Hamburg workers came together to create the *Bildungsverein für Arbeiter* (Workers' Education Club) – following similar examples in Leipzig or Berlin. This involved workers and craftspeople and encouraging proletarian awareness and culture through education.
14. In May 1875, after the Gotha Congress was held, the Socialist Workers' Party of Germany (*Sozialistische Arbeiterpartei Deutschlands*, SAPD), the forerunner to the German Social Democratic Party (*Sozialdemokratische Partei Deutschland*, SPD) – the name used from 1891. One of the SAPD's most prominent figures, the master carpenter August Bebel, labelled Hamburg as 'socialism's capital'. Almost two decades later, in 1890, the city had 84 active trade unions made up of 40,000 workers. Six years later, its port workers went on strike for eleven weeks to defend their rights and were joined by 16,000 workers. This was the first big mobilisation of the local workers' movement.
15. In 1890, 57 per cent of the Hamburg population earned less than 800 marks a year, putting them below the poverty threshold. These working people even developed a specific dialect, called *Kedelklopppersprook*, widely used among the steamship crews that docked at Hamburg and the regulars at the Reeperbahn. This could be used to communicate despite the noise caused by the work being carried out in the area. It consisted of placing the first consonant of a syllable at the end and adding an 'i' to it. Rondinelli, *Ribelli, Sociali e Romantici*, p. 26.

The huge expansion of the workforce led to a kind of residential segregation. The better-off trading families began to move to the suburbs, settling in larger and more comfortable houses. The dwellings they left behind now housed the working families that had just moved to St. Pauli. Additionally work was done to expand the port area, 'consisting of building new quays and railway stations on the south side of the river Elbe to be able to adapt the warehousing of goods',[16] as well as developing a complex of warehouses along the city centre's canals (the *Speicherstadt*, built between 1884 and 1888). The port-renewal projects led to the demolition of 20,000 homes, greater numbers moving to the working-class ghettos (the *Gängeviertel*) and subsequent overcrowding. The additional destabilisation of living conditions in the slums was symbolised by haphazardly erected wooden buildings surrounded by maze-like alleys, the two-bedroom (and kitchen) houses into which six or seven people were squeezed and those residents who opted to share their living space by renting beds per hour. All of the difficulties described were consequences of the local authorities' lack of interest in rehousing affected families.

Different protests took place in the district, such as the two months of protests when 15,000 casual port workers took on the security forces (in May 1890 and November 1896). The reason for this was the 'unacceptable' working conditions and wages they suffered. As well as resisting the police, pickets did other actions, such as cutting boats' mooring so they would drift off, making leaks to sink steamships, attacking police-protected scabs going to work and besieging employment offices. This backdrop of tension did not end until 6 February when the trade unionists in the 1982 Dockers League (Verein der Schauerleute von 1982) put an end to the strike. The use of violence was condemned by the SPD, which repudiated the struggles taking place in the working-class districts. According to the Social Democrat leaders, their inhabitants were part of a lumpenproletariat inclined towards 'violence, rebelliousness, drunkenness, prostitution, and unemployment'. Because of

---

16. Ibid., p. 26 and Petroni, *St. Pauli siamo noi*, p. 23.

these stances, when the members of Social Democrat unions came to the neighbourhood to collect membership fees (on Sundays), they had to do so accompanied by plainclothes police and in the midst of insults and threats.

There was a lack of sanitation in the poorer suburbs. As a result of contaminated drinking water a cholera epidemic caused 8,000 deaths in Hamburg in 1892. This led the Town Hall to intensify the demolition programme it had begun. For the authorities the proletarian districts were a breeding ground for 'moral hazard and social disorder'.

While, on the one hand, the port facilities were modernised to turn Hamburg into a nerve centre for international trade; on the other hand the authorities showed no interest in improving the popular classes' living conditions. This increased the contrast between bourgeois and working class – including prostitutes' – living conditions in Hamburg in a period of great social inequality (at the end of the nineteenth century). They two social groups lived in close geographical proximity, as did refined theatres and proletarian ghettos, but their lives were increasingly different.

In the district on the outskirts of Hamburg a handful of members of Hamburg-St. Pauli Turnverein, most of whom were also members of the local bourgeoisie,[17] founded *Sankt Pauli*. The club did not play its first match until 1907,[18] as until then it did not have enough players to form a team, even though the first references to its football date back to 1899 – coinciding with the beginning of football's gradual popularisation in Germany. For four years its members – from the club's games and sports section (created in 1896) – had been playing unofficial friendlies. However, obstacles emerged in the first matches. Games were played on an uneven pitch, across the middle of which passers-by walked while

---

17. In those years playing football was seen as 'an elitist affair lacking any ethical or philosophical value', a reason why it did not become a mass sport until it spread among the urban working class. Rondinelli, *Ribelli, Sociali e Romantici*, p. 26.
18. That year the team played two matches as part of a gymnastics festival, both against the same team: the Aegir swimming club. While the first ended in a 1–1 draw, in the second St. Pauli thrashed the swimmers 7–1.

players were training or playing a match. Among the club's pioneers were Henry Rehder, Amandus Vierth, Heini Schwalbe, *'Papa'* Friedrichsen, his son Hans Friedrichsen and *'Nette'* Schmelzkopf. One of this group – Amandus Vierth – encouraged his team to wear a dark-brown shirt and white bottoms for the first time on 21 May 1909. Since then, the club always has been identified with the *braun-weiße* colours.[19] Financial problems also arose. In 1908 the group made a loss of 79 marks – a considerable figure in those days.

Despite beginning its activities in 1899, *Sankt Pauli* was not officially founded until 1910. (Relatedly the club's official image today reads 'non-established since 1910'.)[20] Its first official match was in the *Kreisliga Groß-Hamburg* on 15 May 1910, in which it playing under the name St. Pauli Turnverein. It was not until 1924 that it definitively adopted the name FC St. Pauli, doing so because of regulations that forced football clubs to be separate from gymnastics associations when they registered. Regardless of this administrative issue, in the first half of the twentieth century the club's activity focused on sports such as gymnastics and athletics.

Football came to *Sankt Pauli* a long time before taking concrete form as FC St. Pauli. In 1895, a year after St. Pauli was officially annexed by Hamburg, the first season of a league organised by the Hamburg-Altona Football Association (a body had been formed in 1894 by eight teams in the area) was played. League matches were held in Hamburg's only suitably equipped spaces: the Exerzierweide,[21] the Heiligengeistfeld ('the Holy Spirit's field') and on an

---

19.   As time has progressed, the brown and white has been combined with other colours, such as black and red. The brown-white colour scheme is uncommon among football strips. There are only six other teams in the world that use it: Argentina's Club Atlético Platense, Poland's RKS Garbarnia Kraków, the USA's Brown Bears, Norway's FK Ørn-Horten and two other Hamburg clubs (FTSV Komet Blankanese von 1907 e.V and SV Billstedt-Horn 1891). C. Nagel and M. Pahl, *FC St. Pauli. Das Buch: Der Verein und sein Viertel*, (Hamburg: Hoffman und Campe, 2009).

20.   [Translator's note]: *non*-established refers to the anti-establishment side to the club.

21.   This pitch, equipped as a stadium in 1890 on some land previously occupied by the Prussian army as a parade ground, hosted the final of the first German football tournament. This was on 31 May 1903 when VFB Leipzig defeated DFC Prague 7–2 and was proclaimed the first champion in the history of German football. Before

enclosure close to the gym. In those years Hamburg was a pioneer in spreading football across the country. Unsurprisingly, therefore, in May 1903 the city hosted the final of the first football tournament in Germany, which saw FC Prag take on VfB Leipzig in front of 2,000 spectators.

St. Pauli had to wait until 1907 to have enough footballers to play matches, but that summer it played the first two matches of its history. The ball had literally begun rolling but at the same time matches were informal, lacking rules and regulations. In the following (1907–8) season the number of matches played increased to eleven, of which seven ended with victory for the white-and-brown team. In those first years for the club its opponents were teams from Hamburg or surrounding districts. An increase in members and players made it possible and necessary to create B and reserve teams in the following season (1908–9).

In the autumn of 1909, St. Pauli Turnverein joined the Football Association of Northern Germany (*Norddeutscher Fußball-Verband*, NFV), which mainly consisted of the C teams of the clubs competing in the first division. The club was put in the third district – Hamburg/Altona – and it did not become a fully fledged league member until the spring of the following year. In St. Pauli Turnverein's debut, on 30 January 1910, it beat SC Germania 1887 by 2 goals to 0. A worthy victory bearing in mind that St. Pauli only fielded ten players. Meanwhile, the club's B team lost its debut against Eimsbütteler Turnverein.

There seemed to be no end to new developments. In the same year St. Pauli played matches away from Hamburg for the first time ever. These were two friendlies, both ending in defeats for the club: one at Cuxhaven, a conurbation at the mouth of the Elbe River

---

being adapted, it was a grass field used by different teams for football matches. Not for nothing the same space included up to nine playing fields. Moreover, it was the headquarters for clubs such as FC Altona 93, SC Sperber Hamburg, FC Viktoria Hamburg, SC Germania Hamburg and HFC 88. After the First World War the space stopped accommodating football matches as the existing clubs had already built their respective stadiums.

in Lower Saxony;[22] another in Denmark[23] – the club's first international experience. On 22 April 1910, a few days before it was formally founded (on 15 May), the club, which then had five teams, was officially accepted as a fully fledged member of the NFV.[24] That year, in which St. Pauli Turnverein played in the third division of Hamburg-Altona's District III, it played 28 matches, with disappointing results: 20 defeats, six victories and two draws. The trend continued for the rest of the 1910–11 season, frustrating the club's hopes of promotion. This led to the departure of many players who signed for teams that guaranteed greater competitiveness. Flight by players reached its peak in December 1912 when 57 out of St. Pauli's 230 players left the club. It was while this exodus was taking place that the First World War (1914–18) broke out. International tensions had sharpened due to the assassination in Sarajevo of the heir to the Austrian throne, Archduke Franz Ferdinand, by Gavrilo Princip, a member of the pro-Serbian group Young Bosnia. The attack was the pretext for the Austro-Hungarian Empire to declare war on Serbia. The ensuing war was met enthusiastically by many ordinary Germans as well as the political class – including the Social Democrats, who voted in favour of war credits. Nevertheless, the initially feverish '1914 spirit' began to subside when a stalemate in hostilities developed after the Battle of the Marne (6–13 September 1914), when French troops (commanded by Marshal Joffre) halted the German advance. The hope of a *Blitzkrieg* (lightning war) was quickly dispelled. October that year witnessed the prolongation of the war on the Western Front (becoming a war of position). This development meant food shortages and hunger in the rearguard, which rebounded into social conflict.

---

22. In Lower Saxony's capital St. Pauli played against a squad of the city's sailors, who beat the visitors 5–0.

23. In the Nordic country the club played two matches against Svendborg – from southern Funen and created in 1901. In both, the *Sankt Paulianers* were thrashed: 6–0 and 6–2.

24. It was only on 15 May 1910 that a section specifically devoted to football was created within the club's *Spiel und Sportabteilung* department. Rondinelli, *Ribelli, Sociali e Romantici*, p. 70.

Paradoxically the Great War benefited St. Pauli, which won promotion to the second division after several clubs pulled out of the league due to lack of players. Of the 300 registered clubs in the northern league (NFV) before the First World War only 140 remained in it at the end of the conflict. This is not strange if we bear in mind that two million out of the nearly ten million fatalities caused by the fighting were German. The conflict had other devastating effects on people. Food shortages led to the introduction of rationing, and hunger led to riots (such as in 1917). In a wave of social agitation the revolt by sailors at the ports of Kiel and Wilhelmshaven[25] provided historic images, for example when 40,000 workers, soldiers and sailors met at Heiligengeistfeld, in November 1918, to declare the Socialist Republic of Hamburg. Despite the declaration having wide support it did not lead to the creation of a revolutionary government.[26]

Germany's defeat in the First World War led to the abdication of Kaiser Wilhelm II of Prussia and the introduction – after the

---

25. As a result of the victorious Bolshevik revolution in Russia and in the midst of attempts to bring about a truce, on 29 October 1918 the crew of the fleets quartered at these two places mutinied. This was against orders from Admiral Reinnard Scheer (commander of the Kaiserliche Marine) to prepare for an imminent naval battle against the British fleet in the English Channel. The German sailors did not want to give up their lives in a war they believed was already lost and refused to obey their officers. They then took control of events through the revolutionary committees they had created. The mutiny began aboard the ships *Thüringen* and *Helgoland*, moored at Wilhelmshaven, the headquarters of the German fleet. Their example spread to other coastal garrisons and also to the country's interior. In Hamburg some sailors managed to get hold of a torpedo boat and control the port area after clashing with patrol guards. Yet the rebellion was neutralised by coinciding with the end of the war (after Socialist Chancellor Friedrich Ebert ordered troops to demobilise).

26. This episode was not the only of its kind in the country. Years before, in 1906, a struggle broke out against a government measure that became known as *Wahlrechtsraub* (theft of suffrage), which increased the fee charged for gaining citizenship. This led the SPD to call a political strike for the first time in its history: a day that became known as Red Wednesday (*Der Rote Mittwoch*). In Hamburg a march by 30,000 people managed to get into the Town Hall, which led to a violent police response. Social Democrat members tried to calm down tensions. Meanwhile the port workers raised barricades and threw stones at the security forces, while they looted jewellers and other businesses in the city centre. In the end one police charge after another ended the riots. Two demonstrators lost their lives from being hit by police sabres, while dozens more got injured or arrested. Fifty of those arrested were given between five and ten months in prison.

failed Spartacist uprising *(Spartakusaufstand)* – of the Weimar Republic, in the summer of 1919, thus ending the Second German Empire. In the elections to the National Assembly held that month the SPD-led coalition won an absolute majority. This put an end to the 'left-wing adventure' that was expressed in the conflict between communists and social democrats.

Altogether the socio-political changes also affected the city's and the country's football teams. Many could not cope with the impact of war fatalities and their sporting history came to an abrupt end. Others, however, opted to merge. Consequently, on 2 June 1919 the clubs Hamburger FC 1888, Sports-Club Germania von 1887 and FC Falke joined forces to form Hamburger Sport Verein (HSV), which would be FC St. Pauli's main sporting rival. HSV's strip included – among other colours[27] – the red and white characteristic of the Hanseatic League.[28]

When the war ended, the disappearances and mergers of clubs meant that out of the 60 football clubs there had been in the Hamburg area, only ten remained. The membership total for the surviving teams was 1,400 – down from 8,000. In those years *Sankt Pauli*, like others, fielded teenage players, such as Richard Sump who made his debut at the age of 15 (in 1915). To cope with this situation the white and brown team even considered a merger with Favorite Hammonia, which did not take place in the end.

The following year, 1919, was dramatic for St. Pauli in sporting terms. After managing, for the first time in its brief history, to

---

27.   Included in its shield are white and black: the colours worn by SC Germania – one of the teams that merged to form HSV. Additionally the shield's diamond shape recalls the traditional symbol of the city's sea traders.

28.   This was the federation between northern German cities such as Lübeck and Hamburg and German traders from the Baltic Sea, the Netherlands, Norway and Britain. Created in 1158 to protect and promote common trade interests, it obtained important trading privileges. The *Diet* or *Hansetag* – a kind of council made up of delegates from different member cities – governed it. It began disintegrating in the fifteenth century as a result of Dutch and British maritime power. It languished after the Thirty Years' War (1618–48) until its privileges were definitively revoked after Adolf Hitler's rise to power in 1934. See A. Cowan, *Hanseatic League: Oxford Research Guide* (Oxford: Oxford University Press, 2010), and J. Schildhauer, *The Hansa: History and Culture* (New York: Dorset Press, 1988).

play in the top flight of German football, it ended the championship at the bottom of the table. That year, 13 teams competed in
the tournament and *Sankt Pauli* won only one game (2–1 against
second-to-bottom team SPVGG Blankenese von 1903 – from the
similarly named district in west Hamburg). St. Pauli lost all of its
other matches, including by a humiliating 9–0 against SC Victoria.
It was not all bad news that year: after paying 35,000 marks, St.
Pauli gained ownership of the Heiligengeistfeld ground.

A few months earlier, on 5 February, St. Pauli's games and sports
section held its first meeting since the Great War. Until then, gymnastics had been the most practised sport at the club but football
was gaining more and more enthusiasts. This did not just happen
at St. Pauli. There were social and political tensions in the Weimar
Republic (1919–33), and a succession of revolutionary outbursts
took place between 1920 and 1923, such as consecutive strikes on
the St. Pauli docks.[29] But it was then that football became a mass
sport in Germany and almost as popular as boxing. Its increased
popularity was particularly pronounced among the working class,
which since the 1920s had enjoyed more leisure time. Clearly
playing the sport also grew. By 1920 the DFB had 756,000 members
– almost five times more than before the First World War. It was

---

29.   From August to September 1923, St. Pauli's dockers led different industrial
disputes. Increases in the prices of basic products, which reached a high of 662.6 per
cent, and unemployment stirred discontent, which turned into violent revolt. Clashes with the security forces were accompanied by looting of food shops. In response
to these events, the Hamburg SPD told workers to go back to work, and the Communist KPD, surprised by the mobilisations, failed to join them. The government
under Chancellor Gustav Stresemann decreed martial law to re-establish order. This
came into effect on 26 September, while 'proletarian defence' governments had been
formed in Saxony and Thuringia. Because of the magnitude of the events the government mobilised the army. In Hamburg, on 23 October, around 2,000 armed men
attacked 20 police stations. All of this was part of an insurrectional plan dreamed
up by the KPD's Thälmann, who was ignoring his own party's instructions. In the
days prior to the insurrection the call to act had been spreading by word of mouth
around St. Pauli's port and factories. On the chosen day the workers went on to the
streets. Cut off from the rest of country and badly equipped, they were overcome by
the police. The workers' resistance lasted three days. The subsequent repression was
extremely harsh. Hamburg's communist organisations had their activity suspended
and property confiscated. On 23 November the KPD was banned as an organisation.

then when the first big-name footballers emerged, such as Max Breunig, the FV Karlsruher midfielder, and Hans Kalb and Heiner Stuhlfauth, respectively a midfielder and goalkeeper for 1. FC Nürnberg.

Other factors converged to spread football's popularity. First there was a notable improvement in the players' quality of game. This was associated with the gradual introduction of the eight-hour working day (between 1918 and 1923), which facilitated footballers' training. It also was aided by the abolition of both an income tax paid by sports entities and a levy for broadcasting sports events. With regards to political factors, the demise of the anti-socialist laws in 1890 and the rise of the SPD helped football to spread by providing bigger facilities for workers to meet and create their own clubs (such as SK Frisch 04, SC Lorbeer 06 and SC Hansa von 1911 – all three in Hamburg). Additionally, dockers had their own teams, such as BSG Hamburg-Südamerikanische Dampfer and SC Hamburger Seeleute.

So St. Pauli's rise coincided with this first boom in German football. And it did so with a small change in its football kit: from 1920 its players wore a white shirt and long brown shorts, a kit that the players would wear for three decades.

Meanwhile, Hamburg was in full political turmoil. After the strikes by port workers[30] there was an unsuccessful attempt, in October 1923, to forcibly take over the city by the Communist Party of Germany (*Kommunistische Partei Deutschlands*, KPD). This became known as the Hamburg Uprising. The communists wished to capitalise on the discontent of workers by imposing a strategy aimed at taking the latter's demands beyond the factory. They wanted the streets to become a common space where

---

30. The most notable example was the demonstration in March 1921 by Hamburg's dockers, which left Heiligengeistfeld to reach the cranes at the Blohm and Voss shipyards. After occupying the firm's facilities and raising the red flag over the office building, the police confronted the workers and reimposed order. Overall the repression caused 19 deaths and over 40 injuries. Two years later a strike was called at the port against the 'Great Inflation' and unemployment, which ended with the workers looting the quays and the boats moored there. Rondinelli, *Ribelli, Sociali e Romantici*, pp. 35–6.

workers' struggles would come together with the demands of the unemployed masses. One of the party's leaders was Ernst Thäl-mann,[31] from the KPD's most left-wing section. He 'personified the communist ideal of the revolutionary worker' and 'was the extreme opposite of an intellectual'.[32] The failure of the workers' insurrection meant, as well as a hundred fatalities, that Communist Party members were repressed and the organisation banned. That year was the first in which the Weimar Republic managed to lessen the impact of the First World War on society. From then on, the country enjoyed a period of political and economic stability. The 'Golden Twenties' benefited from the devaluation of the mark and an inflow of foreign capital.

31. There were three tendencies in the Hamburg KPD: a moderate one led by teacher Hugo Urbanhns; the so-called 'right-wing sector' with an intellectual leaning and that advocated joining social-democrats in a coalition government ('united front'); and the Thalmänn-led section, in favour of direct action, which was the bigger fraction in Hamburg. The failure of the revolutionary attempt in the Hanseatic city forced the KPD to go underground. Later, in 1924, the Red Front Fighters' League (*Rote Frontkämpferbund*) was created. This had about 100,000 members and became the party's armed wing. Its role was to protect demonstrators and strike pickets and block Nazi squads from acting in proletarian neighbourhoods, making it a kind of 'working-class army'. In October 1928, Thalmänn supported a solidarity strike at the Hamburg docks in support of the British miners' strike at the time. A year later, the Red Front Fighters' League was banned by the Prussian interior minister, Albert Grzesinski, an SPD member.
32. Thälmann became an institution in the Hamburg communist movement. He was born and grew up in the port area. There he worked in different insecure jobs, first as a machinist in a fishmeal factory and later in a laundry. He was called up at the beginning of the First World War and fought on the Western Front. In 1917 he joined the Independent Social Democratic Party of Germany, joining the pro-Communist wing that merged with the KPD three years later. In December 1920 he joined the KPD's Central Committee. As a result of his political activity he was sacked from the company he worked for. In October 1923 he actively participated in the Hamburg Uprising, whose failure forced him underground. In February 1925 he was made president of the Red Front Fighters' League. Months later he was elected as KPD leader. He was the party's main candidate in the 1932 presidential elections, in which the Communists had as a slogan, 'a vote for Hindenburg is a vote for Hitler. A vote for Hitler is a vote for war.' On 3 March 1933 Thälmann was arrested by the Gestapo. After eleven years in the Bautzen prison he was taken to Buchenwald concentration camp where he was shot dead, on 18 August 1944, under direct orders from Hitler. R.J. Evans, *La nascita del Terzo Reich* (Milan: Mondadori, 2006), p. 273. See also R. Lemmons, *Hitler's Rival: Ernst Thälmann in Myth and Memory* (Lexington: University Press of Kentucky, 2013).

But despite the economic boom nationally, St. Pauli was typified by poverty and insecure living conditions, which resulted from hyperinflation. As if that were not enough, the 1929 New York stock exchange crash then hit the German economy. Withdrawal of North American capital from the country left many companies without credit. Factories had to reduce production, which led to an increase in unemployment.[33] Hamburg suffered from a big decline in the circulation of goods through its port. A collapse of different local industries and a shortage of food and fuel worsened people's plight. In a country once again plunged into an economic and political crisis – made worse by increased unemployment and the war reparations imposed on Germany by the victorious side in Versailles – many citizens chose to shun the traditional moderate parties and vote for extremist parties such as the Nazi National Socialist German Workers' Party (*Nationalsozialistische Deutsche Arbeiterpartei*, NSDAP) or KPD, which thanks to Thälmann became the 'party of the unemployed'. This was shown by the strong electoral growth enjoyed by both organisations in the interwar years.[34]

---

33. In January 1933 unemployment in Hamburg reached 30 per cent – compared to 22 per cent in the rest of the country.
34. In the September 1930 elections the Nazi Party won 18 per cent of the vote, making them the country's second biggest political force. Just two years later, in June 1932, in the second round of the presidential elections the NSDAP obtained 38 per cent of the vote. This was the first time that they had won a parliamentary majority. On 5 March 1933, three months after Adolf Hitler became chancellor, the Nazi Party won 47.2 per cent of the vote. In all, 17,277,180 people cast a vote for them in the elections to the *Reichstag* (German parliament) and the party became the main political force there. A few days earlier, Hitler scrapped the Constitution and suspended civil liberties. Then he began mass arrests of Communist and Social Democrat members.

3

The Club's Early Years

In the same period St. Pauli became an 'elevator' club, meaning it went up and down from different football divisions, chalking up top-flight promotions and relegations. Disappointments and celebrations were a constant occurrence. For that reason the period became popularly known as the 'yoyo years'. All the same, it was then that the club's administrative structure was consolidated. In the 1923–4 season, the sports team definitively opted to leave Hamburg-St. Pauli Turnverein to become an independent football team. It was then that the selection of St. Pauli's board of directors was formalised. In its first meeting, held on 5 May 1924, trader Henry Rehder, one of the club's pioneers, was chosen as president. He was accompanied on the board by fellow trader Johny Barghusen, and the ex-player and civil servant Amandus Vierth. We can say, therefore, that 1924 was the year in which *Sankt Pauli* was actually constituted as a football club, as its separation from gymnastic activity was completed. The decision was hastened by the German Gymnastics Association's policy of prohibiting its members from taking part in other sports' matches and clubs.

The 1924–5 season was the first in which the club competed under the official name of *Fußball Club Sankt Pauli* (FCSP). The entity was linked to the local bourgeoisie, while the local working-class community supported the teams in the Workers' Gymnastics and Sports Association (*Arbeiter-Turn- und Sportbund*, ATSB).[1] Indeed, in those years the DFB refused membership

---

1.   This was founded in 1893 in Gera, in the east of Thuringia state. The federation changed its name in 1919 when incorporating sports such as athletics and soccer. Until 1914, the workers' clubs refused to enter competitive tournaments but changed their stance after the Great War. The ATSB involved 1.4 million sports practitioners

to the workers' clubs, to whom it contemptuously referred to as 'gangs of independent workers'.[2]

It might sound surprising now that during the interwar years footballers in worker-related teams, such as Komet Blankenese and Billstedt-Horn – two historic Hamburg teams that still exist today – kicked and violently tackled St. Pauli players. Yet for the other teams the footballers in white and brown represented a right-wing bourgeois club.[3]

Until 1933 the club participated in different interregional leagues. Between 1922 and 1926 it played in the Nord-deutsche League; the following year in the A-Klasse Hamburg – a lower-level tournament. The team was built around young players, such as the skilled Richard Rudolph 'Käppen' (1895–1969).[4] As we suggested previously the period was crucial for the club's future as, finally, in 1924, its members left the shelter of the gymnastics association to form *FC Sankt Pauli*. The team's historic eleven was made up of Sump, Bergemann, Hadlich, Spreckelsen, Röbe, Ralf, Nack, Solt-wedel, Otto Schmidt, Schreiner and Jordan. Finally the run-ins the

---

across seven mainly northern districts. It was linked to the SPD, which led 32,000 members to be excluded for being Communist Party members. With the Nazis rise to power, most of its clubs disappeared, while some leading members, such as Karl Bühren and Max Schulze, fled to the USSR. In 1936 the Gestapo arrested other SPD cadre. The SA occupied the school it had created in Leipzig and confiscated its funds and assets. After the Second World War the ATSB did not manage to rebuild its structures across the country. Indeed it was not until 1993 that it was registered as a federation, and it was definitively dissolved in 2008. To know more about the ATSB's genesis and evolution see A. Kruke, *Arbeiter-Turn-und Sportbund (1893–2009)* (Bonn: Archiv der sozialen Demokratie der Friedrich-Ebert-Stiftung, 2012) and T. González Aja (ed.), *Sport y autoritarismos: La utilización del deporte por el comunismo y el fascismo* (Madrid: Alianza Editorial, 2002), pp. 123–6.

2. Hesse-Lichtenberger, *Tor! The Story of German Football*, p. 37.

3. Komet Blankenese, a team created in 1907, was linked to the left thanks to its working-class base. Consequently, since that decade, it was subject to constant surveillance by the authorities, which saw it more as a political association than a sports club.

4. '*Käppen*', as he became popularly known, had been born in 1895. He worked in Hamburg manning a barge down the Elbe. He was discovered by a club member while playing football at school. As well as playing at *Sankt Pauli*, he had several club responsibilities, such as being treasurer and technical assistant. He also took charge of scouting and signing up young players that excelled in talent.

club had with different sporting bodies led to the official founding, on 5 May 1924, of FC St. Pauli – officially registered as FC St. Pauli von 1910.

The next year, which also saw the first striptease in St. Pauli and the police discovering that drugs were being trafficked locally,[5] the team ended sixth with 17 points. The glory that year went to its arch-rival, HSV, which was proclaimed champion. St. Pauli's key player was its right-winger, Berni Schreiner, a young journalist who usually played with a handkerchief in his hand, which he never lost despite his speed.

In the 1927–8 season the Hamburg team returned to the North German League. It only played there for a year because in 1928–9 it took part in the Toes Round (*Runde der Zehen*, with 'Toes' referring to the number ten – the amount of teams competing). This tournament was created because several northern clubs were unhappy about the fragmentation of football into different local leagues. The change became known as the *Fußball-Revolution* (Football Revolution). They had also come together to avoid being disadvantaged vis-à-vis the southern teams. St. Pauli was joined in the Toes Round by Hamburg SV, Holstein Kiel 07, SV St. Georg and SV Victoria Hamburg. By creating the new league the Northern German Football Association had to negotiate with these clubs. At the end of discussions, an agreement was reached to make several reforms to the competition system. As a result, six major leagues began playing in the 1929–30 season. In this fleeting adventure of the 'ten chosen ones' St. Pauli ended the season in sixth place after winning five out of nine matches, and losing four. Its goal balance was zero, having scored 37 goals and let in 37.

After a restructuring of the competition, St. Pauli played the 1929–30 season in the *Bezirksliga Hamburg*, a kind of local second division. The team managed by Richard Sumps strolled through the tournament, coming top, five points ahead of the

---

5.   In one operation the security forces seized 114 kg of heroin hidden in a cemetery. Shortly after, St. Pauli became the second biggest crime hotspot in Europe after London's Whitechapel. Petroni, *St. Pauli siamo noi*, p. 36.

runner up. It was a winning team featuring footballers like Alex Guiza, Jonny Salz and Oschi Stamer. In March 1931, St. Pauli beat Eimsbütteler TV and was pronounced champion of northern Germany. This was the most important victory in the footballing career of Otto Wolff, a forward for St. Pauli, who would became a central agent in the Nazi repression in Hamburg.[6] That year a significant change took place in the club's directorate. For professional reasons Henry Rehder moved to Berlin and was replaced by the historic figure Wilhelm Koch – an ex-goalkeeper at the club. A 1933 board meeting chose Koch to be club president (*Vereins-*

---

6. Born in Kiel (Schleswig-Holstein) in 1907 to a middle-class family, Wolff gained a degree in economics at the University of Hamburg. Between 1940 and 1945 he became economics advisor for the Hamburg region NSDAP. In 1940 he was appointed head of the Reich commissar's Economics Department in Norway. Ten years earlier he had joined the Nazi Party, and in 1943 joined the SS (*Schutzstaffel* or Protection Squadron, a Nazi paramilitary organisation). During the Second World War he directed expropriating Jewish property and commissioning forced labour. Furthermore, he collaborated with the head of the Neuengamme extermination camp – 15 kilometres to the south east of Hamburg. During the war there were 100,000 prisoners in the camp, of which 40,000 were killed. Wolff was one of the highest-ranking NSDAP officials in Hamburg. He took advantage of his position to acquire two Jewish family properties between 1939 and 1942, and attained the rank of regiment leader (*Standartenführer*) in the SS. In sporting terms, he wore the St. Pauli shirt from 1925 to 1935. In the 1939–40 season he went back to play for the club on the right wing. After the war he was imprisoned by the allies. He was freed and reincorporated into society in April 1948. Then he founded an insurance company KG Otto, which was partnered by the ex-governor of Hamburg Karl Kaufmann. In the 1950s he combined his professional activity with matches for the St. Pauli veterans team. In 1951 he was even put forward to be club vice-president. Two decades later, in 1971, he was made a life member of the association. He died in 1992. Because of his past in the Nazi Party, in 2010 the St. Pauli General Assembly voted to strip him, posthumously, of the Gold Decoration (*Goldene Ehrennadel*) that the club had awarded him in 1960. St. Pauli's biggest rival, HSV, also included a prominent Nazi in its ranks: Otto 'Tull' Harder, club forward between 1913 and 1930, and German squad player with fifteen caps. An NSDAP member since 1930, the subsequent year he joined the SS. As a member of the paramilitary organisation he worked as a guard at the Ahlem-Hannover extermination camp. Three years after the fall of the Third Reich, on 24 January 1948, he was tried in Bielefeld for belonging to the SS. He was sentenced to two and a half years prison and fined 50,000 reichsmark (later reduced to 5,000 marks). He was freed in 1951, after being pardoned by the British government, and lived in Bendestorf until he died five years later. On Otto Wolf see Nagel and Pahl, *FC St. Pauli*, p. 90 and G. Backes, *'Mit Deutschem Sportgruss, Heil Hitler!' Der FC St. Pauli im Nationalsozialismus* (Hamburg: Hoffmann und Campe, 2010), pp. 148–57.

führer). At the same meeting Eduard Stülcken was appointed vice president. Additionally the club gained its first sponsors. These were the brothers Carl and Alexander Richte, two businessmen owning several Hamburg theatres and gambling houses, who provided a donation. This contrasted with the plight of many of the city's inhabitants, who lacked financial means. Indeed, 40 per cent of the population was unemployed.[7] Undoubtedly this was the perfect storm for parties putting forward radical political solutions, such as the Nazi NSDAP. In Hamburg their growth became noticeable in 1927. That year they created a squad to fight communists and social democrats on the street and came up with a strategy to control the taverns (*Kneipen*) – the meeting point for the area's sailors and workers. The following year, in 1928, the party gained three seats in the Hamburg assembly. Within four years its electoral support had grown considerably: the Nazis went from having three to 51 seats out of a total of 160. Of course Nazi presence in the institutions was replicated in the streets, where clashes with members of communist and left-wing parties were constant.[8] Between 1924 and 1929, attacks by SA (*Sturmabteilung,*

---

7. The number of dock workers in the city fell from 28,000 in 1923 to 12,500 a decade later. In January 1933, unemployment in Hamburg reached 30 per cent, while it was 23 per cent in the rest of the country. Rondinelli, *Ribelli, Sociali e Romantici*, p. 37.

8. One of the bloodiest clashes took place on 17 July 1932: 'Bloody Sunday in Altona'. In the middle of the election campaign around 800 workers and Communist members (who attended events with lead piping attached to their waists and stones in their pockets) tried to stop a Nazi march and rally in the working-class Altona district. Around 7,000 NSDAP members and sympathisers turned out. In the following clashes 18 people were killed (including two SA members) and a hundred were injured. A subsequent police raid saw the arrest of dozens of communists, four of whom were executed on 1 August 1933. Years earlier, in 1927, conflicts had begun in the streets of St. Pauli. These involved the SA, which aimed to infiltrate the neighbourhood to take over the taverns and thereby attract and recruit workers and Communist and Social Democrat supporters. Finally, in November 1932, the Nazis gained a pub in Breitestraße, a few hundred metres from the port. They were not made welcome in the neighbourhood, however, as was shown by the repeated smashing of the tavern's windows. As a result of this, they had to keep constant guard at its entrance. On 20 December that year the premises were stormed by pistol-carrying Communist members who wreaked considerable havoc and injured several of the bar's customers.

Stormtroopers or Brownshirts) paramilitary squads led to the death of 29 communists across the country. In the next three years the figure reached 92. This was not surprising if we bear in mind that the communists were the only group that confronted the SA on the streets.

Initially the impact of Nazism on FC St. Pauli was insignificant, as it was on other clubs. It was limited to a couple of players, such as the aforementioned Wolff or the young Walter Koehler (an SA member), the odd director that joined the Nazis and Wilhelm Koch reaching the presidency. Koch's Nazi membership was revealed many years later and caused controversy. He was the club's long-est-serving president and the stadium was named after him (the Wilhelm Koch Stadion) for many years in recognition of his work. Yet he had been a member of the Nazi Party from 5 July 1937. This was not an isolated case. That same year one and a half million Germans joined the National Socialists, including staff at the DFB and numerous heads of other sports clubs. All the same, the fact that Koch did not join the NSDAP until 1937 suggests that he signed up more out of opportunism than conviction, which would also explain why he never played a leading role in the party. Despite his Nazi membership, he tried as much as he could to keep the club at a distance from the growing politicisation at the time. For that reason he was reluctant to allow the Nazis to use the club's facilities for their own sporting or propaganda activities. Koch wanted the St. Pauli stadium to only be used for playing football.[9]

In that turbulent period, before the outbreak of the Second World War, German football had been dominated by Schalke – the winner of five titles between 1934 and 1940. St. Pauli competed in the *Norddeutsche Oberliga*, although it also combined playing in

9.   In 1933, soon after Hitler rose to power, Koch took over managing the company he worked in after its two Jewish owners fled to Sweden fearful of Nazism and anti-Semitism, combining this professional activity with being St. Pauli president. This management role ended when, at the end of the war, he was dismissed in the Allied-led purges of NSDAP members in positions of power. Only two years later he was once again chosen as president, a role he continued exercising until his death in 1969.

the *Gauliga Nordmark*[10] and the *Gauliga Hamburg* with competing in other regional contests.[11]

10.   A trophy devised by the Nazi regime in order to restructure German sports, for which Hamburg, Schleswig-Holstein and Mecklenburg-Lüben competed. St. Pauli played in the tournament in the 1934–5 season, coming tenth. Yet the club's biggest success was during the 1936–7 and 1937–8 seasons, when it came fourth. In the 1938–9 and 1939–40 seasons it came fifth and sixth respectively.
11.   The *Gauliga* were competitions intended by the Nazis to restructure German football, created in 1933. They meant the division of the country into 16 *Gaue* (an old German term effectively meaning tribes). In this system the 16 winners of the different tournaments were divided into four groups. The subsequent champions in each group went on to play in the national semi-finals. In the later part of the Second World War this system was replaced by knock-out rounds. Hesse-Lichtenberger, *Tor! The Story of German Football*, p. 66.

PART II

War and Peace:
From the Third Reich to the *Bundesliga*

4

Sankt Pauli under the Swastika

On 28 January 1933, St. Pauli beat Victoria 1–8, with Erwin Seeler notching six goals. That year, however, did not go down in history because of the Hamburg team's sporting milestone. The day after the goal spree, Field Marshal Hindenburg appointed Hitler, leader of the NSDAP, as chancellor. Thus was completed the so-called 'seizing of power'. This had started a year and a half earlier when the Nazis took over the two pillars of state: the administration and the army. Shortly after, on 27 February, a fire at the Reichstag (the German parliament) facilitated passing the Decree for the Protection of the People and the State, which left the Weimar Constitution suspended and 'laid the foundation for a permanent state of emergency'.[1] In that period around 10,000 Communist Party members were arrested. That was the intimidating atmosphere in which, on 5 March, the last multiparty elections were held in the country. In them the National Socialists won 43.9 per cent of the vote.

The Nazis' rise to power meant the persecution of their political opponents. As well as attacking and imprisoning Communist and Social Democrat members, introducing totalitarianism meant spreading state control to all aspects of life – including social activity. Sport obviously could not escape the new authoritarianism under Hitler's chancellorship. The DFB's press officer, Guido von Mengde, demonstrated this by stating: 'Footballers are the Führer's political soldiers'.[2] All of this was quite paradoxical bearing in mind

---

1. As a result of the Reichstag fire a decree was issued to ban the Communist KPD. A month after, the government ordered the dissolution of the SPD and a month later than that, the Social Democrat-affiliated unions.
2. Hesse-Lichtenberger, *Tor! The Story of German Football*, p. 68.

that Hitler was known for his dislike of sport. He only attended one football match in his life (Germany's defeat at the hands of Norway in the 1936 Berlin Olympic Games).

Despite this aversion, Nazi chiefs tried to exploit football for propaganda purposes. For them sport was a powerful tool that they could ill afford to squander. The cult of the body and physical activity were related, according to the Third Reich theses, with racial thinking and the national community – the *Volksgemeinschaft*.

In the Third Reich, St. Pauli, like most clubs, complied with orders issued by the sporting, social and political authorities. Hamburg was not only a city controlled by Nazis but was one of the 'Führer's five cities'. The Nazis picked these for redevelopment so they could show the world the country's competitiveness and modernity. Hamburg would be a mirror reflecting the Third Reich's best image to the outside world. Among the different regeneration projects planned was the building of the 'Manhattan of the Elbe': a landscape of skyscrapers, squares, long avenues, monuments and palaces in a residential area aiming to accommodate 50,000 people.[3] Moreover, on the Führer's own request, the project had to include a new bridge crossing the Elbe and newly designed riversides. This metamorphosis would greatly affect different historical spots, such as the historic St. Pauli fish market and the port area (Hafenstraße). The city would become 'a ticket to tour an Empire open to the world'.[4] Eventually the project was halted by the start of the Second World War, thwarting such plans.

The NSDAP won a majority in Hamburg's Senate in the elections on 8 March 1933. Overnight, all the unions and political associations linked to the SPD were banned. In one year 2,400 members of

---

3. On 1 April 1937, the 'Greater Hamburg Law', which redefined planning for the city, came into effect. Karl Kaufmann, NSDAP founding member and Hamburg *Gauleiter* (Gau leader) since 1928, presented 'visions for a new Hamburg'. Two years later, the architect Konstanty Gutschow was responsible for designing the details of the intervention. The plan envisaged replacing Hafenstraße's overcrowded tenements with *Gau-Hochhäuser*: new offices, hotels and a skyscraper over 250 metres high. Its surroundings would be large enough for 100,000 people. Nagel and Pahl, *FC St. Pauli*, p. 66.

4. Petroni, *St. Pauli siamo noi*, p. 40.

the Hamburg opposition were arrested, demonstrating an iron grip that also spread to the local media.

In the club, however, life continued fairly smoothly. The country's new administration had issued orders as part of the *Gleichschaltung* (the Third Reich's Nazification process to implement a totalitarian system, grouped together in the 'Aryan clause' of the Civil Service Law that came into effect in April 1933). The clause forced the purging of Jews from the civil service, universities, associations and sports organisations.[5] Yet St. Pauli did not follow the regulations to the letter. Unlike other clubs, such as 1 FC Nürnberg or Frankfurt's Eintracht, St. Pauli allowed membership to those of a Jewish background for that year. Club members included the Jewish brothers Otto and Paul Lang who joined St. Pauli to found its rugby section in 1933. The fates of both were different. While Otto managed to flee the country, his brother ended up interned in the Theresienstadt concentration camp.[6] St. Pauli did not incorporate the 'Aryan clause' into its statutes until as late as 1940. The year the decree was issued, seven years earlier, over a quarter of the Jewish com-

---

5. On 1 April 1933, the German Boxing Federation excluded Jews from official fights. On 12 April, Daniel Prenn, a prominent Jewish tennis player, was removed from Germany's Davis Cup team. Also that month, the German Swimming Federation expelled its Jewish members. For its part, the DFB published in Walther Bensemann's *Kicker* magazine an advert in which it declared that 'members of the Jewish race, and people that turn out to be members of the Marxist movement, are deemed unacceptable'. Hesse-Lichtenberger, *Tor! The Story of German Football*, p. 63 and Backes, '*Mit Deutschem Sportgruss, Heil Hitler!*', pp. 50–2).

6. Pioneers of rugby in the region, the Lang brothers came to *FC Sankt Pauli* in 1933 to create a team after being rejected by another club, SV St. Georg, because of their Jewish origins. Otto, born in 1906, left St. Pauli voluntarily it seems. A year later Otto left for exile, migrating – via Antwerp – to South America, where he died in 2003. His teammates had warned him of the very probable reprisals he would suffer after he punched an SS member. Despite dying his hair and changing his name, he decided to flee. Meanwhile, his brother Paul, born in 1908, decided to stay in Hamburg because he had married an 'Aryan' woman. His marriage did not stop him being sent to the Theresienstadt concentration camp. Eventually the younger Lang left the camp after the Soviet army liberated it. He then lived in Hamburg for the rest of his life; he died in the same year as his brother. In 2008, coinciding with the 75th anniversary of the club's rugby section, St. Pauli's directors placed a monolith at Millerntor stadium's main entrance in order to pay homage to the two men. See Nagel and Pahl, *FC St. Pauli*, p. 91 and Backes, '*Mit Deutschem Sportgruss, Heil Hitler!*', pp. 48–50.

munity resident in Hamburg had fled the city. Three years later, in November 1938, coinciding with the pogrom by the SS known as the Night of Broken Glass, the city's synagogue was destroyed and its Jewish cemetery desecrated. The Nazi raid led to the death of nearly a hundred Jews in Hamburg.

In the early 1930s the club overlooked party affiliation, ethnic origins or the religion of its players and associates. As the Nazification process was already in full swing, this stance would today be branded as disobedience, yet at the time it was an unconscious act. All the same, there is a debate surrounding the degree to which the club collaborated with the Third Reich. This revolves around the role of its management and whether it acted out of opportunism or conviction. In this regard, the following information might be revealing: in 1934 there was only one member of the Nazi Party on St. Pauli's board: Walter Koehler, who was in the SA. He was the only direct link between the authorities and the club in those years. Indeed, FC St. Pauli had not shown any nationalistic or militaristic inclination in its early decades, unlike that demonstrated by other football clubs.

Despite perceptions to the contrary, not everyone in Germany sided with the Nazis. This was so at St. Pauli. In the 1930s a group of young people that loved swing (as well as football)[7] was formed

---

7.   In Hamburg followers of jazz, and of artists such as Duke Ellington and Teddy Stauffer, were known as the *Swingheinis* or Swing Kids. They dressed in a particular style. Men wore sports jackets, chequered trousers, white scarves and – the most important accessory – a black umbrella. Women stood out due to their long hair and striking makeup. Their images were a contrast with the uniformed militarism of the Hitler Youth (*Hitlerjugend*). Consequently the nonconformists suffered attacks from the authorities and the Hitler Youth. Unsurprisingly, from 1936 the Reich's Chamber of Culture banned swing. Despite the Second World War breaking out, the Swing Kids still organised private parties and dances – such as one held in an Altona hotel in February 1940. That year Karl Kaufmann, the Hamburg governor, helped set up the Work Group for War Child Protection. It was a body that, despite its name, was devoted to pursuing the Swing Kids' activities. Similarly, in autumn 1940, the Gestapo created a department in Hamburg purely to monitor the same. That October, its agents began arresting their first swing lovers. Their last concert in the city was held on 28 February 1941. This was a performance by Dutch musician John Kristel at the *Alsterpavillon* – a spot the authorities pejoratively called the *Judenaquarium* (Jewish aquarium) and that was destroyed by shelling in 1942. That

at the club. By doing so they entered into direct confrontation with the new authorities.[8] This was because the Nazi leaders[9] derogatorily labelled this music genre *Negermusik* (negro music).[10] This was enough to provoke angry collective complaints at more than one club meeting.[11] The club was characterised by its opposition

---

day, police surrounded the premises and arrested several audience members. At the police station they were beaten up and had their hair forcibly cut. The authorities' repression, rather than weakening the movement, pushed the Swing Kids to take a stronger stand against the Third Reich. See J. Savage, *Teenage: The Creation of Youth 1875–1945* (London: Chatto & Windus, 2007), pp. 378–83 and M. Zwerin, *Swing frente al nazi* (Madrid: EsPop Ediciones, 2016).

8. Although the swing trend was initially restricted to bourgeois youth, from the late 1930s the style became more mixed, classwise. Because St. Pauli was a district with many dancehalls, swing there attracted dozens of young proletarians. This was the case in nightspots such as Ballhaus Alcazar, the Kaffeehaus Dietrich Menke and the Cafe Mehrer, all on the Reeperbahn; together with the Cap Norte club and Café Heinze elsewhere – in Große Freiheit and Millerntor Platz. All these became 'bastions of cultural opposition to the regime'. For this reason, from 1935 the Nazis banned radio stations from playing swing. But some fans of the genre still listened to it secretly on the BBC, an action that after 1939 was deemed a serious crime. From then, the activity was restricted to people's private spaces. In their eagerness to hound swing fans, the authorities ended up arresting 500 young people in Hamburg for being 'degenerates'. Among the local Swing Kids arrested by the Gestapo was Tommie Scheel, who, after receiving a beating, was put into Fuhlsbüttel prison and made to do forced labour; and Kaki Georgiadi – put into solitary confinement for weeks. These were not one-off cases; other peers of theirs suffered repression from the regime: 380 young people were arrested in Hamburg between October 1940 and December 1942. Seen as anglophiles and traitors for listening to 'perverted music', they were tortured, beaten and sent to different concentration camps (such as Uckermark, Neuengamme, Buchenwald, Auschwitz and Moringen). There they had to wear a red triangle to be identifiable as political prisoners. Other Swing Kids were labelled 'effeminate cowards' and sent straight to the front, where they suffered abuses. Despite all this, new Swing Kid groups continued to emerge in the city. See Rondinelli, *Ribelli, Sociali e Romantici*, p. 41 and Backes, 'Mit Deutschem Sportgruss, Heil Hitler!', pp. 97–118.

9. Paradoxically the Reich minister of propaganda, Joseph Goebbels, decided to increase the participation of swing bands during the Berlin Olympic Games in 1936. This was to transmit an image of tolerance and normality. Backes, 'Mit Deutschem Sportgruss, Heil Hitler!', p. 115.

10. The Swing Kids would mock Hitler Youth when they came across them in the street by shouting 'Swing Heil!'. Rondinelli, *Ribelli, Sociali e Romantici*, p. 41.

11. One of these swing fans was a 19-year-old player of in the St. Pauli rugby team. He was not the only one. Passion for the musical genre also was shared by a club football player, Heiner Nelles. The footballer was born in the neighbourhood in 1926 and joined the lower-team levels at the age of ten. At night, the young player would meet up secretly with his friends to listen and dance to swing. During the war,

to the monopoly that the Hitler Youth aimed to have in education and sport. Therefore its board of directors, while trying to comply with regulations to keep the NSDAP leaders happy, did not unconditionally side with the regime. Even though the club was notably 'petit-bourgeois', like most teams in that period, the St. Pauli directors did not like the Nazis' plan to merge all of Hamburg's football teams into one (which would be SV Hamburg Mitte). By opposing this, the club's heads were mainly acting to guarantee the club's continuity and, by doing so, preserve their status. In other words, there was no resistance or heroism but neither was there fanaticism or blind allegiance. We could say that St. Pauli remained in those years a conservative institution that adapted to the period. That would explain, in part, why the club's attitude towards the Nazi authorities was sometimes ambivalent. Throughout it attempted to avoid taking sides and making enemies but did not adapt to every Nazi whim either. That said, from 1933 its directors tried to maintain good relations with the local Nazi power structure. In 1935 the Millerntor stadium hosted different NSDAP propaganda exhibitions. This incidentally damaged the grass on the pitch, which did not fully recover for nearly a year and a half. For that reason, in that period St. Pauli had to play some matches at Altona's Exerzierweide stadium – or the Exer as it was commonly known.

On 16 March that year, Hitler, contravening the Versailles Treaty (1919), announced that the country was rearming and, furthermore, that military service would be reintroduced. The war machinery was being reactivated. Within three years German troops had occupied Austria, annexing it de facto into the Third Reich. Greater Germany was re-emerging.

Away from this pre-war atmosphere, St. Pauli had a good 1935–6 season, made possible by its coach, Otto Schmidt – an ex-player for the club who made his living as a coal merchant. The club won

---

Nelles avoided being drafted to the SS by first signing up to be a volunteer Luftwaffe pilot. See Backes, 'Mit Deutschem Sportgruss, Heil Hitler!', pp. 117–18 and F. Boll and A. Kaminsky, *Gedenkstättenarbeit und Oral History: Lebensgeschichtliche Beiträge zur Verfolgung in zwei Diktaturen* (Berlin: Arno Spitz, 1999), pp. 27–40.

promotion to the first division. The following year, in 1937, the Hamburg team came fourth in the *Gauliga*, drawing on points with second-place Holstein Kiel and third-place SC Victoria. That was its biggest sporting achievement of the decade. The same year, most St. Pauli directors joined the NSDAP, probably believing that this was the best way to serve the club's interests.

The team ended the next two seasons towards the top of the *Gauliga* table in a solid fifth place. Things changed, however, with the outbreak of war in 1939. That year St. Pauli could not avoid relegation. Institutionally the club's directors, despite their initial indifference, aligned themselves with the authorities following a propaganda campaign begun by the Nazis after the occupation of the Sudetes (in October 1938). These territories were part of Czechoslovakia (made up of minor parts of Bohemia, Moravia and Eastern Silesia). They were inhabited by a German-speaking minority and had been claimed by the Nazis during the interwar period.

In the summer of 1939, all men of between 18 and 45 years of age were called up to be army reservists. They all had to be able to fight in future operations led by the Reich's chief of staff. Conscription affected 120 players from different St. Pauli sporting branches, among which were eight starting players from FC St. Pauli's first team. By 1941 the figure had increased to 200 sportsmen.[12] As well as those called up, the club also suffered losses from Nazi repression. An example was the internment of a member of the coaching staff, Peter Julius Jürs,[13] at the Neuengamme death camp, where he

12. The club tried to keep in touch with the players sent to the front (*Soldaten-St. Paulianer*) through liaising with the person responsible for getting the club's publication to them. The paper included a space to print greetings that their families sent to them. Nagel and Pahl, *FC St. Pauli*, p. 78.

13. Jürs was born on 26 April 1889 and joined St. Pauli Turnverein to play football at the age of nine. Three of his eight brothers died during the First World War, while he suffered serious injuries fighting in Russia. In January 1941 he was condemned to death by the second chamber of the Special Hanseatic Court for jeopardising military force, bribery and falsifying documents. Four months later, the state prosecutor reduced his sentence to 15 years. After being imprisoned in Bremen, he was put into the Neuengamme concentration camp until it was vacated on 20 April 1945. Along with the other prisoners, he was taken to Lübeck to be shut into the

came across Otto '*Tull*' Harder – the ex-HSV forward who helped administer the grounds as an SS member.

In the end, Germany invaded Poland at dawn on 1 September 1939. The Second World War had started. For the first weeks of the conflict football was stopped across the country. The Nazi hierarchy had decided to indefinitely suspend all sporting contests. Two months later, matches resumed as the regime wished to transmit to its people a feeling of normality. The war's outbreak led to players going back and forth between playing and fighting at the front. This explains why it was impossible for St. Pauli to keep a stable team – the reason it was not able to play in local championships in the 1940–1 and 1941–2 seasons. In the latter season military teams proliferated, such as FC LSV Pütnitz (Pütnitz Air Force FC) or the SS Strasbourg Sports Union; and the *sanktpaulianer* shirt was worn for a few months by the Czech international Rudolf Krcil, a midfielder who had stood out while playing for Slavia Prague. During the first years of the conflict, the directors were almost exclusively occupied with overcoming the hurdles created by the war and managing the club as best as possible. Meanwhile the city's port became a strategic centre for the German navy fleet. Warships and submarines were built in the local shipyards.

It was precisely in the St. Pauli and Altona shipyards that clandestine anti-Nazi resistance groups operated, such as the *Bästein-Jacobs-Abshagen-Gruppe* – one of the most active in the city.[14] Their most notable actions involved war-industrial sabotage

---

Cap Arcana boat moored at the city's port. Five days before the end of the war, the ship was confused with a troop transporter and bombarded by the Royal Air Force. Jürs, along with 4,000 other prisoners, died during the British air raid. His name is engraved on a plaque for the Neuengamme memorial devoted to the Hamburg resistance fighters killed or persecuted between 1933 and 1945. Nagel and Pahl, *FC St. Pauli*, pp. 88–9.

14. The name came from the group's founders, Bernhard Bästlein, Franz Jacob and Robert Abshagen. After they were freed from the Sachsenhausen camp they set up an armed resistance group. Its structure consisted of 300 fighters (Communists, Social Democrats, independents, and foreign workers), divided into small squads (cells of three people operating independently) that were present in more than 30 factories in the city. Even so, most of their clandestine activity was carried out in Altona and St. Pauli's shipyards and docks. Nearly a hundred workers from the Blohm

in which they managed to slow manufacturing or make it less efficient. They also produced defective materials, destroyed machinery, burned out boilers and put empty capsules in the anti-tank grenades to disable them. All workers that were believed to have voluntarily hindered production were interned in re-education camps or had their wages docked. The group also produced propaganda and gave support to prisoners, many of which were foreign (French, Dutch and Polish) and being forced to produce armaments.

Hamburg had been preparing for the worst for some time. Since the beginning of the war the city had suffered recurrent air raids. For that reason shelters and refuges were ordered to be built. In 1941, the year of the Nazi offensive against the Soviet Union (Operation Barbarossa), the city had around 1,700 such buildings – giving protection to 250,000 people. The following year, a giant bunker was created at Heiligengeistfeld (St. Pauli), next to Feldstraße, to accommodate 18,000 people. This was a large construction that can be seen standing to this day from the Millerntor stadium. A year later, between 24 and 27 July 1943, this bunker was more necessary than ever as a result of the Allies' 'Operation Gomorrah'. This was an offensive that consisted of seven systematic air raids on the city, which destroyed 75 per cent of Hamburg's urban zone and 80 per cent of its port. Around 31,000 people lost their lives – a figure double that of Berlin – and 125,000 were injured, because the British air force dropped 1.7 million bombs on the area. Around 900,000 people were made homeless. In the following weeks the authorities evacuated almost a million people. The devastation was such that Hamburg became known as 'the city of death'.

---

and Voss shipyard joined the group. The group prioritised mobilising workers, giving solidarity to the foreigners forced to work to build a bunker to protect German war production, giving support to Soviet prisoners of war and doing anti-Nazi propaganda and sabotage. On October 1942 the Gestapo found them out and nearly 200 participants were arrested. Despite that the group was crucial at providing a network of resistance fighters that later spread to other northern industrial cities, and which kept fighting until the Allied troops arrived. In May 1944, in the so-called 'Hamburg communist trials', seventy of their members were given the death sentence and executed. See Rondinelli, *Ribelli, Sociali e Romantici*, p. 43 and U. Puls, *Die Bästlein-Jacob -Abshagen-Gruppe: Bericht über den antifaschistischen Widerstandskampf in Hamburg und an der Waterkante während des zweiten Weltkrieges* (Berlin: Dietz Verlang, 1959).

One of the places that was least affected at first by the shelling was St. Pauli, of which only a third was destroyed. This was possible partly because of the placing of two *Flaktürme* (anti-aircraft towers) in the north of the district. However, later attacks on Hamburg, which targeted the Heiligengeistfeld bunkers, damaged parts of the St. Pauli stadium as it is near to the anti-aircraft site. With ruins and missile craters around them, the club's board of directors made the decision to rebuild the ground straightaway. Yet this was not finished until late in 1946 – a year and a half after the end of the war. According to Wilhelm Koch, one of the Allied air raids that wiped out half of the city also damaged the club's main office. However, the worst damage was suffered by the *Glacischaussee* building that usually housed the team, which was razed to the ground. Matches could not be played at the Millerntor for four weeks. But the worst loss was of the club's documents, as the raids led to the loss of the club's archive, which included its membership list.

The club's football results for those years were erratic. In October 1943, St. Pauli managed to beat HSV 8–1. That way it gained vengeance for the painful defeat its eternal rival had inflicted on it just months before (when St. Pauli lost 0–9). Among the footballers that left the club then was Karl Miller, one of the team's best. With good reason he became the first St. Pauli player to be picked for the national squad.[15] The defender, an international between 1940 and

---

15.   A butcher's son, Miller debuted with St. Pauli in the 1932–3 season. At first he had to play secretly because his father had banned him from playing football. Later, however, his dad became one of his biggest fans. In 1935 Miller was selected to play for North Germany. His good performance did not go unnoticed by the all-German team coach Sepp Herberger. In 1940 Miller was called up and stationed at a *Luftwaffe* unit in Saxony. He combined his military activity with playing some matches as a 'guest player' for Dresdner SC. On 7 April 1940 he made his debut for Germany against Hungary, a match that ended in a 2–2 draw. He also played in the German team's last match during the Second World War, which took place in Bratislava on 22 November 1942. Germany's rivals were Slovakia, who beat the home team 5–2. Between 1940 and 1942, Miller wore the national shirt on twelve occasions – making him the St. Pauli player with the most caps. Additionally, Miller starred – together with his teammates – in a film, *Das große Spiel* (The Big Game), which recreated the 1941 German Cup Final between Schalke 04 and SK Rapid. Shortly after, Miller returned to his hometown to play for Luftwaffen-Sportverein Hamburg – the local air-force team. He was promoted to sergeant and later became

1942, played as a 'guest' for Dresdner SC and in the next two years was in Luftwaffen-Sportverien Hamburg (LSV) – the local German Air Force team. The 1943–4 season was characterised by many matches finishing early. The reason was not the danger of bombing raids but lack of footballs. If the ball being used was damaged or lost there were no others available so play had to be abandonded.

At the same time, although the war was increasingly evolving in favour of the Allies, the Nazi authorities continued to persecute those they called the *Asozialen* (antisocial). This group spanned the unemployed to prostitutes, and included people with hereditary illnesses, disabilities or who had shown 'irregular matrimonial and sexual behaviours'. It also included those that had repeatedly travelled on public transport without a ticket! According to the regime's calculations, 40 per cent of St. Pauli residents were antisocial. Homosexuals, transvestites and transsexuals suffered repression. The 'island of happiness' that St. Pauli had been for them was consigned to history due to the ultra-conservative onslaught. In the Nazis' first year in power they conducted 659 prosecutions of 'perversions against nature'. Also notable was their persecution of the Chinese community, whose roots in the district dated back to the eighteenth century, when they came to work as furnace stokers or coal carriers after steam power was introduced. On 13 May 1944 they were victim to the *Chinesenaktion*. This was an operation in which the Gestapo arrested 130 Chinese people or people of Asian appearance that lived in Schmuckstraße – the so-called 'Chinese street' – a road parallel to the Reeperbahn. On that occasion the pretext used by the Nazis to act against this small community was their link with opium smokers, and trafficking of narcotics and

---

gunner. Due to his 'efforts against Soviet Russians' he received the Iron Cross (of the second-highest level). He continued playing at Dresdner FC until, after the war ended, he convinced some teammates to all go to St. Pauli. His main argument to them was that they would get provisions from his father's butchers shop. That is how The Wonderful Eleven, who dominated Hamburg football in the late 1940s and is believed to be the best team in the club's history, came to be formed. Miller retired after the 1949–50 season, aged 37. After hanging up his boots he remained linked to St. Pauli, representing the club on the League Committee. He died in 1967 at the age of 54. Nagel and Pahl, *FC St. Pauli*, p. 92.

contraband. Prostitutes, who had been hounded since the rise of
Nazism, did not escape the raids either. In 1933 the Nazis arrested
1,500 women working as prostitutes. Their leaders' aim, however,
was not to eradicate prostitution but control it.

Yet a few months later the Third Reich became besieged thanks to
the Soviet forces' advance on Berlin. On 30 April 1945, Chancellor
Adolf Hitler took his life in his bunker in the centre of the German
capital. In Hamburg, days later (on 3 May), after an emergency
meeting with governor Karl Kaufmann, Luftwaffe Major General
Alwin Wolz surrendered. He handed control of the city to David
Spurling, the brigadier commanding the British troops. In Reims,
just four days later, general Alfred Jodl signed the German army's
unconditional surrender before the Allies. The war had ended.

5

Postwar Successes and the Magnificent Eleven

The conflict's end was a fact. Little by little everything returned to normal in the midst of the ruins and hardships – including much of the population starving. There was a lack of consumer goods – food and clothing – while epidemics spread among those that were barely surviving housed in ruins and basements. More than twelve million people were forced to flee or were evicted. The Third Reich's military defeat was a psychological blow to citizens that had seen themselves as invincible. The Allied occupation, militarisation and division of the country were followed by the re-establishment of the German government and institutions. In the first municipal elections held after the war, the SPD won in Hamburg and retook control of the city. Indeed they have been in power for much of the twentieth century.

The city's economy was quickly rebuilt, as happened in the rest of the country. This was thanks to the so-called 'economic miracle' that once again, in the 1950s and 1960s, made Germany a financial hub for the continent. The economic good times also had an impact on St. Pauli. The shipyards went back to operating at peak performance and dockers and sailors, with money in their wallets, sought all kinds of amusement in the neighbourhood. In the early 1950s, the Reeperbahn – known as 'the most sinful mile' – flourished, setting itself up as St. Pauli's cultural and social epicentre where 'sailors, creatives, strippers, prostitutes, homosexuals and gangsters co-habited freely'. Undoubtedly it was St. Pauli's golden era. The district was a space of leisure and tolerance where everything normally prohibited took place. Local actor and singer

Hans Albers invoked its essence in his tune 'Auf der Reeperbahn nachts um halb eins' ('On the Reeperbahn at Half Past Twelve') – popularised in 1954 after the film of the same name was released. The song included the words, 'He who on a joyous night has never gone for a good time in the Reeperbahn is a poor soul because he does not know St. Pauli.'¹ This explains why the striptease clubs, the brothels and the pubs became the district's most lucrative businesses. Together they became a big opportunity for some, such as entrepreneur Willi Bartels – known as the 'King of St. Pauli' – who went from working in his mother's butchers to being the pioneer of modern brothels. One of these was the Eros Centre, which opened in 1967 next to the Palais d'Amour, one of the big brothels at that time. Bartels also worked out that he could do speculative business in real estate. Not for nothing, he acquired on the cheap different bomb-damaged buildings: turning them into hotels, restaurants and fashionable nightspots. The port district was transformed into a tourist attraction park aimed at visitors from Scandinavia and the rest of Germany.

The neighbourhood also became the epicentre of an emerging youth music scene. The new generation of young people was not the 'ruins' generation and it wanted to have a good time. It was then, in the 1950s, that the first youth styles surfaced, as a result of their flourishing in Britain and – in particular – the rise of rock'n'roll. In Hamburg two antithetical cultures were formed around music – the true catalyst for youth culture in those years: the 'rockers' and the 'Exis'.²

Relatedly the district's evolution after the war is crucial in order to understand *FC Sankt Pauli*'s more recent history. It was in the postwar period that Wilhelm Koch became one of football's main

1. The original, a waltz composed by Ralph Arthur Roberts in 1912, described the debauchery that took place in the Reeperbahn at night. In 1954 Hans Alber starred in a film of the same name directed by Wolfgang Liebeneiner, which helped popularise the song.
2. Emerging in the 1950s, the *Exis* took their name from the existentialist movement. They were characterised as wearing black clothes, turtle-necked sweaters and long scarves. They liked smoking Gauloises-brand cigarettes and reading French writers such as Albert Camus and Jean-Paul Sartre.

promoters in the city. Gradually the club started its activities again. Thanks to hundreds of volunteers' great efforts the stadium was restored in record time. Therefore, on 17 November 1946, St. Pauli reopened its pitch, playing a friendly against Schalke 04 in front of 30,000 spectators. The match ended with a 1–0 home victory.

The team returned to competitive football in the 1946–7 season, playing in the Hamburg districts' league – a tournament overseen by the British forces occupying the city. Months later, St. Pauli participated in the *Oberliga Nord*, a newly created competition. Its start to the season could not have been better. The team had a string of good matches that produced these dizzying statistics: 22 wins, two draws and only three defeats. Despite this good performance, St. Pauli lost out on the title on goal difference to its nearest rival: Hamburg SC. Its 1–0 home win was not enough to make up for its previous 0–2 defeat. As a result, one goal separated 'the boys in brown' from the title. Despite this disappointment, that team would be remembered by the nickname *Die Wunder-Elf* ('The Magnificent Eleven').

Coming second in the *Oberliga Nord* enabled the club to qualify for the first national tournament held since the end of the war. On 17 July 1948, amid the political crisis caused by the Soviet blockade of Berlin, St. Pauli went onto the turf of the Berlin Olympic Stadium to play in the cup quarter-finals against SG Union Oberschöneweide – the name then for today's Union Berlin between 1948 and 1951. Before 80,000 fans *Die Wunder-Elf* taught the Berliners a lesson with its commanding play. This was demonstrated by the final score of 7–0 to St. Pauli (which included a hat trick by its right midfielder Heinrich Schaffer and two more by centre-forward Fritz Machate, Schaffer's former teammate at Dresdner SC before the war).

In the semi-final St. Pauli came up against 1. FC Nürnberg in a match full of epic moments – at the Neckar-Stadion in Mannheim on 25 July 1948. Even though at half time the Hamburg team was losing 0–2, in the second half it came back to draw – thanks to goals by Heinz 'Tute' Lehmann and Fritz Machate. In extra time, however, a golden volley by Hans Pöschl dashed the sanktpaulianers' hopes. Despite the result, Die Wunder-Elf put St. Pauli at the centre of the German football map. The face of the team was the aforementioned Karl Miller, a footballer born in Hamburg's Neustadt district and butcher's son. Despite making his debut with the brown-and-white squad during the war, Miller played with Dresdner SC, a team with which he won two Tschammer-Pokale – the original name for the DFB-Pokal (DFB Cup) – in 1941 and 1942. Once the war ended, Miller returned to St. Pauli, as well as to his father's shop in Wexstrasse. His return to the shop must be factored in to understand the fine football played by that incredible team. In a period of scarcity Miller offered his teammates extra portions of meat to compensate for their deficient diets. This, together with the security provided by the British occupation of the city at the end of the war, encouraged footballers such as Helmut Schön, Alfred 'Coppi' Beck, Hans Appel and Willi Thiele to play for St. Pauli. Sausages, therefore, were one of the factors that help understand the success of the late 1940s' historic team.

After reaching the semi-final, Die Wunder-Elf continued to make history by qualifying for the national championship in each of the following four seasons. Indeed, in the 1948–9 season FC St. Pauli was once again Oberliga Nord runner up. In the first of those years, the Federal Republic of Germany (FRG) was created, officially sanctioning a division that would last until reunification in 1990.

The 1950–1 season coincided with the end of rationing, which had been in effect since 1938. Now the German championship group was split into two. The winners of each group would play each other in the final to win the title. That year St. Pauli ended last in its group and therefore had to play the following season in the Oberliga Nord. The team was greatly disappointed when it came third and missed going back up a division. Just before, Miller had left the club, and, at the age of 37, retired from professional football. That was a turning point in the club's history. The Die Wunder-Elf's glory days had come to an end. Despite the club's decline, the players achieved one more important triumph. Thanks to their game, local residents came closer to the club, allowing the club to put down roots in the neighbourhood.

The 1950s, when the FRG joined NATO (the North Atlantic Treaty Organization) and triggered the signing of the Warsaw Pact, ended with a golden climax. In the summer of 1959 the Millerntor stadium hosted a unique game, pitching players from several Hamburg clubs against Santos FC. The latter, Brazilian, team was doing its first European tour that year in which it played 22 matches in nine different countries. Throughout the tour the *alvinegro praiano* (black and white beach) team netted a record 78 goals. The club's main forward, with 28 goals, was a young man aged 17 who months earlier had been crowned world champion in Sweden: Edson Arantes do Nascimento, otherwise known as Pelé. Yes, on 11 June 1959 Pelé went on to the turf to take on a mix of Hanseatic players from clubs like Altona 93 or SC Concordia von 1907. That day, around 15,000 spectators enjoyed the Brazilians' game and their numerous goals. The local team brought together Banse, Martens, Herder, Boekenberg, Mueller, Vormelker, Sanmann, Gronau, Gorska, Voss and Pörsche. That night Pelé scored Santos' first goal in the seventh minute. The others were by Coutinho (who scored a hat trick) and Dorval (who netted two).

6

The New Millerntor Stadium

In the 1960s the club went through several changes while the league system was being restructured. The most important, beyond any doubt, was the building of its new stadium. In 1963 Hamburg hosted, as it had done ten years earlier, a new edition of the *Internationale Gartenschau Ausstellung* (International Gardening Exhibition). To accommodate the exhibition grounds the Town Hall requisitioned the old St. Pauli stadium – built in 1946 and located opposite the old fire station. In exchange, the municipal authorities backed the construction of a new sports complex to be located a few hundred metres from the old stadium. This would be in the Heiligengeistfeld, FC St. Pauli's historic epicentre, although moving the stadium to a municipal park elsewhere in the city had been considered at the beginning.

By 1960, work had started on a venue with a capacity of 32,000 spectators, later reduced to 20,269. The reduction was due to the pitch's lack of a drainage system, leading to a series of interventions that did not end until the stadium's renovation in 2007. Despite these hindrances, FC St. Pauli's new Millerntor stadium was eventually unveiled on 29 July 1961. This was for a friendly match in which the *braun-weiß* team played the Bulgarian CDNA Sofia (later CSKA Sofia), with the home side winning 7–4.

At that time the Millerntor stadium was the most modern sports complex in the city. Yet the club needed to overcome the aforementioned problem of pitch drainage, worsened by the city's high rainfall levels. To do so those in charge of looking after the turf chose to make several hundred holes in it and fill them with sand just before a home match against VFV Borussia Hildesheim (on 21 February 1962). The measure was repeated in May but with unwanted results. Clearly far from overcoming the hurdle, the pitch became a sandpit and object of ridicule. Unsurprisingly the joke on the terraces was that the team had become *Sand* Pauli. When player Heinz Deininger became injured – breaking his ankle during a friendly – due to the pitch's poor state, the club's directors reacted angrily, refusing to return to the venue unless the required drainage took place and the grass was in the required condition. For this reason, in June 1962, after reaching an agreement with the local authorities, St. Pauli moved its matches to the Hoheluftstadion – owned by SV Victoria – which was then the oldest ground still standing in the city. The brown-and-white team's exile did not end until 10 November 1963. That day, the club's players returned to the Millerntor Stadion to take on VfL Wolfsburg.

The new stadium's inauguration coincided with a rise in crime in the district, which was linked to the growing prostitution and entertainment industries. It was then that some local gangsters became well known. One was Wilfrid 'Frieda' Shultz, the Godfather of St. Pauli, who went from being a warehouse assistant to owning restaurants in the Reeperbahn and being a partner in hotels and discotheques. In 1959 he took over gambling in the area after the US Mafia helped remove the Italians running a protection racket. In St. Pauli, Frieda's word was gospel. He was tried on 25 occasions but was given only four minor convictions and had good relations with the city's upper classes. In the 1980s, when drugs burst into the neighbourhood, he retired, dying of cancer in 1990. His criminal gang had to coexist with others. These included the GMBH cartel: a ring of pimps (Gerhard Glissmann, Michael 'Mischa' Luchting, Walter Beagle Vogeler and Harald Voerthman). They operated in St. Pauli in the 1970s and 1980s, controlling brothels, peep-show venues, restaurants, casinos and clubs. Other gangs were the Nutella Bande, led by 'Tommy Karate' Born, who took on the GMBH over controlling prostitution; Das Chicago, the third St. Pauli gang which became prominent in the 1980s due to the rise of cocaine; the gunmen 'Wiener' Peter and Werner Pinzer – the St. Pauli assassin; or bikers groups such as the Hamburg section of the Hell's Angels (which was shut down by the police in the 1980s). These groups formed alliances or fought between them from the 1970s, and the gang warfare continued into the following decade over control of weapons and drugs such as cocaine.

7

Creation of the German League

The 1960s were crucial to the evolution of both German football and St. Pauli. On 28 July 1962, DFB members met in Dortmund for their annual convention with the joint aims of appointing their new president and establishing a nationwide professional championship. They chose Hermann Gösmann as president and overwhelmingly backed the new championship: 103 voted in favour, 23 against. A year later the project took form and made possible the first *Bundesliga* championship in the 1963–4 season.

The plan of merging the different regional tournaments into one went back a long way. In 1932 the DFB president at the time, Felix Linnermann, proposed creating a *Reichsliga*. The initiative, however, clashed with the interests of the regional associations who did not want a national tournament because it would reduce their influence on the sport. The tug-of-war that took place between them and the federation had as a backdrop the argument about football's professionalisation. While the DFB originally wanted to keep football as an amateur activity, from October 1932 it tacked sharply to legalise professional football. This measure was overturned by the Nazis when they came to power a year later, so that the aforementioned *Gauligas* – 16 regional championships – were reintroduced.

Six years later, in 1938, the creation of a *Reichsliga* was considered again. This resulted from the *Anschluss* (incorporation of Austria into Nazi Germany, which took place on 12 March that year). The rethink also happened due to Germany's disappointing performance in the World Cup in France. Its humiliating elimination in the quarter-finals by Switzerland, in the Parc de Princes stadium, brought about a deep restructuring of German football.

The authorities again considered the possibility of creating a single competition with the stronger teams, which would help improve German players. If the *Reichsliga* did not happen, the DFB studied the alternative of reducing the number of *Gauligas* from 16 to 5. Nonetheless, all of this was a dead letter after the Second World War broke out. Once again, the project to create a national championship was shelved. Indeed, during the conflict the number of regional tournaments multiplied due to the difficulty teams faced in travelling long distances.

The end of the war led sports activities to be progressively resumed. In the Allied-occupied areas competition returned gradually depending on the state of the infrastructure. In other words it was conditional on whether shelling had damaged the stadiums and made using them impracticable. Yet the Allied division of the country into four areas prevented holding a national league because of the difficulties in obtaining free-movement passes and letters of safe passage.

Football activity definitively yet still unevenly returned across the country from the 1946–7 season. From September 1947 four *Oberligen* were held: Berlin, North, West and South. Meanwhile a fifth (South-West) could not begin for another year because of problems with the French authorities. That was the year in which *FC Sankt Pauli* had won its tournament group phase and then went out in the semi-final against Nuremberg – after a goal in extra time.

Despite the problems resulting from the Soviet Union's blockade of West Berlin on 24 June 1948, the competition continued with few alterations. The start of the Cold War particularly affected the clubs located in the zone occupied by the Russians. These included SG Planitz, winner of the championship in the USSR-controlled sector, which was not allowed to travel to Stuttgart to play in the quarter-finals against Nuremberg on 18 July 1948.

The next year, the FRG was officially created. It was then that the idea of organising a nationwide championship was revisited. However, as already mentioned, the project was not implemented until the early 1960s. Once again it took a World Cup defeat, this time in Chile in 1962, to reactivate the project to create a German league. On that occasion it was the Yugoslav team (managed by Prvoslav Mihajlović and including the players Galić, Radaković and Popović) that beat the Germans 1–0 in the quarter-finals. This new disappointment was a turning point. Indeed, even the *Mannschaft* (German) team manager in Chile, Sepp Herberger, became one of the biggest defenders of creating a national championship: 'If we want to continue to be internationally competitive we must raise our abilities nationally.'

Before the new tournament took shape, West German football was divided into five *Oberligen* (North Germany, South, West, South-West and Berlin). The German Democratic Republic (GDR), however, had a single league. When the *Bundesliga* was created, 46 clubs showed an interest in participating. Of these, only 16 were chosen, according to criteria to do with sport, finance and representativeness. These were Eintracht Braunschweig, Werder Bremen and Hamburg, representing the *Oberliga* North; Borussia Dortmund, 1. FC Cologne, Meidericher SV (now MSV Duisburg), Preussen Münster and Schalke 04 representing the *Oberliga* West; 1. FC. Kaiserslautern and 1. FC Saarbrücken for the *Oberliga* South-West; Eintracht Frankfurt, Karlsruher SC, 1. FC Nürnberg and TSV 1860 Munich for the *Oberliga* South; and Hertha Berlin for the *Oberliga* Berlin. Thirteen of the rejected teams, among them Bayern Munich, made a formal complaint to the DFB. Finally, after years of negotiations and difficulties, the first *Bundesliga* season began on 24 August 1963. The honour of being the new German league's first champion went to 1. FC Cologne.

Meanwhile, because *Sankt Pauli* was not one of the 16 clubs chosen, it was included in the *Regionalliga Nord*, a kind of German second division. In 1964 the Hamburg team came top of its group but then failed to win promotion by coming last in the playoffs. In the 1965–6 season the Pirates once again won the *Regionalliga Nord* but again did not win the promotion they wanted, despite playing well in the playoff. They missed out due to goal difference:

the sanktpaulianers let in two more goals than their rivals, Rot-Weiss (from the state of North Rhine-Westphalia).

The following year, 1967, the club was mired in controversy when its president, Wilhelm Koch, openly accused the club manager, ex-footballer Kurt 'Jockel' Krause, of not spurring on his players enough and not instilling a fighting spirit in them. Yet in the background were the coach's nocturnal visits to a strip club in Große Freiheit (St. Pauli), where he was seen in the company of its owner and several gangsters. It seems that Krause had a 'very close' engagement with the neighbourhood.

That year, on 2 June 1967, a 27-year-old student – Benno Ohnesorg – died from a police bullet on a demonstration. The protest was against the trip to Germany by the Shah of Persia, Reza Pahlavi – the monarch backed by the West who ruled Iran. The visit, together with the presence of US troops in the country, was the spark that ignited the frustration felt by the new generation of youth towards the then-*Große Koalition* (Grand Coalition) government. This had been formed by means of a pact between the Christian Democrat right (*Christlich Demokratische Union Deutschlands*, CDU) and the SPD. The government, furthermore, was led by an ex-NSDAP member (between 1933 and 1945): Chancellor Kurt Georg Kiesinger. Young people's hopes of change were dashed. Disappointment was channelled into what became known as the *Außerparlamentarische Opposition* (APO, Extra-Parliamentary Opposition). This was a heterogeneous grouping of organisations and parties without institutional representation. The failure of the mobilisations against the Emergency Law, which awarded the government special powers, brought on the APO's decline. Its defeat, furthermore, led to the radicalisation of small groups. These include the 2 June Movement, the Red Army Faction (*Rote Armee Fraktion*, RAF) and the Revolutionary Cells (*Revolutionäre Zellen*), which all went underground, opting to pursue armed conflict or urban warfare.

This was the context in which St. Pauli began its decline. The golden age it enjoyed in the 1950s was over. By the end of the next decade there had been a rise in unemployment, due to the bank-ruptcy of several boat companies and the closure of several leisure premises (of which some survived by being turned into discos). Moreover, the AIDS virus had appeared and spread, alongside the aforementioned organised crime. Together the two turned St. Pauli into the place with the worst reputation in West Germany.

PART III

Cult Pirates of the League

8

From the Regional Leagues
to the Second Division

After the *Bundesliga* had been created, St. Pauli continued playing
in the *Regionalliga Nord*. The Hamburg team had had good seasons
but when it came to the playoffs it did not finish the job. Time and
again the story would be repeated in the early 1970s (between
the 1970-1 and 1973-4 seasons). In 1972-3, the brown-and-
white team won its championship and it came second in 1971 and
1974, the latter being the year in which today's nationwide second
division (*Bundesliga 2*) was created. But in each case the end result
meant the club failed to achieve its goal of reaching German football's top flight. FC St. Pauli eventually realised its goal in 1977
when, for the first time in its history, coached by Diethelm Ferner,
it went up to the *Bundesliga*. It had won the championship, four
points ahead of second-place Arminia Bielefeld, after a string of 27
matches undefeated. One of the pillars of the successful team that
season was Walter 'Froschi' Frosch – a defender signed from 1. FC
Kaiserslautern in 1976.[1]

---

1. Frosch played for St. Pauli for six years, scoring 22 goals in 170 matches. In
his first season at the club he helped them win promotion to the *Bundesliga*. The
following year he was out of action for several months due to injury, preventing
him from stopping the club being relegated. In 1982, coinciding with Michael
Lorkowski's arrival on the coach's bench, Frosch left *Sankt Pauli* for Altona FC (von
1893), the club at which he hung up his boots in 1985 aged 35. Frosch's legacy at St.
Pauli goes beyond his sporting successes. For a start, he picked up a record number
of yellow cards in a single season (18 in his debut year with St. Pauli). Frosch
also had a reputation for being a compulsive smoker – smoking (it is said) up to
60 cigarettes a day – and alcoholic, drinking a record of 30 beers in a day. In 2010,
when St. Pauli celebrated its centenary, fans chose him as one of the century's ideal
eleven. After five operations against cancer, the ex-player died of a heart attack on 23
November 2013. See C. Viñas, 'Walter Frosch. El rebelde impertinente', *Panenka*, 27
November 2013.

Winning promotion to the *Bundesliga* coincided with the district being at its peak. To celebrate St. Pauli's promotion, Mariano Pérez, owner of well-known Reeperbahn brothel, the Café Lausen, treated the whole team to a trip to Mallorca. While there, the club played a friendly against RCD Mallorca that ended in a 1–1 draw. The away team stayed at the Hotel Sofía in Palma, where they were offered a complimentary drink. The players thought it was fruit juice but it was actually sangria. Later that day, during the match, the *Sankt Pauli* coach had to point out where the goal was to some of his players – such as young Rolf Peter '*Buttje*' Rosenfeld who had never drunk alcohol before. Also surprising was the attitude of several players who tried to score from outrageous places on the field. Behind their desire to score was the promise by the Café Lausen owner of treating players that scored to a 'special visit' to one of his nightspots.

St. Pauli made a promising start in the new league, including winning 3–1 against Werder Bremen at a packed Millerntor stadium thanks to two goals by Dietmar 'Didi' Demuth. However, its adventure in the first division only lasted one season. Its 16-strong squad was too small to meet the challenge of playing top-flight German football. And this was not helped by the injury suffered by its powerhouse Frosch.

But the most notable aspect of St. Pauli's first experience in the *Bundesliga* was its directors' decision to play 12 out of 17 home matches in stadiums different to its own. Claiming that this would provide greater revenues for the club, matches were played in none other than the Volksparkstadion: home of HSV – St. Pauli's arch rivals. Undoubtedly it was a very controversial decision. And it was a disaster from a sporting point of view. The team only picked up 7 points – after winning two games and drawing three. The other matches ended in defeat.

A saving grace was a 2–0 home win on the sixth match day of the 1977–8 season, against Kevin Keegan's Hamburg. That brought one of the season's few big cheers. It was 3 September; the *Sankt Paulianers* took the lead thanks to a 30th-minute goal by striker

Frank Gerber.[2] Despite having clear chances to increase its lead, it was not until the 87th minute that midfielder Wolfgang Kulka sealed victory with a second goal. On the terraces the few hundred St. Pauli fans that had travelled to the game celebrated in style, half in a state of shock, half in ecstasy. So too did the players who had been duly spurred on by the *Sankt Pauli* coach before the match. Diethelm Ferner had told them, 'Lads, they don't take us seriously here', reminding them of the local newspaper headlines the day before, such as 'We will win 8–0!' (*'Wir gewinnen 8:0!'*), which predicted a thrashing by HSV.

Putting rivalries to one side, HSV was at the time one of the fashionable clubs in German football, and deservedly so. It had won the German Cup in 1976 and the European Cup the following year. Furthermore, it included the aforementioned Kevin Keegan, winner of two Golden Boot awards (in 1978 and 1979). So this was not just any victory for St. Pauli. It was also the first time that a Hamburg derby had been played in the *Bundesliga*, and as such it raised expectations greatly. Around 50,000 spectators attended the match, an unheard-of feat at the time, and one only repeated 32 years later. The locals' game was so flawed that even their own supporters cheered on the St. Pauli players – something unthinkable today. Around 9,000 St. Pauli supporters turned out for the next game, when average attendance was little more than a thousand.

But despite this worthy victory, St. Pauli lost 22 matches in its first *Bundesliga* season. As well as being a brief stay, it was financially problematic. The temporary move to the Volksparkstadion did not generate the expected revenues. Less spectators turned out than was hoped and profits were minimal. That season, St. Pauli ended at the bottom of the table with just 18 points – having scored 44 but let in 86.

---

2. Gerber ended the season as the team's top scorer with 16 goals. Years later, in June 2002, he returned to St. Pauli to join its management. The team's poor progress meant that the ex-forward would end up as head coach for the Pirates from December that year, replacing Joachim Philipkowski. Despite not being able to avoid relegation, he managed the team for the 2003–4 season in the *Regionalliga Nord*. After a string of bad results, and with the club facing further relegation, a narrow 1–0 defeat at the hands of Rot-Weiss Essen in March 2004 sparked Gerber's sacking.

Relegation led the club to play in the *Bundesliga Nord* again. In the 1978–9 season, the team ended the championship in sixth place. Financial problems, however, put a question mark over the organisation's survival. One of the factors behind such a delicate situation was the drop in attendance at the stadium. While the average number of spectators in the 1977–8 season was 13,776 people, in the subsequent period the figure fell to 2,396. In the middle of the club's 70th anniversary, several sponsors told club chiefs that they would stop working with St. Pauli (including funding the club through advertising). This, they said, was to avoid being associated with 'a pathetic club'. Their withdrawal led to players going on to the pitch wearing shirts with patches covering the old sponsors' logos. This, added to an accrued debt of 2.7 million marks, took FC St. Pauli close to bankruptcy.

Because of the club's inability to honour payments the DFB refused to renew its professional licence, automatically relegating it to the amateur *Oberliga Nord* – the third division of German football. The team's coach heard about the DFB's refusal on the radio. He immediately rang the federation's HQ in Frankfurt to confirm the news. Both he and the squad were in a state of shock, which was followed by the team letting in four goals in its next match (against Preussen Münster). Several players decided to leave because of the club's financial and relegation problems. The club, like its neighbourhood, was clearly in decline. Its critical financial situation made it necessary to put together a team with young amateur footballers (coached by Werner Pokropp, a St. Pauli player in the 1960s).

The club's precariousness reached unexpected levels. Players had to use their own transport for away games – for instance when travelling to Hannover to play against Arminia – and were even responsible for driving the club's dilapidated coach to games a long way away. On another occasion, St. Pauli rented a coach in such a bad state that its players were intoxicated or dazed by the fumes from the exhaust pipe. Often these trips were paid for by supporters wishing to share the journey with the squad in the *Mannschaftsbus* (team bus). And this was all because of the debts the club had with different coach companies. The club's lack of resources inspired unexpected creativity from its management. The club even sold cakes made by club members to raise funds. At times the sale of these products and coffee exceeded ticket sales. In the autumn, Pokropp was replaced as coach by Kuno Böge, the former Holstein Kiel manager. In the end, despite some defeats, the team came tenth and avoided relegation.

Undoubtedly that season became the tipping point. Something was changing at St. Pauli. The fact that it was on the verge of disappearing because of financial hardship brought forth a change of mindset. In 1980 St. Pauli began its gradual transformation – a metamorphosis that led it to become a *kult* club. But changes were not limited to its sporting side. During the 1980s, the neighbourhood underwent significant convulsions as a result of real estate speculation and the evolution of the sex industry the area was associated with. Readjustments that 'pushed away those that had been at the fore of a century of life in the neighbourhood: the sailors and workers'. These changes were also linked to the reconversion and automation of the shipbuilding industry, which would lead to a notable shrinking of the workforce.

9

Transition from Neighbourhood
to *Kult* Club

The 1980–1 season brought hope back to St. Pauli fans. Kuno Böge's disciples qualified for the final of the amateur championship, having won their group. Despite losing that match against FC Cologne, the new enthusiasm did not dwindle. The team had come top in the regular championship – a feat that would normally mean automatic promotion – but that year the DFB had decided to restructure the competition and suspended promotion from the *Oberliga* to the second division. The federation made up for this by offering St. Pauli the chance of travelling to play a series of friendly matches in Africa, which is how the *sanktpaulianers* got to tour countries such as Kenya, Tanzania and Somalia. The person then responsible for managing the players was Michael Lorkowski, who had replaced Böge as the man in charge of the first team. With their new coach, FC St. Pauli came sixth in its qualifying group.

Germany at the time was marked by the end of the socialist-liberal coalition government – due to the crisis triggered by NATO's deployment of West German missiles – and the chancellorship of Helmut Kohl (CDU general secretary). This was the context of the 1982–3 season, when FC St. Pauli once again had promotion within its grasp. Twelve points ahead of its nearest rival, the *Sankt Paulianers* approached the playoff with confidence. But they lost three of the six playoff matches, very likely because of the youth and inexperience of its players (whose average age was 22.3). This made it impossible to go up a division and the team stayed in the *Oberliga Nord* for another year.

The club's luck seemed to change in the next season (1983–4) when St. Pauli finally went up to the *Bundesliga 2* at the expense of the Werder Bremen amateur team, which had actually finished the footballing year two points ahead of its Hamburg rivals but could not enter the promotion playoff because it was a subsidiary. Once again, St. Pauli's stay in the all-German second division was short-lived. The *Sankt Paulianers* were relegated by just one point and ten goals. That was the difference between the team and FC Homburg directly above it in sixteenth place. Once again, the white-and-brown team found itself in the *Oberliga Nord*. Its precarious financial situation did not allow it to adequately prepare for this division. The team was relegated, but despite that the fans felt proud of their team, built around players who were born in Hamburg, such as André Golke, Jürgen Gronau and Stefan Studer (curiously having learned the game in HSV's lower-level teams.) The team had character and gave its utmost on the pitch. Not for nothing players became known popularly as *Die Jungen Wilden* (the young savages).

In the end, led by Lorkowski, St. Pauli managed to reach the promotion playoff. This time, unlike on previous occasions, the *Sankt Paulianer* players did not go wrong. In the key match, against Rot-Weiss Essen, St. Pauli prevailed with a convincing 3–0 win. That was the last game for the German coach on the bench of the Hamburg club, ending his era with the success of gaining promotion to the *Bundesliga 2*.

The club's sporting and financial situation, however, was nothing to celebrate – quite the opposite. The 1980s witnessed one of the FC St. Pauli's most significant economic crises. The danger of the club disappearing was real. Clearly all this had an impact on the sports budget. There was no money to sign prominent players and the club had to form a squad packed with youngsters. There was even a drop in the number of spectators at matches. Nevertheless, in the middle of the decade things began to change. It was then that the club went through its transition from a traditional club to cult club, an era that coincided with the boom in the squatting-linked autonomous movement.

The origins of the squatters' movement in Hamburg go back to 19 April 1973, when number 39 Ekhofstraße was occupied in protest at the building of 450 luxury flats in the district (Hohen-felde). At the beginning, the occupation stirred a significant wave of solidarity across the city, with meetings being held to discuss both the need for protests and the projects that were now to be done in the neighbourhood. They also led to a youth centre being built, which became an important meeting place for local young people who did not have a space like this.

This was the first occupation in the city, following the example of those carried out in Berlin and Frankfurt. It clearly caused a major problem for the institutions. They criminalised the movement by accusing it of being a cover for terrorists and criminals, and subjected it to continual police harassment.[1] Eventually, on the morning of 23 May, nearly 600 police evicted the Ekhofstraße squatters. Seventy activists were arrested, of which 33 were accused of belonging to or supporting a criminal organisation. Despite the eviction being successful, the occupation was an inspiration for the diverse squatting phenomenon that emerged in Hafenstraße a decade later.

It was precisely that street of abandoned mansions next to the port that became the epicentre of St. Pauli's transition to a cult club. In 1981 a group of activists occupied eight of these buildings. Their pioneering action turned Hafenstraße into a symbol of resistance for the German autonomist movement. Soon there would be a proliferation of squats, independent bookshops, people's kitchens, 'infoshops', non-conventional beer-houses, concert halls and gal-

---

1. Squatting has its roots in the duality that the German radical movement developed in the 1970s as a result of a series of strikes against overtime in factories. On the one hand there were the 'Mollis' – punks and activists advocating and practising direct action – and on the other the 'Müslis', defenders of passive resistance and with positions close to those defended years later by the Greens. The first group developed a way of life based on the do-it-yourself principle. Furthermore, they defended radical social transformation through a 'chain insurrection'. The Situationist movement's influence could be seen from their style: jeans, black bomber jackets, balaclavas or bike helmets. They dressed this way to avoid being identified by the police and also to create a homogenous and intimidating group. After incidents in Berlin's Kreuzberg neighbourhood in December 1980, these autonomous activists began to be called the Black Bloc (der Schwarze Block). Rondinelli, Ribelli, Sociali e Romantici, p. 51.

leries. These were all different expressions of an alternative way of life. But the decade was a turbulent one, full of tension and clashes with police. In 1986 the police besieged the buildings, destroyed furniture and property, and evicted six occupants. At that time all action was met with a counter, and a demonstration of 2,000 people was improvised. This was not the first or last of its kind. Soon marches supporting the Hafenstraße squatters were held in other cities and even other countries (such as the Netherlands and Denmark). Anti-police riots took place within these. The high point of the solidarity action was on 20 December when 12,000 demonstrators marched through Hamburg's streets. This kind of public pressure did not cease until, in autumn 1987, the squatters reached an agreement with the Town Hall consisting of 'drawing up a contract that gives residents some security against possible evictions and harassment by police'.

That year the football season ended with St. Pauli in third place – that is, with the chance of gaining promotion. Back on the first match day of the 1986–7 season, a group of around 60 Hamburg punks and autonomists went to a match at the Millerntor stadium for the first time. 'FC St. Pauli was ideal' for them, basically because the ground was less than a kilometre from the Hafenstraße. Their presence, furthermore, happened to coincide with team coach Willi Reimann's desire to promote an 'alternative football' built from 'commitment, passion, a fighting spirit, and the heart'. To achieve this, he could not have had better allies than the Hafenstraße fans, as they became commonly known. The presence of these young *Sankt Paulianer* fans – visibly antifascist and linked to the squatters' movement – was not at all liked by other teams' fans who insultingly labelled them as *Zecken* (spongers or parasitical ticks). The term was proudly reappropriated by the Pirate fans, as demonstrated in their hallmark chants: 'We are *zecken* | Anti-social *zecken* | We sleep under the bridge | Or in social missions' *('Wir sind Zecken | Asoziale Zecken | Wir Schlafen unter Brücken | Unt in der Banhofsmission')*.

Also that season, St. Pauli and HSV drew each other in the second round of the cup. It had been eight years since the two teams had met in an official competition. Despite St. Pauli hopes, the match – played on 19 November 1986 – was not another proud moment in the club's history. Rather, it was the opposite. St. Pauli was knocked out 6–0 and HSV reached the final. The *Sankt Paulianers* were spurred on by the result, however, and followed their defeat with twelve unbeaten matches. This led them to come third and qualify for the promotion playoff. Their opponent, over two games, was FC 08 Homburg, the green-and-white team from Sarre that had ended second from bottom in the *Bundesliga*. The first (away) game was a disaster, with St. Pauli losing 3–1. It was forecast that the return match would be a blistering one, not just because of the fans who packed out the stadium but because the game was played in the middle of June. If the relegation/promotion match had any particular importance it was because it was broadcast live, by the RTL TV network. This helped start and spread the 'St. Pauli legend' across Germany. People had an image of the 'historic losers' who, despite winning 2–1, failed to win promotion. Around 18,500 rebel outsiders, despite the outcome, did not for a second cease to cheer on their team and wave hundreds of flags. At that time this was an atmosphere without parallel in the *Bundesliga*.

Such joy in defeat showed the uniqueness of St. Pauli and its fans. While others would have sunk into depression after missing the chance of promotion by losing at home, the *Sankt Paulianers* celebrated the match. The most important thing was not the final score or any sporting success. At St. Pauli, at least, these had never been a priority. Nor did fans have regrets. Quite the opposite: they displayed their happiness for the club having attempted promotion without losing the St. Pauli soul.

If becoming a cult club that depended on its autonomist and punk followers[2] and media coverage, it was also shaped by trans-

---

2.   The impact of punk rock on the section of fans that emerged in the 1980s was considerable. The meeting points for many of these supporters were the concerts of local groups such as the Slime. These took place in the Markthalle, Onkel Otto and

formations affecting the district, such as the collapse of the local sex industry caused by the AIDS explosion at the time.[3] As already mentioned, generally St. Pauli was in full decline. It went from having 31,000 inhabitants in 1970 to having 22,000 in 1985. All of this helped reduce rents and increase the squatting of empty houses, which drew students, artists and other young low-earners to the area. In the long term, however, their arrival meant the development of a bohemian and alternative community that would end up increasing demand for housing and push prices back up. This gentrification led to a deep metamorphosis of St. Pauli's urban fabric.

Cobra clubs. The alternative music scene and youth subcultures played an essential role in the emergence of the many young punks that started to actively support St. Pauli at that time. This trail was clear even from the musical selection played through the Millerntor speakers, which included punk/Oi! bands such as the British group Cock Sparrer. One of their tracks, 'We're Coming Back', is played before the start of the second half. Hamburg's own punk music first emerged in 1975 with the band Big Balls and the Great White Idiot. They became known after their first LP *Big Balls* (Teldec, 1977) – a version of the famous Sex Pistols album *Anarchy in the UK* that was baptised 'Anarchy in Germany'. The group, made up of Peter Grund (drums, vocals), 'Baron Adolf Kaiser' (vocals), Wolfgang Lorenz (guitar) and the brothers Alfred and Atli Grund (bass and guitar, respectively), was characterised by its extreme and transgressive live performances. In these, its lead singer dressed in a Nazi uniform. Later they were joined on the scene by others, such as Slime, The Buttocks and Razzia. From 1979 the Hamburg punk scene was centred on the *Fischmarkt* area thanks to the opening of clubs hosting concerts in the genre: for instance, Krawall 2000 became a flagship venue. But everything ended when a punk crew from Osnabrück city insulted a group of prostitutes, leading their pimps to intervene and unceremoniously destroy the club. After that episode, the punks moved to Karolinenviertel, an area to the north of St. Pauli that included places such as the Rip-Off record shop, the Markstuben pub, and the Klick cinema. Later, the punk scene took root in other working-class areas such as Schanze and St. Pauli itself. In the first years in which punk blossomed in Hamburg the landmark bands included FTE Buttocks (founded in 1978) and the Coroners (in 1977), which became very popular as a result of a punk version of a classic German Christmas carol *Ihr Kinderlein Kommet*. The forming of a Hamburg punk scene was helped by the city's links with Britain, enabling us to see why Hamburg developed a more independent and stronger punk scene than the rest of the country. Petroni, *St. Pauli siamo no.*, pp. 70–1.

3.   The impact of the epidemic on the neighbourhood was clear from the different clubs and brothels that had to shut down. Having lost their work, many of the prostitutes working in them ended up committing suicide, while others died of the disease. The first death from AIDS in Hamburg was on 29 October 1983. In August 1985 there were nearly 40 cases of the virus in the city. Rondinelli, *Ribelli, Sociali e Romantici*, p. 49; Petroni, *St. Pauli siamo noi*, p. 106.

In just five years – the period spanning the mid-1980s to 1991 – *FC Sankt Pauli* became a landmark team, a real virtue for a team whose highest position in the *Bundesliga* was tenth in the 1988–9 season. Let's rewind a little to the beginning. In 1984 the team had got back up to the second division. It did not manage to stay up, but then it spent two seasons in the *Oberliga* and gained promotion in 1986. Finally, in 1988, St. Pauli returned to the highest German division.

Putting the club's sporting trajectory to one side, that season Millerntor reaffirmed itself as a stadium where you could have a totally different footballing experience. Its fan base was consolidated and the Hafenstraße-Block continued to grow. Meanwhile, in September 1987, the board of directors took to the federation the proposal to change the club's name. Their wish was for it to be renamed *FC Deutscher Ring St. Pauli*. In other words, the name of the club's sponsor – a local building society – would be added. In the end, the DFB rejected the proposal. Despite the controversy over this, the team reached the end of the season with a chance of promotion. St. Pauli, under coach Helmut Schulte, only needed a draw at the SSV Ulm 1846 ground to seal its return to top-flight German football on the last match day of the championship. The game, played on 29 May 1988, was decided after a great 25-yard strike from midfielder Dirk Zander. That 29th-minute goal was the only one of the match. The victory at the Donaustadion triggered an outpouring of joy in St. Pauli. For only the second time in its history the *Sankt Paulianers* would play in the first division. That night around 6,000 people went to Hamburg airport to welcome the players – some of whom ended up being carried aloft by fans. It was chaos. Dozens of cars and motorbikes escorted the footballers' coach to the Reeperbahn – the epicentre of the celebrations.

Promotion meant increased interest in the club, which coincided with the progressive transformation of the Millerntor terraces. Joining St. Pauli's lifetime supporters – occupying the same spot week in, week out and with little interest in politics[4] – were a group

---

4. In the first half of the 1980s a quarter of St. Pauli's fans were women. K. Langosch. 'Fußball und Frauen-Warum Nicht?', *Hamburger Abendblatt* (18 November 1986), p. 21.

of young people who, according to the veterans, made a lot of noise and dressed strangely. As already mentioned, these new fans mostly came from the punk and autonomist movement. This was clear from their coloured Mohicans, and their leather jackets full of patches. It was from then that FC St. Pauli became known as a club 'with an alternative and anti-system lifestyle'.

The 1980s was a socially troubled time for Hamburg. Since the late 1970s the city, and particularly the St. Pauli neighbourhood, had been feeling the effects of a bad recession. Young people suffered from dropping out of school, unemployment and a lack of affordable housing that meant they were unable to leave their family homes. Stagnation and lack of opportunities 'were the conditions leading young people to seek an alternative way of life'. Many such people were students that had to leave their studies and then found it difficult to find work and housing. They were the seed of the city's autonomist movement.

All the same, the importance of this and the squatters' movement in Hamburg would not have been what it was without the impact of another movement. This was the anti-nuclear struggle, which emerged in response to the energy policies introduced after the 1973 oil crisis – including the adoption of nuclear energy to solve the energy crisis. Events taking place in Brokdorf were important in this regard. The government had decided (in the 1970s) to build a nuclear energy plant in this municipality – located in the Unterelbe region (less than 70 kilometres from Hamburg). In response, a protest movement – with significant involvement from the radical left – emerged, calling a protest on 30 October 1976. Around 8,000 protesters attended, some of whom occupied the area where the plant was to be built – to be violently evicted by the police. Buoyed by their success in mobilising, the organisers called a second demonstration on 14 November, which over 40,000 people joined and which ended in clashes between activists and state forces (who fired tear gas from their helicopters).

Eventually a judge found irregularities in the plant construction project regarding the elimination of toxic waste. This led the work, which had been carried out since 1976, to be halted. Four years later, however, the building work was restarted, sparking new protests. After the parliamentary elections of October 1980,[5] the SPD – in conjunction with the CDU – confirmed that the construction of the plant would continue. In response, a new demonstration of 8,000 people attacked the plant surroundings and even set fire to one of the water cannons used by police. The success of this direct action helped keep up the resistance, which now included throwing petrol bombs at the electricity company responsible for the plant as well as its directors' homes. Yet this kind of protest split the anti-nuclear movement. One wing of it aimed to strengthen its position by negotiating with the government, and the other – the autonomist wing – wished to keep the movement as an independent and self-determined force.

This debate was the backdrop to the demonstration planned to end outside the SPD's extraordinary conference in Hamburg city centre on 2 February 1981. The police deployed 2,500 officers to guarantee the safety of the 370 Social Democrat delegates attending the event. When autonomist activists tried to get to the centre and convention hall, unrest broke out, including the breaking of windows of banks, luxury hotels, insurance companies and sex shops. Violent clashes with the police also took place. In all, nearly 300 protesters and police were injured. The autonomist movement was gaining strength and made a clear statement of intent in the

---

5. That summer a big mobilisation took place, this time in the municipality of Gorleben (Lower Saxony or the Wendland) to avoid the construction of a radioactive waste storage plant. Drilling to test the ground's suitability had begun in 1979, and to stop it the anti-nuclear movement called a demonstration for 3 May 1980. Nearly 5,000 people turned out and occupied the land declaring the formation of the Wendland Free Republic (*Republik Freies Wendland*). The activists set up a community of around a thousand people with their own self-organised parliament, church, market, clinic, canteen, hairdresser, greenhouse, kindergarten and even solar-powered showers. This was unprecedented in the country. On 3 June 1980, on its 32nd day, around 8,000 police officers cleared the camp. The legal argument for the eviction was the supposed violation of several laws (such as the state's Forestry Law, as well as the Land Law and Registration Law). The eviction proceeded without incidents as those occupying had opted for passive resistance. The Wendland episode became a turning point for the German autonomist movement. See G. Zint, *Republik Freies Wendland* (Frankfurt: Zweitausendeins, 1980).

declaration read at the end of the protest: 'Our strength [...] comes from our political and strategic ideas, from our communication structures, from our ways of life [...] If the law threatens our life, then we have the right to break the law.'

Soon after, a march was called on 28 February 1981, which turned out to be a mass protest. Over 100,000 people marched to the Brokdorf gates to protest the restarting of building. Due to the possibility of new incidents, 30,000 German police were brought in to protect the plant area. Furthermore, they prevented several coachloads of activists from Berlin, Stuttgart and Munich from getting to the area.

On 26 April 1986, the accident at the Chernobyl nuclear plant (in Ukraine) took place, affecting nearly 600,000 people. After the disaster, anti-nuclear mobilising regained momentum across Germany.[6] One of the protests was against the building of the Wackersdorf nuclear reprocessing plant opposite the Brokdorf plant. The resistance against the plant building gave a big boost to the West German autonomist movement, reinforcing an independent political pole that was able to fight on other fronts.

In 1981, Hamburg witnessed social convulsion and the growth of oppositional movements (such as the antipatriarchy, antifascist and anti-militarist movements). In the autumn, the first squatting took place in empty houses on Hafenstraße and Bernand Nocht Straße – two streets next to the docks on the north side of the Elbe (i.e. in the middle of the St. Pauli district). These uninhabited buildings

---

6. On 7 June a march was called which Hamburg autonomists joined. A convoy of coaches, vans and cars tried to reach the gates of the Brokdorf plant. The police tried to block the nearly 10,000 people en route but people broke through the lines, leading to clashes. Eighteen helicopters and special police units took on what the media labelled 'chaoten'. The following day, 800 anti-nuclear activists gathered in St. Pauli, in the Heiligengeistfeld at the foot of an anti-aircraft tower, and were kettled and arrested. The detained – of which there were more ecologists than anarchists – were taken to different Hamburg police stations. That night, barricades were raised and burned in Hafenstraße in protest against the arrests. On 8 June, while the anti-nuclear protesters were still under arrest, St. Pauli was playing at Millerntor the first leg of the play-off to win promotion to the second division. The match, against ASC Schöppingen, ended with a 3–1 home victory – a score that enabled the *Sankt Paulianer* squad to go up to the *Bundesliga 2*. Petroni, *St. Pauli siamo noi*, p. 101.

provided unsatisfied young people (the unemployed, punks, anarchists) with environments in which to live, socialise and develop community projects. They incorporated in them people's kitchens, experimental theatre workshops, alternative libraries and concert areas. Before being occupied, the premises – owned by the Town Hall – were earmarked to become offices as part of a substantial urban renewal project for the docklands. This was to be completed by 1989 to coincide with the port's 800th anniversary. To carry out this intervention, the Senate and the SAGA (*Siedlungs-Aktiengesellschaft Altona*) construction company joined forces. In 1985 they did the paperwork and inspections required for the buildings to be declared uninhabitable, justifying their demolition. That March, a large police operation accompanied inspection of the first three houses in the area.

The squatting in Hafenstraße, which soon spread to the Altona and Hohenfelde districts, was inspired by the similar movement that developed in Berlin in the late 1970s and early 1980s.[7] But

---

7. In 1980–1, the first wave of occupations took place – a total of 160 (mainly in East Berlin). In that period a public-financing scandal emerged in relation to the Bautechnik AG company, owned by architect Dietrich Garski (the reason why it became known as the Garksi Scandal). Several of Berlin's elected officials were involved in the tax fraud, as was the local Berliner Bank. At the time, 100,000 Berliners were homeless. The scandal aided the spontaneous occupation of properties taking place in Berlin neighbourhoods such as Kreuzberg, where buildings shelled and abandoned in the Second World War were taken over. The new occupants organised themselves in '*Instandsetzung*' – a German word that means both occupation and repair. On 12 December 1980 the police performed roundups to stop a new wave of squatting. This led to a riot, known as the '12/12 riot', which inspired solidarity actions and helped spread the movement across the country. During the confrontation with police the autonomist activists won – for the first time – the support of many local residents. Using the slogan 'Legal, illegal, I don't give a shit' ('*Legal, illegal, scheißegal*') 3,000 people organised themselves autonomously in a community. It was a phenomenon that soon spread to other German cities such as Munich, Frankfurt, Cologne and Hamburg. Almost a year after the Berlin crackdown, on 22 September 1981, eight squats were evicted in the city. In the clashes that followed a young man, Klaus Jurgen Rattay, died, hit by a bus while running from the police. That was a turning point. Support for the movement was dwindling and the authorities came up with a new strategy. To avoid more violent episodes they would try and reach agreements with squatters to regularise renting of their building. The last eviction in Berlin took place in 1984. See Geronimo, *Fire and Flames: A History of the German Autonomist Movement* (Oakland: PM Press, 2011), pp. 99–106 and Petroni, *St. Pauli siamo noi*, pp. 65–7.

Hamburg quickly established itself as a benchmark for the squatters' movement. It attracted punks, anarchists and young alternative activists from other cities. They were able to introduce an alternative way of life to the city in bookshops, bars, cafes, concert halls, art galleries and social centres that they themselves created and managed. A whole community experience that 'rejected the little that the mainstream was able to offer them, to develop their own forms of alternative life with minimal interference by the state'.[8] They were society's outsiders who saw themselves reflected in Italian movements of the 1960s linked to the extra-parliamentary communist left (such as Lotta Continua[9] and Potere Operaio[10]). These youth did self-organisation and direct action (strikes, squatting and street fighting) and became known as 'autonomists'. The magazine *Autonomie* played a prominent role in the movement. Published from 1975 to 1985 – at first edited in both Hamburg and Frankfurt – *Autonomie* had as its main subjects the legacy of Nazism in Germany, revolutionary developments in Iran, the anti-nuclear movements, repression, the Italian autonomist project and a class analysis of imperialism in the industrialised countries. The magazine acted as a bridge between the 1968 student revolts and the 1980s autonomist scene.

The Hamburg authorities' desire to avoid a repetition of the Berlin squatting led to the passing of the so-called '24-hour regula-

---

8.   Davidson, *Pirates, Punks and Politics*, p. 74.
9.   Organisation founded in Turin in November 1969 by workers and students. Its main leaders were Adriano Sofri, Giorgio Pietrostefani and Enrico Deaglio. It became a political party after its 1975 conference. Poor election results and criticisms inside the party led it to dissolve a year later. Many of its cadres would end up in a range of parties – from the Italian Socialist Party to the Greens, Rifondazione Comunista or the Radical Party. To know more about its trajectory see A. Cazzullo, *I ragazzi che volevano faré la Rivoluzione 1968–1978: Storia de Lotta Continua* (Milan: Mondadori, 1998).
10.   A far-left group active between 1967 and 1973, and flagship organisation for 'operaismo' – the Marxist tendency structured around conflict in factories and the figure of the 'mass worker'. Standing out among its main theoreticians were two of its founders: the sociologist Toni Negri and the physicist Franco Piperno. The organisation suffered a split In June 1973. Part of its discourse was picked up by Autonomia Operaia. See A. Grandi, *La generazione degli anni perduti: Storie di Potere Operaio* (Turin: Einaudi, 2003).

tion', which made it impossible to occupy a building in the city for longer than this amount of time. At first this meant that squatting would initially remain underground. To attempt to normalise their situation squatters made a public proposal to avoid evictions and negotiate the use of premises through what they called 'administrative autonomy'. Although a study found that the costs of regulating the buildings would be much lower than demolishing them, the Hamburg Senate rejected the squatters' proposal.

It was not until the next elections, held in summer 1982, that negotiations were resumed to avoid new evictions. Finally the local government, then headed by Social Democrat mayor Klaus von Dohnanyi, agreed to the so-called '1983 Truce', which guaranteed the right to reside in the premises until 1986. In that period relations between the authorities and squatters oscillated between dialogue and cordiality, on the one hand, and repression and conflict, on the other.[11] The fact that SAGA accepted mediation with squatters' lawyers made it possible to agree to put back resolving the dispute until 1986.

Hafenstraße thereby became one of the epicentres of the German autonomist movement. Unlike its Berlin counterparts, who were mainly students and middle-class youth, the Hamburg squatters came from the so-called lumpenproletariat – that is, from humble working-class origins. This background also explains the relationship between the Hafenstraße squatters and football – a sport linked to the working class since its popularisation in Britain in the late nineteenth century. In the street next to the docks there was

---

11. In January 1985 the authorities drafted a plan that included forced inspections, declarations of unfitness for habitation and demolitions of Hafenstraße buildings. In April the Senate decided to go ahead with the evictions and demolition, setting 9 May as the date to begin this. The squatters gave a symbolic response. A delegation of Hafenstraße residents dug a war axe into the front door of a senator's home. Over the coming months the police ramped up the pressure on Hafenstraße. On 1 August, while attempting to arrest a young man, they clashed with around 50 punks. The incidents were so serious that the police brought in the Mobile Operational Unit (*Mobile Einsatzkommando*) – a police tactical unit. As a result of the unrest, 16 members of the security forces were injured. Petroni, *St. Pauli siamo noi*, p. 92.

much political agitation, such as to win support for the RAF[12] prisoners who had been on hunger strike since 1984 in protest against their solitary confinement.[13] Other agitation, the following year, was against the murder in Frankfurt of the young antifascist Günter Sare, on 28 September, while demonstrating to prevent a National Democratic Party of Germany (*Nationaldemokratische Partei Deutschlands*, NPD)[14] meeting in a municipal hall in Frankfurt

---

12.   In the 1980s, different media outlets did not hesitate to claim that RAF members were hiding out in Hafenstraße buildings. The rumour was started, on 16 October 1985, by Hamburg police's head of intelligence services Christian Lochte.

13.   The solidarity campaign with the RAF prisoners consisted of organising several mobilisations, most of which ended in clashes with the security forces. Activists blockaded the entrances to the port with burning barricades and threw stones at the police and fire brigade. Meanwhile demonstrations reached Hamburg city centre and caused massive damage to the shop windows of luxury goods stores. Faced with this, a CDU senator publicly stated that Hafenstraße had become a 'lawless area'. Petroni, *St. Pauli siamo noi*, p. 92.

14.   A neo-Nazi organisation created in Hanover on 28 November 1964 and led by the ex-CDU member Friedrich Thielen. The party was formed by different forces nostalgic for National Socialism, such as the German Imperial Party (*Deutsche Reichspartei*) the Patriotic Union (*Vaterländische Union*), Strong Together Germany (*Gesamtdeutsche Partei*), the German Party (*Deutsche Partei*), the League of Expellees and cadre from the most reactionary wing of the Free Democratic Party (*Freie Demokratische Partei*) led by Heinrich Fassbender. In 1965 the NPD stood in the federal elections, winning 2 per cent of the vote but no seat in the Bundestag. The creation of the CDU and SPD grand coalition led many disillusioned conservative voters to turn to the NPD. From 1966 it had MPs in seven regional parliaments. In the 1969 federal polls it won 4.3 per cent of the vote with judge Adolf von Thadden – a German Imperial Party member – as its main candidate. [Translator's note]: Adolf von Thadder has been revealed as a likely MI6 spy. In the 1970s the organisation went into decline and became politically marginal. From the beginning of the 1990s the NPD was led by Udo Voigt, a former air force captain, who relaunched the party after the drift towards national conservatism under his predecessors (Martin Mußgnug and the particularly extreme Günter Deckert). In 2005 Voigt reached an electoral agreement with the German People's Union (*Deutsche Volksunion*, DVU), the *Deutschlandpakt*, which helped the organisation regain parliamentary representation. Four years later the alliance broke down. In 2011, however, the DVU merged into the NPD. In the 2014 European elections the NPD – from that year led by former army sergeant Frank Franz – won a European parliamentary seat (with 1 per cent of the vote). From 2001 the party faced different legal proceedings to make it illegal. The first was by the Gerhard Schröder (SPD) government. None were successful. The Constitutional Court rejected them arguing that they endangered the state's network of undercover agents (*V-Mann*). The NPD had around 5,500 members and 350 elected representatives. The party has a discourse that is racist, anti-immigrant, anti-Semitic, Islamophobic and revisionist, and aimed

(Bürgerhaus Gallus).[15] There were also the 'port days' (*hafentage*) that became one of the German autonomous movement's most important gatherings. Pretty soon Hafenstraße emerged as a symbol for the international squatters' movement and, in doing so, helped the rebirth of the city neighbourhood (*Kiez*).

Nonetheless, the situation in the area changed sharply in 1986 when the security forces began harassing its residents – then around a hundred – coinciding with the end of the agreed truce. Both squatters and other activists – mainly grouped in the *Initiative Hafenstraße* solidarity network – responded by carrying out direct actions and publicising the role and aims of the squatters' movement, in order to influence public opinion.

On 28 October 1986, 500 police officers were deployed in Hafenstraße to evict 13 SAGA properties. To prevent the evictions those occupying the buildings dug in on the rooftops, from where they threw all kinds of objects at the riot police (rocks, bricks, metal balls, gas canisters, rubbish and paint). As the doors were reinforced inside, the police needed to bring in several locksmiths and protect them with shields. Once inside the building, the police used tear gas while they threw the squatters' furniture and personal objects out of the window. That night 3,000 people demonstrated in support of the squatters, and tried to re-enter the properties (but were stopped by the security forces). In the early hours, local authority offices and SAGA's HQ were set on fire and doused with stink bombs. While these incidents were taking place, activists set up the Hafenstraße Initiatives Support Committee, through which

---

to be equated with the Austrian FPÖ. See R. Ackermann, *Warum die NPD keinen Erfolg haben kann: Organisation, Programm und Kommunikation einer rechsextremen Partei* (Berlin: Budrich Unipress Ltd., 2012); A. Röpke and A. Speit, *Neonazis in Nadelstreifen: Die NPD auf dem Weg in die Mitte der Gesellschaft* (Berlin: Christoph Links, 2008); and R. Suso, *La claveguera marró: L'NSU i el terror neonazi a Alemanya* (Manresa: Tigre de Paper, 2016), pp. 323–44.
15.   His death, caused by the impact from a police water cannon, was the fifth caused by the police in a demonstration. In Hamburg, in the following days, dozens of autonomist activists and punks protested over Sare's death by attacking several police stations with Molotov cocktails, raising barricades and destroying different shops and banks. Petroni, *St. Pauli siamo noi*, pp. 93–4.

different campaigns were implemented to help local residents get to know the squatter community. With the same aim, 70 informative activities were held across the country in November and December.

In the middle of this, on 9 November, Hamburg Senate elections were held in which the SPD vote fell by 15 per cent in St. Pauli and 9 per cent in the city. A few days later, early in the morning on 21 November, five police units arrived to evict the Ahoi bar. Tensions escalated. The Initiatives Committee called a demonstration in solidarity with the Hafenstraße residents. More than 12,000 people turned out and marched along central streets in Hamburg. Visible among the throng was a block made up of a thousand punks, anarchists and autonomists. They walked in formation, dressed in black with balaclavas or bike helmets, behind a banner that read: 'Solidarity with Hafenstraße. No evictions, no demolitions, enough police terror!' Armed with sticks, the protesters in this 'black bloc' prevented the police from surrounding the demonstration and forming cordons on both sides. The protest eventually ended in a riot when the entourage went past Hamburg's prison. It was then that the police tried to immobilise the lorry with the organisers' speakers to put an end to the action. The city became the stage for pitched battles between autonomists and riot police units. Demonstrators managed to regroup and the march reached St. Pauli, ending in front of the houses threatened with eviction. There, a dozen hooded squatters welcomed the protesters from the roofs. *It was a true show of force.* An action that achieved its goal: to hold off the expulsion of the residents of squatted properties. To round it off, at the end of the year, and to coincide with the deadline for the evictions to have been carried out, an 'international day of resistance' was coordinated. The call was backed by hundreds of activists across Europe.

Meanwhile, the Initiatives Committee organised a new day of action – 'Day X' – to support Hafenstraßbe squatters' demands and pave the way for new occupations. As a result, on 23 April 1987, 30 simultaneous actions were performed across the city. These

ST. PAULI

included an occupation of Radio Hamburg by a group of students;
the storming of different shopping centres, banks and offices of the
authorities; breaking the windows at the speaker of Hamburg parliament's private residence; and distributing movement flyers and
painting murals in different city areas. The following day, the local
press printed headlines such as 'Terror in Hamburg'.

Additionally, on 19 July 1987, previously evicted buildings were
reoccupied. This was a new gesture of defiance towards authorities
that were overwhelmed by the drive shown by the autonomist and
squatters' movements. The Senate tried to negotiate with squatters, offering them rental contracts. Yet the Hafenstraße delegates
demanded the definitive scrapping of eviction and demolition
plans as well as being reconnected to the power grid. The pressure
the movement put on the authorities, as well as its determination to
not give up on actively defending the squatted places, would culmi-
nate in what became known as the 'Barricade Days' in November
1987.[16] This episode forced the authorities to forget their eviction
plans and ensure the stability of the Hafenstraße squats.

Practically all those occupying the freed spaces were young
people that participated in existing activist groups (anti-nuclear,[17]

---

16. That day, the entrances to the docks were blockaded by activists using
barricades made of tyres, furniture, metal, road signs and parts of broken down cars;
10,000 police were brought in from different parts of the country. A police cordon
was formed around St. Pauli to cut off the squatted buildings. The attempt failed as
5,000 activists managed to reach the occupied properties, avoiding police controls
by moving around in small groups. Finally, on 16 November, six days after the end
of the ultimatum given by the authorities, the interior minister gave the police the
green light to perform the evictions. Yet the action was halted at the last minute
because Hamburg's mayor had not been informed about it. With repression off
the table, the squatters and authorities reached a compromise: the activists would
take down the barricades in exchange for getting rental contracts for the disputed
properties. Petroni, *St. Pauli siamo noi*, p. 116.
17. The anti-nuclear movement was one of the foundations from which St. Pauli's
new political and cultural scene was built. The movement emerged in the 1970s and
spread nationally. It incorporated groups of students, farmers and young residents of
the areas next to nuclear plants. The first protests took place in 1975 against a project
to build a plant in the Wyhl municipality (Baden Württemberg); 20,000 people
occupied the land on which the plant was to be located. Afterwards there was a series
of protests: Kalkar (1976), Gorleben (1977), Brokdorf (1981) and Wackersdorf
(1986). On 8 June 1986 a demonstration was called in Heiligengeistfeld, Hamburg,

84

anti-militarist, ecologist). Some even combined this engagement with playing sport. The most notable of these was a group of football-loving 18–25 year olds. They had been kicking a ball around since they were little and – despite criticisms from some of their comrades – they were not willing to stop playing 'that bourgeois sport'.[18] That was what led to the spontaneous creation of FC Hafenstraßbe – a team made up of young squatters from the iconic St. Pauli street.

In those years, most of the team's members were HSV supporters. This was unsurprising because, as mentioned, the Hanseatic team was experiencing a golden age in sporting performance. After winning the cup and coming second in the league in 1976, the Hamburg club enjoyed years of international triumphs. It won the Cup Winners' Cup (in 1976–7) beating Anderlecht 2–0 in Amsterdam. Then it won the European Cup (1982–3) by defeating Juventus 1–0 in Athens.[19] With a string of victories like this it was difficult not to be attracted to the team. Things were not all rosy however. HSV's triumphs coincided with the growth of neo-Nazism on its

---

to protest against the police having prohibited people from joining the Brokdorf anti-nuclear mobilisation the day before. In the new protest the police arrested 860 people during twelve hours of 'Hamburger Kessel' (Hamburg kettling). The crackdown was, according to then Chancellor Helmut Kohl, in response to 'provocation by criminals and anarchists'. Four days later, close to 50,000 people demonstrated in Hamburg against the arrests. The anti-nuclear movement was perceived as a real threat by the authorities. This was why the Bavarian First Minister, Franz Josef Strauß, warned of an imminent 'civil war caused by violent anarchist criminals that want to create chaos to benefit Soviet intervention'. See Rondinelli, *Ribelli, Sociali e Romantici*, pp. 50–1 and Geronimo, *Fire and Flames*, pp. 85–97.

18.   Until the mid-1980s left-wing militants saw football as 'suspect' and 'distracting the masses from pursuing political and social objectives [...] Going to the stadium was seen as something suspicious, like someone who went to a brothel. Saturdays, when matches were played, should be for political discussions and demonstrations', in Rondinelli, *Ribelli, Sociali e Romantici*, p. 92.

19.   The match took place on 25 May 1983. After the victory over the Italian team, the HSV fans flew back to Hamburg. The flight and hotel cost them 200 marks. After landing, the punks that had gone with the team went to a concert along with other fans. In the middle of the performances, a group of neo-Nazi skinheads with baseball bats turned up and fought them. For many of these HSV fans this was a turning point. They could not go on sharing the terraces with those who had assaulted them. Petroni, *St. Pauli siamo noi*, p. 97.

terraces (in the Volksparkstadion). The sight of extreme rightists in the west stand's (*Westkurve*) block E during the 1980–3 triennium intimidated the young Hafenstraße-linked fans.[20] They could not bear the aggressive atmosphere. 'On the terraces you wouldn't hear "*Ole!*" any more but "get out!" [*"raus"*] and "*Sieg heil*", said a veteran punk who attended HSV matches then. Another former HSV follower linked to the Hamburg punk scene said, 'the situation started getting dangerous in 1981 and unbearable in 1982'. Many decided to stop going to the stadium, fed up with the presence of extreme rightists and the club directors' tolerance of them. Despite all of the complaints fans made to the club, its directors did not do anything to eradicate neo-Nazi symbolism from the stadium.

Despite the disappointment this caused, the young squatters, punks and autonomists continued to play in the neighbourhood team they helped create. For a while they did not want anything to do with professional football. They were still upset by what was happening in their old club and the inaction of those running it. The youths' distancing from the club was gradual but steady. Then, during the 1985–6 season, a group spontaneously decided to check out what was then called the Wilhelm Koch Stadion in which the district's team played, St. Pauli: a historic team that, as we have seen, was meandering unceremoniously between the lower divisions of German football. Others, however, preferred to go and watch Altona 93 or SC Victoria – two even more modest teams in the area.

All of the young people that had abandoned their childhood club to get to know others could feel their appetite for football returning. Going to Millerntor was a new and different experience. It was a close, humble, unassuming and unpretentious neighbourhood

---

20.   Neo-Nazi groups also were visible on the Hamburg streets. In 1980 a shelter for Vietnamese refugees was set on fire, killing two people (Ahn Lan Do and Ngoc Nguyen, 18 and 22 years old, respectively). The words 'foreigners out' were painted on the door of the building. The police identified three members of the German Action Groups (*Deutsche Aktionsgruppen*) as responsible for the assault, led by lawyer and Holocaust denier Manfred Roeder. See Suso, *La claveguera marró*, pp. 195–6.

team, and had practically no far-right fans. Playing with your mates was fine but it did not give you the same feeling as being on the terraces. Little by little, the new faithful grew in size, encouraged by word-of-mouth and friendship networks. Millerntor became a meeting point 'where you could have a good time and enjoy football with friends and some beers'. What most surprised them was the friendly and relaxed atmosphere they found in the St. Pauli ground. This was nothing like the atmosphere of tension and intolerance they had experienced at the Volksparkstadion. It was all a gradual and totally unplanned process. And, in the words of one of the mentioned fans, it was 'very natural, coming from pure fun, experiencing football as it was meant, and as something close – from the district we lived in'.

By the mid-1980s that trickle of support grew. And although they were still a minority, they made themselves noticed. And in what a way! They hung a pirate flag on the *Gegengerade*, the stadium's lateral stand, and made football chants that mixed political slogans with caustic humour. Examples include 'Fascism never again, war never again, Third Division never again!' (*'Nie wieder Faschismus, nie wieder Krieg, nie wieder 3. Liga!'*), and 'Who are the rats that betray us? The Social Democrats! Who will never betray us? St. Pauli! (*'Wer hat uns verraten? Sozialdemokraten! Wer verrät uns nie? Sankt Pauli!'*). They also started doing happenings – the forerunner of the organised '*tifos*' (choreographies) by fans. In these, 'the new fans put into practice fun guerrilla [*Spaßguerilla*] actions using left-wing activist Fritz Teufel's protest forms and tactics based on sarcasm and irony to provoke and tease'. All of this surprised both the club's veteran fans and its fan club members, which were the team's support base at the time. They were mainly dockworkers and youth linked to the '*Kutten*' phenomenon,[21] who had never

---

21. Having fans with the *Kutten*-style was common in most German clubs at the time. These were associated with rockers and motorbike gangs. An appearance characterised by wearing sleeveless jean jackets with team patches and badges. The *Kutten* style did not spread to nearby countries and therefore remained an exclusively German phenomenon. These fans tended to congregate in the working-class stands where they would perform choreographies that were spontaneous and unplanned

notably taken political stances on the terraces. Most of them would describe themselves as apolitical and the odd one would sympathise with the right.

Clearly the club administrators did not welcome the presence of the new 'odd-looking kids' behind the benches. They therefore gave instructions to prevent 'that pirate flag' from entering the next game. On the next match day, there was an exchange of words between half a dozen club security guards and the young fans. In the end, as recalled by Volker (one of the activists), the pirate banner was allowed in after one of the fans reminded those trying to block them of who they were dealing with. 'We are from Hafenstraße and you know what we do? If you don't want trouble, you know what to do.' Fearful of the reputation of daring youth hardened in countless battles with the police, the security guards, who were older and wanted an easy life, allowed the flag in. When in the next match a dozen more pirate banners appeared on the terraces, displayed by other fans out of solidarity, the club's transformation had started. It was becoming an example – later an international one – of rebel football. It was starting to be a cult club and no longer a depoliticised district team. The transformation was made possible by different factors coming together:

> [the] relative success of the team that at that time went [...] from the *Oberliga* to the *Bundesliga* in a space of five years; the evolution of local rivals HSV – in sports terms and the social and political composition of its support; socio-economic and cultural changes taking place in the *Sankt Pauli* district; and the development of the far-left political scene in Germany.[22]

---

because they lacked structure and leadership. They were small gangs of friends who would meet in the stadium and in some cases formed official fan clubs. Their presence was biggest in the most industrialised cities, such as Dortmund, Stuttgart, Berlin, Frankfurt, Kaiserslautern, Gelserkirchen and Hamburg, which showed their working-class leaning. Despite having no political inclination they did exhibit sexist, xenophobic and homophobic attitudes, which brought them close to the far right. Violence by the *Kutten* – often spurred on by alcohol consumption – was limited to the football stadiums and to brawling with rival fans and pinching their scarves and caps. Petroni, *St. Pauli siamo noi*, p. 77.

22. The German left's most orthodox sector – that linked to the May 1968

If we add to this the handful of young fans that one fine day decided to leave their lifelong club to join *Sankt Pauli*, we have all of the elements that converged to produce the club's metamorphosis.

Among those youths were punks, such as Raupe, Stevie and Doc Mabuse. Years later, Doc Mabuse claimed to have introduced the skull and crossbones on the Millerntor terraces. But the truth is that the pirate flag had already become quite a symbol within Hamburg's squatters' movement. Indeed the first flag unfurled in the stadium had previously adorned the walls of the *Volxküche* (also known as the *Vokü*). This was a centre – at number 116 Hafenstraße – that had opened in the winter of 1982 and operated as a people's kitchen and meeting point for local squatters. It was its flag, which itself had been robbed from a wall at the Hamburger Dom (a fairground in Heiligengestfeld), that Mabuse had removed and stapled to a broomstick to take to the St. Pauli stadium. For the Hafenstraße punks, the skull and crossbones – or Jolly Roger[23] – was a symbol of defiance. A symbol of 'freedom and resistance to authority' which continued the legacy of those pirates who – like punks – lived beyond the fringes of the law and dared challenge authority. The flag would soon be visible among squatters in Amsterdam, Copenhagen and Berlin. The link between corsairs and squatters is not so strange if we bear in mind that Hamburg, as well as being a port city, has its own pirate tradition. Prominent in this was the leg-

---

explosion – looked down on football. For its members the sport represented the proletariat's lowest spirit. Soccer was a pastime dreamed up to distract the attention of society's lower layers and not entertainment for intellectuals. For the German left, those that watched football were just as suspicious as those that frequented the brothels. Rondinelli, *Ribelli, Sociali e Romantici*, p. 96; Petroni, *St. Pauli Siamo noi*, p. 112.

23.   The term derives from the French 'Jolie Rouge' and was used by the *FC Sankt Pauli* fans to name the symbol they had been identifying with since the early 1980s: the skull (*Totenkopf*) and crossbones used by pirates. During the Second World War it was used by different military divisions such as the British submarines and Third Panzer Division of the SS. Years later, the name was adopted by one of St. Pauli fans' key bars, near to the stadium. Originally the red flag with skull and crossbones was raised by pirates when certain death was coming. The pirates that pioneered using the Red Jack were English ones, from 1694. Later, after the Spanish War of Succession in 1714, many corsairs returned to piracy and some kept the red flag because it symbolised blood. Rondinelli, *Ribelli, Sociali e Romantici*, pp. 86–7.

endary figure of Klaus Störtebeker, the pirate of the Elbe,[24] whose hideout was in the Swedish locality of Visby. He became renowned for seizing Hanseatic ships and sharing the loot with the locals.[25] Yet, in 1401 he was captured after having been betrayed by a crewmember. He was then tried in Hamburg for piracy – alongside 73 of his sailors – and sentenced to death. He had his head cut off on the marsh-like island of Grasbrook, opposite the city.[26]

For centuries, Störtebeker's figure has had mythical status, fed by different legends. He has become a popular figure among Hamburg's militant leftists who see him as waging a 'medieval class struggle' against the opulent Hanseatic League. The pirate was also remembered in Hafenstraße when, in 1985, in the middle of the tensions over its squats, the Störtebeker Centre was created. This had received financial support from the Greens and became a meeting place for the antifascist movement. Punks did not forget the city's most renowned pirate either. The band Slime[27] named a

24.   In fact Störtebeker was a nickname regularly used in Lower Saxony that meant, 'he who downs a tankard in one go' (echoing pirates' ability to consume a lot of beer). Later the Störtebeker name was adopted by other freebooters and fugitives as a *nom de guerre*. Legend has it that the ship's shaft was pure gold and was cast to fit the top of St. Catherine's church in Hamburg. Rondinelli, *Ribelli, Sociali e Romantico*, p. 103.

25.   In the late fourteenth century, the House of Meclenburg created a crew of privateers – the *Vitalienbrüder* – whose objective was to roll back the power of the royal Danish fleet. They took on the Danish ships in order to guarantee that supplies reached the besieged city of Stockholm. Once the conflict ended, some of the crew's captains (such as Störtebeker and Godeke Michels) turned to piracy, focusing their activity on Hanseatic League vessels. After 1390, the League had forcibly imposed its domination of the commercial routes across the Atlantic Ocean and Baltic Sea. Those pirates that challenged the power of the Hamburg authorities became known as 'equal participants' ('*likedeelers*'). They did not follow any hierarchy and were free to take the decisions they wanted. Petroni, *St. Pauli siamo noi*, pp. 12 and 112.

26.   One of the most common legends about him was that when Störtebeker heard about his sentence he asked the city's mayor for as many members of his crew to be freed as steps he could make once decapitated. Hamburg's highest authority agreed to this. After being decapitated the pirate captain's body rose and walked in front of eleven of his men until the executioner tripped him up. Despite this feat, his men were finally executed.

27.   Group formed in Hamburg in 1979 by Michael 'Elf' Mayer on guitar, Eddi Räther on bass and Peter 'Ball' Wodock on drums, and joined by singer Dirk 'Dicken' Jora months later. Slime was one of the city's pioneering punk bands alongside the aforementioned The Buttocks and Coroners. In their early years, Slime rehearsed

song after him in his honour.[28] In 2010, the year of *FC Sankt Pauli*'s centenary, a 600-year-old skull was stolen from the Hamburg History Museum. It is believed to have been Störtebeker's. During the time it disappeared, the police got to question members of different St. Pauli fan clubs, believing that they might be behind the theft. Eventually the police recovered the skull from two homeless people that had taken it in the hope of selling it.

The decision by the first Hafenstraße fans to bear the flag with the skull and crossbones was therefore full of historical connotations and symbolism. The pirate flag raised on a broom paraded from the *Gegengerade* turned the club and its fans into the 'Pirates of the League' (*'Freibeuter der Liga'*). A nickname for *FC Sankt Pauli*'s fans and players that, together with that of the 'Pirates of the Elbe', has endured to this day.

With regard to those who introduced the flag at the club, one of these – Doc Mabuse – ended up disillusioned with St. Pauli. He believed that the club was becoming too commercial and no

---

in the old bunker, when they also played – along with The Buttocks – in the Neuengamme youth detention facility, built on the site of the Nazi concentration camp of the same name. Among their most notable songs are 'Deutschland Muss Sterben ... Damit Wir Leben Können' ('Germany Must Die... So We Can Live'), 'Wir Wollen Keine Bullenschweine' ('We Don't Want Any Fucking Cops'), 'Polizei SA/SS' ('Police SA/SS'), 'A.C.A.B.', 'We Don't Need the Army' and 'Hey Punk'. If there were a single reason why Slime became a popular band it was the police seizing copies of their first LP, *Slime I*, after a raid on the Rip-Off shop in 1982. The shop owner, Klaus Maecks, was accused of 'sedition and inciting crime' after being mistaken for Slime's record producer. After bringing out three more LPs the band dissolved in 1984, but then reformed in 1990. The group reappeared live on 7 September 1991 before 15,000 people as part of the *Viva St. Pauli* festival. This was the first time that Slime had played since Germany had been reunified. Almost all of the band's members were HSV supporters, as indicated by their song 'Block E' – referring to the Volksparkstadion's most lively stand. The exception to this was their lead singer, who was an FC St. Pauli fan – the reason why the band has often performed in concerts organised by fans of the *Sankt Paulianer* club. For more on the band's musical career see D. Ryser, *Slime: Deutschland muss sterben*, (Munich: Wilhelm Heyne Verlag, 2013).
28. The song 'Störtebeker' was included on the *Alle gegen alle* album released in April 1983 by Aggressive Rockproduktionen. Here is a fragment: 'He was born 600 years ago | to be a great pirate | he was strong, proud and brave | a second Robin Hood | he robbed from the rich to give to the poor | but the rulers showed no mercy | and they took his head | Störtebeker we won't forget you | Störtebeker, we drink to you | Störtebeker, you were the best man of your time.'

longer different from others, and for that reason stopped going to the Millerntor. You could no longer meet up with the players (such as Michael Dahms, Andrew Pfennig, Jürgen Gronau, Stefan Studer, Peter Knäbel and Volker Ippig) for a chat, a beer and a post-match discussion. This used to happen in the Clubheim – the small bar under the stand opposite the *Gegengerade*. Even a commercial brand has been made of the *Totenkopf* (skull and crossbones). That is why Mabuse, the veteran punk and 14-year Hafenstraße resident, left St. Pauli. First he moved to Berlin's Kreuzberg district; later he returned to Hamburg to live in a trailer park, in Altona's Gaußstrasße. Although he burned the original flag that he took to the Millerntor, one of the windows of his trailer still is decorated with a black Jolly Roger. Now, however, like other veterans from those years, Doc Mabuse prefers to go and see the games of more modest teams such as Altona 93 – a closer and (according to him) less commercialised team. Still, after so many years football remains an important part of his life.[29]

Doc Mabuse was one of the St. Pauli followers from the Hafenstrabe squatters' and autonomist associations that were responsible for introducing a new way of cheering the team at the Millerntor. Indeed, this way was the embryo for the new '*tifo*' culture developed by fan groups from the last decade of the twentieth century. The arrival of the group on the stands changed forever the experience at matches by creating a vibrant atmosphere. One of the first novelties they introduced were songs – some full of irony – that have become fixtures among St. Pauli fans. These are not only in German but also English and French. One of the most renowned is the popular '*Aux armes*' that the *Sankt Pauli* fans often intone at the beginning of matches. Paradoxically it originates from the song '*All'armi*' – the Italian fascist anthem of the interwar years. The song was adapted three decades later, in the 1980s, by Marseilles *ultras* (organised and fanatical fans) who popularised and spread it on football terraces.

---

29. M. Sonnleitner, 'Der Mann, der den Totenkopf ans Millerntor brachte. Doc Mabuse: Scheiß auf Knoppers', *11 Freunde*, 27 January 2012.

Perhaps surprisingly, *Sankt Pauli's* fans were among the first on the continent to sing the famous 'You'll Never Walk Alone' – which was imported from Liverpool (and not from the Celtic club they are twinned with). The fact is that the port connection between Hamburg and the English city helped its arrival, as well as new trends, fashions and new ways of cheering on teams. The trips these young football lovers made was crucial to St. Pauli being the first German team to sing the Anfield classic.

As well as transforming the way of cheering on the team, the Hafenstraße fans also helped strengthen the ideological side of the club's support. The adoption of St. Pauli by its local autonomists and squatters was not planned. The opposite was the case: spontaneously and gradually the young people who went to the squats started going to the matches at Millerntor. In that regard, as we described, word of mouth among circles of friends, the role of the pioneers (such as Doc Mabuse's punk crew) and the familiar atmosphere in the stadium helped bring in other young Hafenstrasße residents or regulars. 'With a local team, spending an afternoon in the stadium seemed to be fun [...] whether to have a beer and a good time with friends or to see a good football match. Or both things!'[30]

That was how, in the 1986–7 season[31] (key in the club's history), the Hafenstraße FC St. Pauli followers grew to nearly 60 members. Their location in the ground stayed the same: behind the coaching-team's benches in the middle in the *Gegengerade* (the stand that had been in Millerntor stadium since the start, in 1961). It was the space that quickly became known as that of the 'Black Bloc' or 'Hafenstraße Bloc'. The Hafenstraße fans chose to be in the *Gegengerade*. This was instead of the north stand (*Nordkurve*) – the most working-class section at that time and where fan groups like the *Veteranen* would be. This was a conscious decision as, being

---

30. Davidson, *Pirates, Punks and Politics*, p. 80.
31. The year 1987 was the last without fencing around the Millerntor pitch, which allowed spectators to move freely around the venue's different stands. If the match was undecided, some fans would take advantage of this to stand behind the opponent's goal to annoy the goalkeeper. Petroni, *St. Pauli siamo noi*, p. 99.

newcomers to the stadium, they did not want to impose their ways on the traditional fans. It also had to do with the punks and squatters' desire to have their own area inside the stadium. And, as other sources suggest, a space where you can see the football well. Whatever it was, the fact is that their jackets and black hoods made them quickly recognisable.

The group gradually grew in size to 200 people. This was thanks to the arrival of new followers who, despite not participating in the daily life of the squatting community in the port area, sympathised with their worldview and way of seeing football. Others were attracted by the songs and the introduction of what became known as the '*tifo* culture'. The growth coincided with the team being promoted to the *Bundesliga* after being runners-up (behind the Stuttgarter Kickers) in the second division.

That season also saw the return to the squad of goalkeeper Volker Ippig, probably the player that most identified with the new philosophy at the club. This footballer with blond, unkempt hair lived in a Hafenstraße squat and participated in a cooperation project with Sandinista Nicaragua.[32] He was a perfect St. Pauli 'antihero'. The

---

32. Born in 1963 in Lensahn (Schleswig-Holstein), a small municipality 100 kilometres from Hamburg. After first playing for TSV Lensahn at the age of 18, he signed for FC St. Pauli. Ippig made his debut with the club's B team against OSC Bremerhaven in September 1981. In less than a year he had become the first team's reserve goalkeeper thanks to the trust put in him by coach Michael Lorkowski. Three times a week Ippig would take the bus to Hamburg until the club's vice-president Otto Paulick offered him his house to get settled in the city. He made his debut with the first team against TSV Plön in a match in which he scored an own goal. He left the club in the 1983–4 season to pursue other activities. These included working in a nursery for disabled kids and six months' voluntary work for a brigade building a health centre in the Nicaraguan municipality of San Miguelito. At the time, the Central American country was engaged in a revolutionary process after the Sandinista National Liberation Front led the overthrow of dictator Anastasio Somoza. Ippig went back to Germany in 1985 and rejoined the team, then managed by Willi Reimann. He built a cabin in his village of birth and combined living there with his stays – over three months – at the Hafenstraße squat. He liked spending time with the community's artists, students, punks and activists. He cycled from the Hafenstraße to training and his celebrations, in which he raised his fist at his Hafenstraße friends, turned him into a real icon for the *Sankt Paulianer* fans. Because of this he became commonly known as 'the punk in goal' ('*Punk im Tor*'). It was even the case that T-shirts were produced with the slogan 'Volker, hear the signal' ('*Volker, hör die Signale*'), which played with the first line of the German version

1988-9 season was the first in which a television network, RTL, broadcast all of the championship's matches, coverage that coincided with the club returning to top-flight football, helping spread the 'St. Pauli myth' across the country. The Hamburg team was the division's 'exotic guest'. Its uniqueness was exploited by the media using all kinds of labels for St. Pauli. Jörg Wontorra, a TV presenter who then was sports director for Radio Bremen, went as far as describing the club as the '*Bundesliga*'s brothel'.

With a deteriorating stadium, lacking professional structures and with a young team inexperienced in top-league football, St. Pauli was a likely target to be relegated. Yet, despite ending the season being defeated 5-1 by Bayer 05 Uerdingen, St. Pauli had obtained a comfortable tenth place – the club's best in the *Bundesliga* in its history. The Hamburg people responded to this and an average of 20,909 filled the Millerntor terraces weekly. This was an impressive figure that was only surpassed that year by Borussia Dortmund, Bayern Munich and VfB Stuttgart.

Meanwhile, the clubs' finances had become critical. The organisation's debt rose that season to 3.8 million marks. In order to turn its fortunes around and save the club, the management came up with a plan. On 4 January 1989 club Vice President Heinz Weisener announced that the club had taken a project to the Hamburg Senate that consisted of building a big multipurpose complex at the Millerntor accommodating 50,000 spectators – all seated. This Sport-Dome would have a hydraulic roof, retractable stalls, an ice-

---

of the communist anthem 'The *Internationale*'. In the winter of 1992, after suffering serious injury to his neck vertebra, he retired from football – after having kept the FC St. Pauli goal on 100 occasions. This sparked depression and the ex-player withdrawing from the world until, in 1999, he went back to the club to coach its lower-level teams and goalkeepers in the first-team squad. Five years later, he left the club after clashing with fans after defending the keeper Carlster Wehlmann's signing for HSV. After a period training VfL Wolfsburg's goalkeepers, he began managing, in 2008, the team for which he had first started playing: TVS Lensahn. He also combined running a school to train goalkeepers with being a mooring supervisor at the Hamburg docks. See G. Joswig, 'Fußball hat mein Leben gerettet!', *11 Freunde*, 5 April 2013; L. Wöckener, 'Der Torwart, der jetzt Hamburgs Hafen hütet', *Die Welt*, 3 January 2014; and E. Peinado, *Futbolistas de izquierdas* (Madrid: Léeme Libros, 2013), pp. 119-23.

hockey rink, a swimming pool and an underground car park for 4,000 vehicles.

In order for the project to be viable the venue would have to host 200 sporting events a year. Furthermore, it considered building an adjoining hotel and shopping centre. The plan was backed by a group of Canadian investors who wished to erect a similar venue to Toronto's SkyDome. The total construction cost would be 500 million marks. Furthermore, the project was expected to have a developmental and social impact on the whole district (and not just the area around the Millerntor). While the work was being performed, St. Pauli would have to play its matches at the Volks-sparkstadion (HSV's ground). To make up for the inconveniences incurred the club would be paid 10 million marks. In short, the idea was to turn the Millerntor stadium into a modern complex capable of hosting major international events. According to the club's directors, the new facilities would allow the club to overcome its shortfall and become financially independent.

The broader context to the proposal was the commercialisation process that German football had started. The same season, the DFB sold the league championship broadcasting rights to a private company, the UFA, which resold them to the private RTL network and the public ARD and ZDF networks. Different experts say this began the progressive commodification of German football.

Predictably the Sport-Dome was met with rejection from citizens and the club's more aware fans, none of whom had been consulted regarding the project. Rapidly neighbours and fans joined forces to try and stop it from happening. Their campaign took on an explicit slogan from the beginning: 'St. Pauli, yes. Sport-Dome no!' ('St. Pauli ja, Sport-Dome nein!'). On 11 March 1989, supporters that were against the project decided to launch a boycott to make clear their disagreement with the board's decision. They gave out 6,000 leaflets at the entrances to the stadium asking fans to remain silent for the first five minutes of the match that day (against Karlsruher SC). Although the action did not last more than four minutes, it served to demonstrate that much of the club's social base did not approve of building the Sport-Dome. After the match a demonstration was held, which 1,500 people joined.

A second protest was called to coincide with St. Pauli's match against Bayer Leverkusen, which was to take place on 7 April. People were to meet at Sternschanze station and march from there to the Millerntor. But the day before, under pressure from fans, the FC St. Pauli president, Otto Paulick, announced that the project was being withdrawn. This backtrack by management was perceived as a victory for fans and reinforced the 'St. Pauli' myth. It was 'the first practical and united action through which the network of fans started to interact with the club's corporate structure, extoling values such as anti-commercialisation and neighbourhood ownership'.[33]

Some fans saw this 'extra-sporting' triumph as more important than a team victory. However, their euphoria soon vanished. On 20 May 1989, FC St. Pauli played against Bayern Munich at the Olympiastadion. As usual, *Sankt Paulianer* fans travelled to the away game. But at the stadium 30 police units subjected the 2,000 away fans to thorough searches. During the time the police escorted them, the St. Pauli fans were controlled in all their movements and were prevented from drinking beer. Worse, those wearing boots were forced to take them off as police alleged that these were potential 'weapons'. This humiliating treatment led a group of fans to ask St. Pauli for space to publish its response in the club's regular match brochure. However, such an article was never printed. This pushed several fans to decide to create their own mouthpiece: the *Millerntor Roar!* (*MR!*)[34] fanzine that became *Sankt Paulianers'* independence voice.[35] Its first, 16-page edition was published on

---

33. Rondinelli, *Ribelli, Sociale e Romantici*, p. 113.
34. The publication took its name from a club fan group created in 1986 that was characterised by trying to establish a combination of support for the team with anti-racist politics. The last edition of the *MR!* fanzine was published on 18 April 1993, coinciding with the match between FC. St. Pauli and SC Freiburg. It announced the launch of its two successor publications: *Unhaltbar* (with markedly political content) and *Der Übersteiger* (which combined football and music with politics). Rondinelli, *Ribelli, Sociali e Romantici*, pp. 116 and 119.
35. The emergence of *MR!* was due to the impact of punk subculture on the

29 July 1989, coinciding with the build-up to the FC St. Pauli vs Werder Bremen match, with a circulation of 500 copies. It was fully produced and photocopied in a squat in Davidstraße. Soon, given the good reception fans gave it, its print run increased to 3,600 copies per edition, leading it to become the country's bestselling football fanzine. As well as producing the publication, its writers also developed initiatives, such as that put forward in the 1990–1 season against the DFB's decision to both increase the proportion of seating in the Millerntor and give the police major powers to control fans.

Beyond that controversy over overzealous policing, 1989 ended in an unexpected way. On the night of 9 November people began to spontaneously knock down the Berlin Wall before astonished *Volkspolizei* (GDR police). The wall had been raised in 1961 on the orders of the East German Communist Party (*Sozialistische Einheitspartei Deutschlands*, SED). Between August 1961 and 9 November 1989 it had divided East from West Berlin. In that period, at least 86 people died trying to escape to the FRG. The wall included additional security systems, such as barbed wire surroundings, trenches and surveillance towers. The East German authorities alleged that it was an 'antifascist protective wall'. Its demolition in 1989 was the first step towards the country's reunification and the end of the Cold War.

The new Germany, which the Reunification Treaty created officially on 3 October 1990, meant the GDR joining the FRG to form the world's third richest state. Nevertheless, subsequent economic restructuring revealed the existing inequalities between West and East Germany. Helmut Kohl's Ten-Point Programme proposed

---

Millerntor terraces. In sporting terms, *MR!* demonstrated the influence of the Italian *ultra* model. Across the Alps from Germany the first fanzines linked to the *ultra* movement appeared in the mid-1980s. The pioneering publications were *Urlo di carta* and *Tam Tam e segnali di funo*, which had been published by the Cosenza fan crews since 1985. FC St. Pauli fans were also inspired by British fanzines such as *The End* and *When Saturday Comes*. New fanzines later joined these and *MR!*, for instance *Splitter, Pipa Millerntor, Blödes Volk, Nachgetreten, La Gazzetta d'Ultrà, Basch, Der Chaote, Hossa and Kiezkieker* (appearing in 2011 with a print run of 600). Rondinelli, *Ribelli, Sociali e Romantici*, pp. 116 and 188.

replacing the planned economy with a market one. A privatisation process thus accompanied the transformation, leading to the dismantling of the former-GDA's industrial and productive fabric and higher local unemployment. Furthermore, the purchasing power of 'easterners' (*'Ossis'*) was declining as a result of unifying exchange rates and their firms' low productivity – a third lower than in West Germany. Together these factors drove the former East German territories to suffer hardships.

Unemployment, insecure living conditions, and lower wages than those received by their western equivalents, encouraged the idea that easterners were 'second-class citizens'. In the east, both people's economic plight and the collapse of the socialist GDR led to the emergence of right-wing extremism and xenophobic outbreaks – helped by German patriotic fervour over reunification.

Discontent and frustration were channelled by different neo-Nazi parties, such as the NPD, the DVU[36] or The Republicans (*Die Republikaner*, REP).[37] Headway was also made by neo-Nazi organisations such as the Free German Workers' Party (*Freiheitli-*

---

36. A political party that developed from an association created in 1971 by the millionaire Bavarian advertiser Gerhard Frey. Centred on Munich, the party gained a seat in the Bremen parliament in 1987. It also reached the Schleswig-Holstein institutions in 1993 after obtaining 6.2 per cent of the vote. Five years later the DVU won 12.9 per cent in the Saxony-Anhalt polls. These were fleeting successes as in most cases its MPs were not re-elected. In 2004, the party signed a cooperation agreement – the *Deutschlandpakt* – with the NPD that hit the buffers at the end of the decade due to electoral competition between the two parties. Eventually, in January 2011, the DVU joined the NPD and, on 26 May 2012, was officially dissolved. A year later Frey died, in Gräfelfing at the age of 80.

37. A political party founded in Munich on 26 November 1983 by several Bavarian Christian Social Union leaders that were unhappy with the party's official line under Franz Josef Strauß. Initially the Republicans defined themselves as nationalists, conservatives and anti-immigration. But in 1985 journalist Franz Schönhuber – an ex-member of the Nazi Party and SS – was made president and led the party towards extreme nationalism (tying to ape the success of Jean-Marie Le Pen's *Front National*). In West Berlin in 1989, REP won a 7.5 per cent share of the vote and eleven seats in its parliament. Also that year the party obtained 7.1 per cent of the vote, and six seats, in the European elections. After reunification the party's Berlin vote share was only 3.1 per cent. In 1994 Rolf Schlierer replaced Schönhuber as leader. Under the new leader *Die Republikaner* distanced itself from extremists. Yet that change led to a drop in electoral support for the party, which in the 1999 European parliamentary elections fell to 1.7 per cent. Since 2014 Johann Gärtner has been party president.

che Deutsche Arbeiterpartei, FAP),[38] German Alternative (*Deutsche Alternative*, DA)[39] and the Nationalist-Revolutionary Workers' Front (*Nationalistische-Revolutionäre Arbeiterfront*). They called for scrapping the right to asylum, introducing compulsory military service, deporting foreigners, separate schooling for males and females and discriminatory treatment against gays and people with AIDS.

Meanwhile, in Hamburg in 1990 the local authorities cancelled the rental agreement they had with the Hafenstraße residents, claiming that illegal activities were taking place in their buildings. The courts later ratified this cancellation, in 1991. It led *Millerntor Roar!* to launch (in its twelfth edition) a solidarity campaign with the slogan 'Hamburg without the Hafenstraße is like the *Bundesliga* without St. Pauli'. Moreover, the fanzine encouraged people to join a demonstration in support of the affected residents on 9 February that year. Visible on the march – beginning at Gerhart-Hauptmann-Platz and involving 3,500 people – were banners reading, 'You'll never walk alone'. Around 1,500 police escorted the demonstration to avoid incidents. The campaign's manifesto included an

---

38. The FAP was created in 1979 and was small before gaining notoriety in 1983 when Michael Kühnen and dozens of other members from the Action Front of National Socialists/National Activists joined it. In 1987 the FAP had 500 members – many of whom were neo-Nazi skinheads. Its membership grew further after German reunification, when it made an unsuccessful attempt to ally with the NPD. It stood in both the 1987 federal elections and 1989 European elections but obtained insignificant results. When Kühnen announced his homosexuality it shook the organisation. In 1989 he was replaced as leader by Friedhelm Busse and a wave of members resigned from the party – mainly in support of Kühnen. On 24 February 1995 the German Federal Constitutional Court outlawed the FAP. It was judged that the aim of the organisation was to overthrow the country's democratic system and defend Nazism and violence against refugee centres.

39. An organisation created in 1989 by Michael Kühnen (after being expelled from the FAP for being gay) and heir to the National Gathering (*Nationale Sammlung*) that was quickly banned by the Interior Ministry in February 1989. DA was characterised by its glorification of the Third Reich and anti-immigrant discourse, and became the violent wing of the neo-Nazi movement. In East Germany it was called *Nationale Alternative* and led by the skinhead Ingo Hasselbach. Frank Hübner replaced Kühnen as leader of the organisation. In 1992, DA was outlawed after an arson attack on a refugee centre in Mölln (Schleswig-Holstein). By then it had 340 members spread across Rhineland-Palatinate, Saxony, Bremen and Berlin.

explicit conclusion: 'If there were even a small chance of keeping Hafenstraße, like the chances of our FC St. Pauli's getting a goal, we know that those who fight may lose but those that do not, have already lost! FC St. Paul will not retreat and Hafenstraße will remain.'[40] Some of the club's first-team players participated in support activities.[41] Some even were photographed wearing the official shirt in front of murals in solidarity with Hafenstraße.

In sporting terms, the 1990–1 season – the last in which the championship was exclusive to West German teams (but held after reunification) – was another disaster for St. Pauli. At the end of an erratic year, the *Sankt Paulianers* had won only six games and 27 points – leaving it in 16th place in the league. The only positives that year were a victory in the first match of the season against Hertha BSC at Berlin's Olympiastadion,[42] and a home victory against

---

40. Petroni, *St. Pauli siamo noi*, p. 139.
41. The fanzine organised other initiatives. In 1992 Andreas 'Boller' Jeschke, a recent signing at St. Pauli, stated in an interview that he did not have a single book at home. The fanzine's editors then promoted among readers the campaign *Bücher für Boller* (Books for Boller) to collect books for the player. Minutes before a match at the Millerntor, several fans handed books to the player. Years later, Boller confessed that he had not had the chance to read any and that they were in a box in his garage. Rondinelli, *Ribelli, Sociali e Romantici*, p. 118.
42. The trip to the Olympiastadion, on 9 August 1990, was expected to be complicated for the *Sankt Paulianer* fans due to extreme belligerence towards them from the local hooligan Hertha Frösche crew. As a result, autonomist movement members in Berlin's Kreuzberg district suggested that they go with St. Pauli fans to the stadium. On match day, hundreds of antifascist from the capital received, at Kreuzberg's Kottbusser Tor, the Pirate fans who had travelled from Hamburg, Frankfurt and Göttingen. When the fans reached the surroundings of Hertha's ground, they came across local fans doing fascist salutes. On the terraces the local crews shouted at the St. Pauli fans: 'unemployed, unemployed'. The visitors taunted them back with: 'taxpayers, taxpayers'. The match was a good comeback for St. Pauli. The team won 1–2 thanks to goals by the Czech Ivo Knoflíček and Slovak Ján Kocian, both thanks to assists from André Golke, and that way reversed the Berliners' lead – scored by Uwe Rahn. A triumph on the first day of the championship put St. Pauli provisionally at the top of the *Bundesliga*. When the match finished, the police escorted the *Sankt Paulianer* followers to Kreuzberg. Once there, they celebrated the win at a party organised in a local squat. The return match, played on 5 March 1991, was pretty unique. St. Pauli's directors decided to hold it at HSV's Volksparkstadion, with the idea of being better able to separate both groups of fans there. The choice of stadium did not go down well with *Sankt Paulianer* fans. Indeed, *Millerntor Roar!* instigated a boycott of the match, organising an alternative Fan Demo Party at the

Bayern Munich.[43] Despite these odd successes, St. Pauli ended up having to win the playoff match against the Stuttgarter Kickers – third in the second division – to not be relegated. After the home and away matches both ended 1–1, a tiebreaker was arranged at a neutral ground. This was held on 29 June 1991 at Parkstadion de Gelsenkirchen – Schalke 04's stadium. A 3–1 win by the Stuttgart team sent St. Pauli down to the *Bundesliga 2* after three seasons in top-flight German football. Even though relegation was likely, this was a massive disappointment, as was shown by the tears on the field from players such as charismatic keeper Volker Ippig, and off the field from the 15,000 fans that had travelled there. After three years the *Bundesliga* dream had vanished in the worst possible way.

Nevertheless, the season was interesting from a social point of view. The club, after a campaign initiated by *Millerntor Roar!*, officially banned any racist, fascist or discriminatory mention in followers' chants, banners and flags.[44] Thus, FC St. Pauli became

---

Gegengerade. As a result nearly 1,500 fans followed the match listening to the radio from the Millerntor terraces. The game – commonly known as the 'phantom match', ended in a 2–2 draw. Petroni, *St. Pauli siamo noi*, pp. 145–6.

43.   The match, played on 2 March 1991, ended in a 0–1 *Sankt Paulianer* victory, thanks to an angled shot by midfielder Ralf 'Colt' Sievers in the 43rd minute – 15,000 open-mouthed Munich fans could not believe it. The St. Pauli fans that had travelled there were euphoric. That season Bayern would end up in second place – three points behind the champions, 1. FC Kaiserslautern. Much of the merit for the Pirate's victory went to its goalkeeper Volker Ippig – maker of several 'miracle saves'. To commemorate that sporting feat the *Fanladen* produced a special shirt for followers that travelled to Munich with the words '*Ich war dabei!*' ('I was there!'). The exploit is still remembered today. Petroni, *St. Pauli siamo noi*, p. 140.

44.   On 1 April 2006, St. Pauli was visited by Chemnitzer FC, a team from Saxony that was followed by an infamous group of neo-Nazi hooligans: the HooNaRa (Hooligans-Nazis-Racists) – led by Thomas Haller and founded at the beginning of 1990. In the hours before the game, the visiting extremists attacked several hairdressers run by members of Hamburg's Turkish community, while chanting '*Sieg Heil*'. In the stadium they exhibited red flags with white circles, that is, symbols similar to banned *swastikas*. Symbols that St. Pauli security guards removed among shouts of 'Jewish pigs'. During the match the 200 Chemnitz fans made extremist chants such as, 'We are building a train from St. Pauli to Auschwitz' and, 'Fenerbahçe, Galatasaray, we hate Turkey'. The following year the HooNaRa, which included around 30 Nazi fans, officially disbanded after several legal cases and the death of Rico Malt, Haller's successor as leader. See S. Dobbert and C. Ruf, 'Nazis im Fußball: Die Rassisten sind immer da', *Der Spiegel*, 17 February 2007.

the first German club to officially veto racist or other discriminatory behaviours. The decision was taken after an episode that took
place on 18 October 1991. During a match against VfL Osnabrück,
a group of *Sankt Paulianer* neo-Nazis made chants such as 'foreigners out' against Turkish-origin fans in the stands. Some of the latter
shouted back 'fascists out' and were assaulted by a group of eight
Nazis. The incident led the club to take a decision, unanimously
backed in the members' general assembly held on 28 October, of
vetoing all forms of racism, fascism, xenophobia or discrimination
in slogans, banners, flags or behaviour in the stadium. Pressure
from fans was crucial to the organisation deciding to eradicate the
scourge of racism from the club.[45] Relatedly, a month later, on 26
November, FC St. Pauli took on Galatasaray in a friendly, involving goalkeeper Harald 'Toni' Schumacher, to which thousands of
Turkish fans came. The event helped establish links between the
club and this particular community.

The affair is key to comprehending not just the club's change
in mentality (beyond its politically aware supporters) but also the
expansion of its support base. Also central was a musical festival
held before the start of the following season. On 7 September
1991, the Viva St. Pauli Festival was held. This was a counter-cul-
tural event organised by the Hafenstraße autonomist and squatter
movement. Its aim was to collect funds to pay the debts accrued
(from paying fines and legal assistance, and totalling 30,000 marks)
by activists in these movements. The organisers' aim was for the
festival to take place in the St. Pauli stadium, an idea that was
rejected initially by the club's directors – fearing acts of vandalism
during the concert. Nevertheless, after the initiators insured the
event (the cost of which was extraordinarily high – nearly 20,000
marks) the club gave them space for the event to be held at the
Millerntor.

The activity lasted a whole weekend and included some of the
best-known rock and punk outfits in Germany, such as Die Toten

---

45.   The first to demand that the club adopt a clear stance over the racist incident
were those producing *Millerntor Roar! Petroni, siamo noi*, p. 146.

Hosen, Slime, Extrabreit and Rio Reiser. Around 15,000 people came from across the country and it became a milestone for its generation, with no incidents taking place. The autonomist movement ended up collecting more money than was strictly needed. Consequently it decided to hand out the surplus amount among other organisations, and 8,000 marks were given to the St. Pauli Evangelist Church to buy a van. The church had shown solidarity with Hafenstraße and was doing important social projects with local children.

The festival also became a turning point in terms of the club developing a mass following. It helped root the club in its district through fans getting involved in different social projects, such as those with first- and second-generation migrant families. Yet not all of the Hamburg squatters' movement supported the festival. Criticisms were raised in an assembly of the Rote Flora – a historic city building that had been squatted for two years.[46] Critics censured

46. A property occupied in November 1989 in Schanzenviertel – St. Pauli's northeast. The building was built in 1888 as the Tivoli-Theatre (soon after, renamed the Concerthaus Flora) to host a variety of entertainments (including concerts and even operas). It was one of Hamburg's few theatres still standing after the Second World War. Indeed, it still held performances until 1943, when it was shut because of the conflict. After being used for a while as a warehouse, it was refurbished and, in 1949, reopened its doors again as a theatre. From 1953 to 1964 it was used as a cinema with 800 seats. Subsequently it housed a 1000 Töpfe department store until, in 1987, it stopped being used for commercial purposes. Then music producer Friedrich Kurz planned to adapt the building to become a music venue. However, local residents and autonomist groups rejected the proposal. Subsequent (violent) protests caused the investors to pull out of the plan. In August 1989 the authorities offered a six-month rental contract to activist groups. Eventually, on 23 September, the Rote Flora was squatted and opened as a cultural centre. 'Flora for all' was the slogan used during that period. At the start of the following decade the squatters were served with an eviction notice. Behind this decision was the intention of creating flats in the building. In January 1991 the court ruled the contract annulled, saying that 'presumed criminal activities' were taking place inside. Afterwards the occupiers and the Town Hall tried negotiating a new lease, but when activists turned this down the Hamburg Senate decided to sell the occupied building to employer Klausmartin Kretschmer (in March 2001). Ten years later, with the building still occupied, the contract that prevented Kretschmer from reselling the building expired. Fearful that this would lead to eviction, the occupiers responded with the campaign 'Flora bleibt unverträglich' ('Flora Remains Incompatible'). When the building's demolition was announced, on December 2013, serious incidents occurred. Finally, in January, it was announced that the centre would not be pulled down. In all, Rote Flora has

the festival for being too commercial and making people pay to enter.

That season, 1991–2, the championship underwent restructuring in order to incorporate the ex-GDR teams. Accordingly the second division was split into two groups: North and South. The Hamburgers, with Argentinean Gustavo 'Cepillo' Acosta[47] in their line-up, managed to qualify after a previous round in the North group, where it was a challenger for the title. In the end, despite forward Markus 'Toni' Sailer netting 15 goals, the team ended up in fourth place, four points behind KFC Uerdingen 05 – who won promotion.

The reunification-related transition season – from 1992 to 1993 – went no better, as the club came 17th. Indeed, it was one point away from automatic relegation, which that year affected seven teams because of the league's reorganisation. This meant that St. Pauli had to play in cities such as Leipzig, Rostock, Jena and Chemnitz – all in the eastern regions. As well as being a long way away, what was most worrying about these matches was their local

---

become a symbol of the squatters' movement – not just locally but internationally.

47.   A player signed from the Buenos Aires club Ferro Carril Oeste and thereby the first Latin American to play for FC Sankt Pauli. Acosta had made his professional debut in his country in 1985. A German businessman had travelled to Argentina to sign Juan Eduardo Esnáider but that player had just reached a deal with Real Madrid, leading to Acosta being offered the chance to play in Europe. He lived in Hamburg for a year and a half without much luck. An injury meant the midfielder only played 16 games for St. Pauli (in which he scored three). In an interview the player looked back at his first days as a Pirate team player: 'After signing my contract in the stadium, the St. Pauli president said to me "I'll show you Hamburg". He took me to the port, where he showed me, as if it were a tourist attraction, its streets – including Herbetstraße – with all those pretty girls in the windows, and we ended up in a cabaret where they did a sex show. Days later, on my debut, the fans welcomed me with Argentina and Che Guevara flags behind one of the goals. They always used them when I played in the team.' It is perhaps not odd then that, years later, Acosta stated, 'despite being there only for a small amount of time, they showed me a different way of seeing the world'. The next season Acosta went to SV Lurup, another Hamburg team – for whom he played for just a year, before signing for Unió Esportiva Lleida – the club he played for from 1994 to 1996. He then played at Cádiz CF and Deportivo Independiente Medellín, where he hung up his boots in 1998. Y. Vera, 'La incredible historia e St. Pauli: Club social y deportivo', *No/Página 12*, 17 April 2014.

socio-political context, which at the time saw extreme right-wing parties booming. After assessing the risks, the *Fanladen* decided not to do the trips, which became known as the East Boycott.

St. Pauli came fourth in 1993–4, just two points away from reaching the *Bundesliga*. It was a good omen of what was to come in the next season; after which St. Pauli won automatic promotion to the top flight of German football. The club was managed by Uli Maslo and had as its top goalscorers Jens Scharping and Russian Yuri Savichev – with twelve and ten goals respectively. The prize was shared, however, with Hansa Rostock, one of the *Sankt Pauli-aners'* biggest rivals. In the last match of the championship, played on 18 June 1995 against FC 08 Homburg, St. Pauli needed a win to be able to compete again in the *Bundesliga*. Three minutes from the end, the referee – Bodo Brandt-Chollé, who was refereeing the last match of his career – blew for a penalty. But the *Sankt Paulianer* fans thought he had indicated the end of the match and invaded the pitch. The action, which could have led to the club losing the match 0–3 and therefore staying in the second division, ended with no penalty. After removing thousands of supporters from the playing area, St. Pauli vice president, Christian Hinzpeter, crossed the turf to announce by microphone that the referee had told him the match had ended with a home victory of 5–0. Now the party could start.

The start to the *Bundesliga* could not have been better: a 4–2 victory against 1860 Munich at the Millerntor. The day after, the press published a table worth framing on a wall: FC St. Pauli was top. But, as is well known, happiness is short-lived in the house of the poor: the *Sankt Paulianers* would spend the last championship games anguishing over whether they might stay up. Their eventual 15th place ensured that they would play in the first division the following year. On the seventh day of the league, on 29 September 1995, some serious incidents occurred during the game against Hansa Rostock. The Pirates' supporters were attacked inside and outside the stadium by home supporters.[48] Undoubtedly the

---

48. This was not an isolated incident. The professed hostility between the groups of fans resurfaced in the 2009–10 season, when the Hansa Rostock followers threw

match further worsened the acrimonious rivalry between the two northern teams.[49]

The process of increasing St. Pauli's support, through the cult status the club attained through actions like prohibiting far-right symbols on the terraces, came to a temporary halt in the mid-1990s. The parenthesis, in which Hamburg's alternative scene and radical left was also affected, resulted from charges of rape brought against a member of a well-known German punk band. In response to the accusations, some prominent local movement activists and club fans defended not condemning the accused until there was reliable evidence and he was convicted. This led to activists breaking from or distancing themselves from the movement and affected attitudes towards the club. It was a reflection of the state of Hamburg political activism, where unspeakable episodes took place, such as butyric acid attacks on the *Fanladen*. The issue created some conflict within the alternative scene, but this was overcome after it was accepted that mistakes had been made. This allowed the club to continue to develop its social base, accompanied by fans' greater participation in the everyday life of the club.

In the 1996–7 season the team ended at the bottom of the table, taking it down to the *Bundesliga 2*. The club's coach, Uli Maslo, had just been replaced by his assistant Klau-Peter 'Ka Pe' Nemet, who took over six matches from the end and did not manage to win one. The change did not serve to overturn the club's spiral downwards. Relegation to the second division further weakened the club's financial situation. The club performed a set of changes that revealed its directors' lack of judgement and sporting project. Many criticisms were made against the way the club was being run

---

lit flares at the stands occupied by St. Pauli supporters. Similar disturbances had happened the previous season, when *Sankt Paulianers* were attacked by rival fans at Rostock train station. Davidson, *Pirates, Punks and Politics*, p. 63. See also S. Toporan, 'Die Chronologie des Hasses', *Hamburger Abendblatt*, 4 March 2009.
49. This extreme animosity inspired the screenplay for the film *Schicksalsspiel* (Match of Faith), made in 1993 by Bernd Schadewald. The story described a Romeo and Juliet-type romance between a St. Pauli fan (Roland) and a Rostock waitress (Conny) with the backdrop being the incidents between the two sides. Davidson, *Pirates, Punks and Politics*, p. 148; Rondinelli, *Ribelli, Sociali e Romantici*, p. 127.

by club president, architect Heinz Weisener. However, he had the support of the most veteran fans, who called him 'Papa Heinz' and worshipped him as a kind of patriarch. This was because at several times of serious economic difficulty he had used his personal wealth to save the club.

All the same, a group of fans unhappy with how the organisation was being managed became club members and formed the Interested Members' Group (*Arbeitsgemeinschaft Interessierter Mitglieder*, AGIM). Its aim was to actively participate in the club's administrative and organisational structures to try and change the club from the inside.[50] Initially the AGIM was set up to push for the St. Pauli B team – at the time playing in the fourth division – to be able to play its matches at the Millerntor. They had stopped being able to do so when coach Uli Maslo had forbidden this to avoid excessive deterioration of the grass. That meant that the youngest *Sankt Paulianer* players played their home matches in districts such as Hoheluft, Marienthal, Rothenbaum and Altona. This was quite a trip for those lads.

Soon, however, AGIM members chose to take on the challenge of trying to counter Weisener's authority and change the way FC St. Pauli was run. In that regard, the changes ordered by the DFB favoured such fans gaining a position of power inside the club. As a result, the AGIM became the fans' most prominent voice inside the club. This was demonstrated in October 1998 when they put a motion to the club's general assembly to change the stadium's

---

50. Its creation coincided with a DFB directive that forced clubs to create an internal control body. That meant modifying statutes, a condition that had to be met to obtain a federation license to be able to compete. To comply with the new regulations the St. Pauli board tried to create a 'proposal board' that would put forward candidates for president. The AGIM, however, did not agree with this solution and defended creating a genuine control body whose members would have to be chosen by the club members' general assembly. In the end an agreement was reached to create a Statute Commission made up of five members from both the president's office and the AGIM. Its role would be to modify the organisation's statutes. The agreement document, passed on February 1997, provided for the setting up of a directorate consisting of seven members elected directly in the General Assembly. Rondinelli, *Ribelli, Sociali e Romantici*, p. 142; Petroni, *St. Pauli siamo noi*, p. 155.

name from Wilhelm Koch Stadion. Their argument revolved around the ex-president's involvement with the Nazis. A book by journalist René Martens, published a year earlier, had revealed the link. Despite opposition from the most longstanding members, the motion eventually passed and it was agreed to replace Koch's name with Millerntor. After the vote, Hans Apel, SPD member and former defence minister in the Helmut Schmidt government, resigned as advisor for the club.

Meanwhile the upheaval continued. In the summer of 1997, Eckhard Krautzun became the new *Sankt Paulianer* manager, but he was sacked in November and his place given to Gerhard Kleppinger. St. Pauli seemed to be reproducing its organisational problems on the field. After three months on the job, Kleppinger too was replaced, in January 1999, this time by Willi Reimann. And it would not be the last change to take place. On 14 March 2000, with the season still in full swing and the team in the lower half of the league table, Reimann resigned. Dietmar Demuth became the new *braun-weiß* coach. St. Pauli suffered that season, once again. They did not ensure relegation was avoided until the very last match. Its rival at the Millerntor on that day – 16 May 2000 – was Rot-Weiß Oberhausen, which took the lead 31 minutes into the game. As things stood, St. Pauli was heading for the *Regionalliga* because the Stuttgarter Kickers, the main team competing with the Pirates to avoid relegation, was at that moment beating Karlsruher SC (from Baden-Württemberg). When the Stuttgart team ended up drawing, the tension at the Millerntor slackened but St. Pauli needed a goal. In the 90th minute, a ball played into the away team's penalty area allowed Croat Ivan Klasnić to stretch to make a cross, which forward Marcus Marin put in the net: 1–1. A miracle had happened. Euphoria in the midst of an epic story, and a pitch invasion to celebrate the draw. St. Pauli ended thirteenth, with 39 points and a goal difference one higher than the Stuttgart Kickers.

10

Fußball Gegen Nazis

The progressive transformation and politicisation of St. Pauli's support happened in parallel to the extreme right infiltrating German football terraces. Hooliganism spread in Germany from the 1960s thanks to the British soldiers housed in NATO barracks in the FRG. British soldiers did not miss out on going to international matches in Germany involving their national teams. Their presence did not go unnoticed, as they were responsible for several incidents – such as pitch invasions and fights with locals. They became the main transmitters of football-related violence within German football. Additionally the away trips by Manchester United fans (to Hanover in 1965) and Liverpool (to Mönchengladbach in 1978) seduced a whole generation of German youth, which very quickly got organised to imitate the British ways of supporting and behaving.

That was how, in the late 1970s, the first groups of neo-Nazi followers emerged in German football. The 1977–8 season, in particular, saw the spread of hooliganism on the country's terraces. Until then German fans had been characterised by their traditionalism. In one of the last match days of the championship there was a stampede in Block E of the Volksparkstadion, where HSV's extremist fans[1] congregate, during the celebrations for having won

---

1. The boom in the skinhead style goes back to the 1980s. The first German skins were linked to the punk scene. The emergence of extreme-right skinheads was encouraged by the rise of extremist football fandom. This happened in Hamburg with the appearance of the Savage Army, a crew of around 500 ex-punks and right-wing hooligans that became the country's first violent fan group. Despite their origins in the punk scene, they embraced the ideas of Michael Kühnen's Action Front of National Socialists/National Activists (*Aktionsfront Nationaler Sozialisten/ Nationale Aktivisten*, ANS/NA). Many leaders of the Hamburg neo-Nazi scene came out of the Savage Army, such as Wacker (an ex-member of the Viking Youthm WJ),

the league. Four fans were seriously injured. From then on, outbreaks of hooliganism became commonplace in German football.
In 1982, for the first time football stadiums saw symbols such as
the *swastika*, Nazi salutes, anti-Semitic chants and xenophobic and
racist political slogans. From then on, groups of extremist followers
linked to neo-Nazi organisations, and the fights they caused, flourished in many German clubs. In Berlin in that period, Hertha BSC's
extremist group – named Zylon B in honour of the gas used by in the
Nazi death camps – set a train alight.[2] That kind of vandalism, far
from being sporadic, became frequent in the German league. This
can be explained by the proliferation of Nazi gangs in the stadiums
during the 1981–2 biennium. These included the Borussenfront –
created in the early 1980s by extremist Borussia Dortmund fans[3]
and led by Siegfried 'SS-Sigi' Borchardt;[4] the Adler Front that
surfaced at Frankfurt's Eintracht and is closely related to the ANS, a
small neo-Nazi group that ordered its members to recruit members
at the stadiums; the Fan-Club Phönix, from Kaiserslautern, which
also had ANS links; Schalke 04's Mighty Blues; Karlsruhe's Destroy-
ers; the aforementioned Hertha BSC's *Frösche*; and other similar
groups in Nuremberg, Munich and Stuttgart. The groups coordinated with each other to do actions against immigrants and their

Grashoff and Burkhardt (all also having been part of the city's punk circles). Petroni,
St. Pauli siamo noi, p. 75.
2. The club, at that time, had other similar groups with an ultra-right leaning, such
as the Spree Randale, Hertha Frösche and the Skins von Eisern Berlin.
3. Its members were convicted on several occasions for committing acts of
discrimination, vandalism and violence. Pressure on them by the police and club,
after they received a formal complaint from the Association of Victims of Nazi
Persecution, helped the Borussia Dortmund gang's decline. Years later, however, the
group was reactivated through attending matches played by lower-level club teams.
4. An industrial salesman who was a member of the ANS/NA and FAP. After the
latter organisation was banned, Borchadt organised *Camaraderie Dortmund*. He has
been convicted for assault on several occasions. Borchadt was a candidate for the
neo-Nazi organisation The Right (*Die Rechte*). In 1982 he founded the *Borussenfront*,
a group of extremist Borussia Dortmund followers linked to neo-Nazi parties such
as the FAP and NPD. In 2014 he won a Dortmund parliamentary seat for the district
of Innenstadt-Nord after obtaining 2,101 votes. His campaign was full of football
nostalgia and used the slogan: 'from the south stand to the Town Hall'. Two months
after taking his seat he resigned citing health reasons. He was substituted by Dennis
Giemsch, one of The Right's main ideologues. Suso, *La claveguera marró*, pp. 359–60.

organisations and businesses in cities such as Hanover, Dortmund, Berlin and Hamburg.

Millerntor's terraces did not escape this trend. Although they were never more than a minority, in the 1980s the club had small crews of neo-Nazi fans – called the United Fanclub and North Side – who would be in the *Nordkurve*. These followers caused several incidents. They did racist chants and displayed icons from the German Empire – as neo-Nazi groups did after explicit Nazi symbols were prohibited.[5] It is no surprise, then, that the Hafen-straße squatters' appearance in the stadium led to many tensions, and that the far-rightists were harassed and chased until they were expelled from the Millerntor stadium.

Most of the neo-Nazi hooligan groups consisted of unemployed working-class youth who, facing uncertainty about their future, blamed their status on having immigrants in the country. The idea was exploited by extreme right organisations to win support. One of these groupings was the aforementioned ANS (led by former army officer Michael Kühnen).[6]

---

5. They regularly hung a flag on the fencing that separated the *Nordkurve* from the pitch including the club colours and the imperial war insignia (*Reichskriegsflagge* – used in the German Reich between 1892 and 1918). Also, the North Side included a big German flag including the group's name in Gothic white letters in the middle.

6. Kühnen began his political path in the Maoist movement. He worked at the Hamburg shipyards where he came into contact with the extreme right. Kühnen joined the National Democratic Youth (*Junge Nationaldemokraten*) and the youth section of the NPD – a Nazi organisation formed in 1964. Shortly after he left the party unhappy with its leaders' approach. He then served in the army, from which he was expelled in 1977 for spreading neo-Nazi propaganda in the barracks. He founded his own organisation, the ANS/NA, which emerged to carry out violent acts and bank robberies. In 1979 Kühnen was arrested and given a three and a half year prison sentence for incitement to violence and racial hatred. After serving his sentence, in 1982 he tried to reorganise the ANS/NA but a year later the Interior Ministry banned its activities. Then he focused his efforts on working with the FAP. All this happened while he moved closer to the views of Ernst Röhm, the founder of the SA. Faced with rumours around his possible arrest, in 1984 Kühnen fled to the French capital, protected by the Federation of National and European Action. He was eventually arrested in Paris and extradited to Germany, where he was sentenced to four years in prison. In 1986, while imprisoned, his homosexuality was made public, which led to him to lose considerable support in neo-Nazi circles. In 1988 he was freed and took advantage of this to create a new group, *Nationale Sammlung*, which was banned by the authorities the following year. Three years later, on 25 April 1991, he died of AIDS.

A turning point in the evolution of German hooliganism was 16 October 1982. In the run-up to a cup match that pitted HSV against Werder Bremen, a group of extremist Hamburg fans – members of The Lions (*Die Löwen*) group[7] – assaulted a 16-year-old away fan, Adrian Maleika. The young man, a member of The Faithful (*Die Treuen*) fanclub, was hit on the head by a brick when fleeing an ambush by HSV '*hools*' near a train station.[8] The attackers were waiting for the rival fans armed with sticks, gas devices and flares. Maleika lost consciousness and died the day after at Altona General Hospital as a result of a brain haemorrhage and fractured skull.[9]

That was the first death from organised violence in German football and the case received a lot of media attention. From then on, the problem of hooliganism affected almost all of the country's clubs. Extreme right-wing groups started to organise with the aim of infiltrating and publicising their ideas in the stadiums. In the early 1980s this led German autonomists (in cities such as Berlin,

7. At the time, most of this group of around 30 people were far-right rockers from Hamburg's Barmbeck neighbourhood. In the Volksparkstadion stands they tended to chant SA songs, do the fascist salute and display NPD symbols. On 19 December 1983, different Lions members were convicted by a Hamburg court for the murder of Maleika. One of the accused was given a two and a half year prison sentence, and another nine months. The other five defendants were aquitted. During the trial it could not be proved who had killed the Werder Bremen fan. HSV had other neo-Nazi groups, such as the Savage Army, a group of neo-Nazi skinheads from the Hamm district that in the 1980s would carry out actions against alternative youth centres, left wingers, members of the Turkish community and places frequented by punks. On 1 May 1982, before a cup tie between Hamburg and Frankfurt's Eintracht, a group of local neo-Nazi hooligans, together with Hamburg and Nuremberg radicals, attacked different Turkish trade union stands. That was the first coordinated action between German neo-Nazi hooligans. Many members of The Lions joined the local section of *Aktionsfront Nationaler Aktivisten*.
8. The tragic incident was able to happen because The Faithful (a group of Werder Bremen fans) that Maleika belonged to got off at the Eidelstedt train station without being given police protection because most away fans had got off at the Stellingen station – one stop before – where the security forces escorted them to the Volksparkstadion.
9. The event encouraged the creation of the HSV Fan Project in 1983, which centred its actions on educating the youngest fans on the perils of violence, political extremism, racism and alcohol abuse. Its example was followed by St. Pauli, which in October 1989 introduced its own 'fan project' – thanks to an initiative by Hafenstraße activist Sven Brux. This was called *Fanladen St. Pauli*, and was backed by the club's then-president, young architect Christian Hinzpeter.

Nuremberg, Frankfurt, Göttingen and Hamburg)[10] to forge greater antifascist unity and resistance against attacks from the neo-Nazi fans.[11]

In HSV's case, the violence and unpunished display of neo-Nazi imagery led the most aware fans to distance themselves from their lifelong club. Many of them, as mentioned previously, ended up on the terraces of the Millerntor (as in those days there was no extreme rivalry between HSV and St. Pauli, or at least not as much as nowadays). Indeed, it was from this point that the political antagonism between the two sets of fans intensified. In December 1984, Hamburg and Borussia Dortmund neo-Nazis attacked several Hafenstraße buildings with Molotov cocktails. This was not an isolated case. Rather, the siege against squatted buildings by neo-Nazi hooligan crews would persist for nearly a decade.[12] This

10. In Hamburg in 1983 the Anti-Fascist Action/National Organisation (AFA/NO) was created, which consisted of members of the Communist League, the KPD and autonomist activists. The national steering body for these groups did not reject the use of violence to stop the neo-Nazis. Furthermore, its antifascist activists extended the fight against the extreme right to opposing capitalism and imperialism. AFA/NO was created as a consequence of the storming of the Federal Congress held by the NPD in the town of Bad Fallingbostel, 100 kilometres south of Hamburg. Around 2,000 antifascist activists besieged the building where the neo-Nazis held their party conference. The action ended with 80 activists arrested and 20 injured. Petroni, *St. Pauli siamo noi*, pp. 78–9 and 142–3.
11. An example was the reaction to the murder, on 24 December 1985, of a Turkish migrant, Ramazan Avci, by a Bergerdorf neo-Nazi group near Landwehr station in eastern Hamburg. Avci was attacked with baseball bats and run over by a car. He died in hospital three days later without having regained consciousness. His corpse was taken to Ankara for burial. On 11 January 1986, 15,000 people protested against far-right violence on Hamburg's streets. The action helped develop links between the antifascist movement and the city's immigrant community. Hamburg's Turkish community also mobilised, with some of its youth creating surveillance and active self-defence squads such as the Champs or Red Bombers. The police arrested five neo-Nazi skinheads as the perpetrators of the homicide but they were released after questioning. Eventually all five were charged with murder and received convictions of three to ten years. A few months later, Hamburg was again the stage of a racist murder. On 24 July, three skinheads from the small neo-Nazi group *Lohbrügger Army* (linked to the ANS/NA) punched and kicked builder Mehmet Kaymakci to death. The perpetrators were convicted to ten years prison and served five of these. Petroni, *St. Pauli siamo noi*, p. 80; Suso, *La claveguera marró*, p. 198.
12. On one occasion Carsten Wacker, a leader of the Hamburg neo-Nazi movement, turned up drunk and aggressive at the Onkel Otto pub in the middle of

led the squatters to organise night-time vigilante groups to avoid more surprises.

Hostility towards squatters was also directed at St. Pauli fans. This was not for nothing as many squatters were regulars at the Millerntor. The extreme rivalry spread everywhere. In 1987, in a concert by the British punk group Toy Dolls at the Markthalle centre in Hamburg, there were politically inspired clashes between HSV and St. Pauli fans. The right's attitude contrasted with that which dominated in the *Sankt Paulianer* stands where you should 'not be racist or homophobic or have a hooligan mentality'.[13] From that point on, the *Sankt Paulianer* followers became a target for hooligans and far-right groups across the country.[14]

A year later, on 21 June 1988,[15] another violent episode featuring extremist fans took place. This time it was because of the UEFA European Championship match[16] that Germany played against the

---

Hafenstraße. Its customers reacted to the provocation and Wacker ended up with a fractured skull. He left warning, 'next week there is a match and we will attack Hafenstraße'. He was referring to the match that would take place between HSV and Borussia Dortmund. On match day 300 neo-Nazis tried to storm Hafenstraße but were stopped by the police. Petroni, *St. Pauli siamo noi*, p. 79.

13. Rondinelli, *Ribelli, Sociali e Romantici*, p. 102.

14. In October that year, coinciding with a match at the Millerntor against SV Darmstadt 98, several incidents were caused by the extremist supporters of the team from the state of Hesse. On their trip to Hamburg they did a lot of damage to the train they travelled in. They continued their altercations at the Altona station they arrived at. Once inside the stadium the police had to intervene using tear gas. However, the most serious incidents happened after the match near the Reeperbahn when a group of Hafenstraße punks confronted the away fans. The resulting brawl ended with a couple of people injured and several arrests. Petroni, *St. Pauli siamo noi*, p. 133.

15. This was the year in which the hooligan phenomenon exploded in Germany. Following the British and Dutch model, widely disseminated by *Fan Treff* – the fanzine that became the platform for extremist supporters' groups across the country – different groups of fans tried to emulate British hooligans' violent behaviour. A year earlier, in 1987, coinciding with the game between Germany and England in Dortmund, several incidents occurred in the city centre when German crews tried to storm British fans. During the ensuing police intervention, 46 fans were arrested. Petroni, *St. Pauli siamo noi*, p. 121.

16. The authorities' concerns over the possibility of clashes between groups of fans during the UEFA Euro 88 in Germany were proved right when England played Germany in Düsseldorf. The English hooligans, who travelled there from Gelserkirchen – where England had played against Denmark – did not encounter

Netherlands at Hamburg's Volksparkstadion. That morning a large contingent of 300 HSV hooligans and other neo-Nazis attacked several Hafenstraße buildings. The far-rightists appeared in the district shouting 'Jews out' and 'death to the red front'. Between the squatters and right-wing radicals were riot police forming a cordon to prevent clashes. Realising they were outnumbered, the police withdrew in the midst of a shower of Molotov cocktails, steel balls, stones, sticks and rockets. According to the police, 60 people were injured (of which 17 were police officers) and the material damage caused was estimated at 100,000 marks. Days before the conflict, the Hamburg-published weekly paper *Stern* published 'gaffes' by the neo-Nazi fans in which they talked about 'cleansing the St. Pauli docks'.

Shortly after, concurring with the first match of the 1988–9 season (played in July), Nuremberg hooligans arrived in Hamburg with the intention of attacking Hafenstraße buildings. Having been warned of the possibility of incidents, around a hundred activists made preparations to defend the buildings, while many bikers rode the surrounding streets to monitor any neo-Nazi movements. Around 9 pm, squatters and hooligans clashed in front of the Albers Eck pub, a few metres from the squats. It took the law-and-order forces an hour to restore normality.

As we described before, in the late 1980s St. Pauli had numerous neo-Nazi supporters. On 12 August 1989, the club lost 0–1 to FC Nuremberg. But the defeat was made worse by racist shouting from *Sankt Paulianer* fans against Souleyman Sané, the visitors' Senegalese striker. For many St. Pauli followers that was incomprehensible and shameful. The editors of *Millerntor Roar!* quickly reacted by producing a leaflet titled 'Players and Fans against Racism', which was publicly supported by all FC St. Pauli's first-team players – headed by Ippig. It was also backed by all of the *Nordkurve* fan clubs, including the Heiligen Geister, the Tornado and the Millerntor, all of which were related to the *Kutten* phenomenon and

---

any kind of policing that would stop them from clashing with local extremist fans.
Petroni, *St. Pauli siamo noi*, p. 121.

had not adopted any political stance until then. The reaction by the *Nordkurve* groups was particularly significant, as the racist shouts against the visiting player had come from that stand. Furthermore, the pamphlet called on the DFB to ban racist chants and symbols in all grounds. Supporters also urged the club to begin the actions required to eradicate this kind of behaviour on its premises. Just a month later, on 16 September, St. Pauli played a derby against HSV. Despite the security operation in place, there were clashes between the two teams' followers. These began when 200 HSV hooligans attacked *Sankt Paulianers*. That day, a group of skinheads had assaulted several people at a punk festival in a central square.

A year later, in the midst of German political reunification and with rightist extremism thriving[17] – putting immigration at the centre of the political debate – extremist away fans caused repeated incidents. Coinciding with the home game against Karls-ruher, nearly 200 fans were involved in a brawl in the Hans Albers Platz, which ended in approximately 60 arrests. A few days later, on 7 March, there were new fights coinciding with the UEFA Cup match between HSV and Juventus. The Hamburg hooligans went scouring the city looking for fans from Turin. But the actual clashes

17.   In the early 1990s the neo-Nazi movement gained new wind, mainly in the former East Germany. It emerged that cities such as Dresden, Rostock, Cottbus, Magdeburg and Berlin had far-right skinhead groups. This was something detectable in the dying days of the GDR from xenophobic or anti-Semitic attacks carried out. An example was the desecration of the Schönhauser Allee Jewish cemetery, built in 1827 in Prenzlauer Berg (a district in East Berlin), which took place on 5 March 1988. Then, six students from the Fischer Kurt School opposite the cemetery were arrested for writing anti-Semitic slogans on several tombstones. The actions of these small neo-Nazi groups, including hooliganism inside football stadiums, was silenced by the East German authorities. One attack by skinheads on 17 June 1987, was on a group of youngsters attending a punk concert in a church. Half a year later, the perpetrators were arrested and were given prison sentences of between 14 months and two years. Between 1991 and 1992, violent acts increased nationally by 54 per cent – from 1,438 to 2,285. Of the victims, 90 per cent were foreigners. Left-wing and alternative young people were also a priority target for the neo-Nazis. On 11 May 1992, punk Torsten 'Lampe' Lamprecht was murdered in Magdeburg, and on 21 November 1992 the activist Silvio Meier was killed at the Samaritstraße underground station in Berlin. A year earlier, in September 1991, neo-Nazi youth besieged a building in Hoyerswerda housing Mozambican and Vietnamese refugees for a week. Petroni, *St. Pauli siamo noi*, p. 141. See also Suso, *La claveguera marró*, p. 214.

were with a group of autonomists, which ended with 120 arrests. A week later, such incidents were repeated corresponding with the match between HSV and Bayern Munich.

The same year, 1990, the World Cup was held in Italy.[18] Taking advantage of the semi-final match between Germany and England, a group of 300 hooligans attacked cops with bottles and firecrackers in front of the Davidwache police station. Shortly after, members of the United group attacked the Jolly Roger bar.[19] A month later, antifascist St. Pauli fans stormed the pub frequented by the *Sankt Paulianer* neo-Nazis. As a regular in the Hafenstraße section recalls, 'The right-wing fans were a problem. At the beginning, there were more of them in the *Nordkurve* than us. Despite that, we grew and grew until eventually we could kick them out of the stadium. Along with their shitty slogans and Nazi symbols.'[20]

---

18. After 1989, actions by neo-Nazi groups multiplied, particularly in the eastern states. The violence and xenophobia ended up on the terraces. Another element that helped this process was the increase in right-wing skins in the country. They could also be seen in clubs such as Berlin FC Dynamo (the forerunner to Berlin FC), Dynamo Dresden, Hansa Rostock, FC Energie Cottbus, 1 FC Lokomotive Leipzig, 1 FC Magdeburg and Eintracht Braunschweig. In April 1990, coinciding with the anniversary of Adolf Hitler's birth, FC Berlin extremists sang neo-Nazi songs during the match between their team and Hansa Rostock. That was the prelude to incidents that led to around 50 injuries and 30 arrests. Meanwhile in the west, extremist supporters changed their look from skin to 'casual' to avoid police controls. The growth led the German government to introduce the National Concept for Security and Sport (*Nationales Konzept Sport und Sicherheit*, NKSS): a series of measures to stop acts of violence, racism and xenophobia in the stadiums. Petroni, *St. Pauli siamo noi*, pp. 130–1 and 173.
19. A key meeting point for the most radical wing of the *Sankt Paulianer* fans. Located at 44 Budapesterstraße, near the Millerntor stadium: 'its walls are covered with stickers from all the Hamburg team's crews. It's a dingy dive with several screens to watch matches. Customers drink beer and the atmosphere is filled with smoke from cigarettes and the joints that some smoke, while rock music can be heard in the background. 'Dump' is the word that comes to mind when you enter. But it is much more than that. The bar is managed by a group of 100 supporters: the Ball Kult. Its proceeds go to Braun Weisse Hilfe, *Sankt Pauli*'s social-initiative section, which among other things organises football championships against racism, pro-integration campaigns, and support for the disadvantaged.' 'Sankt Pauli, fútbol y política en el barrio', *El País* (3 July 2014).
20. Rondinelli, *Ribelli, Sociali e Romantici*, p. 120.

Similar events happened on 8 July when a group of neo-Nazi radicals tried to go to the Reeperbahn, where thousands of people were celebrating the *Mannschaft's*[21] victory over Argentina in the World Cup final. On that occasion, the police stopped the extreme rightists from getting to the Hafenstraße, leading to clashes between police and hooligans and damage to local shops and pubs. As a result of the conflicts, 54 police officers were injured and 88 people arrested. That same day, members of the United Fan Club joined with HSV hooligans to attack the *Fanladen* HQ. Three months later, coinciding with the match Hertha Berlin played at the HSV ground, on 14 October groups of neo-Nazi hooligans went on a spree against Hamburg's shops and bars. This time a demonstration was called to defend St. Pauli, which 2,000 fans and local residents joined. In a seemingly downward spiral, towards the end of the year neo-Nazi supporters of 1. FC Nürnberg and HSV caused similar unrest.

In the first match of the 1990–1 season FC St. Pauli had to travel to Berlin to take on Hertha. The trip obviously entailed risks. At the time, the Hertha following included very active neo-Nazi groupings (such as Endsieg, Zyklon B and Wannseefront, and whose members mostly came from the Brandenburg suburbs – a local far-right heartland). Faced with the possibility of clashes, nearly 400 members of Berlin's alternative scene met in Kottbusser Tor, in the Kreuzberg district, to join up with the 5,000 St. Pauli fans that had come from Hamburg.

Despite campaigns against the violence and its tendency to spiral, the incidents did not stop. In October 1991, slogans against Turkish-origin fans (such as 'Fuck foreigners') were yet again made from the *Nordkurve*. When one of the fans targeted called back 'fuck you fascists!' he was punched. Again, the editors of *Millerntor Roar!*, together with the Hamburg Turkish community, advised the club to prohibit the use of racist language in the stadium. This request was accepted almost straight away. Moreover, in an explicit gesture of solidarity, for the next Millerntor game, held on 3 November against FC Remscheid, the board of directors invited 150 members

---

21. [Translator's note]: nickname for the German national team.

of the Turkish community to come to the ground. That day banners could be seen on the terraces with slogans such as 'Resist racism' and 'Against racial hatred, self-defence now', and you could hear chants such as 'Nazis out' (*'Nazis raus'*). To underline the club's stance and make clear its 'rejection of violence against Turks in Germany',[22] FC St. Pauli played the aforementioned match (on 26 November) against Galatasaray, one of the most key and popular clubs in Turkish football. And at the end of the year, the *braun-weiß* team became the first German team to officially ban racist chants and neo-Nazi flags in its stadium.

The club's clear and firm stance was taken, furthermore, at a complex time socially. In August 1992, race riots took place in Rostock's Lichtenhagen neighbourhood. These were some of the darkest episodes in German history since the end of the Second World War.[23] The following spring, St. Pauli fans that had travelled to the city, and were at the Warnow River estuary, were attacked by 400 neo-Nazi Hansa supporters (as well as far-rightists from Frankfurt, Leipzig and Berlin) armed with iron bars. The attackers chased the *Sankt Paulianers* through the area close to the stadium until the latter got to the train station. Two years later, on 23 Sep-

---

22. On the day that the club invited 150 members of the Turkish community to watch a match at the Millerntor, the banning of using racist language was announced through the stadium's speakers. For more on this, see the German documentary *Und ich weiß, warum ich hier stehe* made in 1991 by the *Millerntor Roar!* fanzine. See also Rondinelli, *Sociali e Romantici!*, p. 129 and Vera, 'La increible historia de St. Pauli'.
23. Between 22 and 24 August 1992, hundreds of skinheads and neo-Nazi party members attacked an apartment block housing dozens of refugees, most of whom were Romanian gypsies. Around 3,000 locals took part and the police stood by outnumbered and eventually left. The centre had to be evacuated on the second day of incidents by special police units sent from Hamburg. Then, the demonstrators moved on to target a building in which 115 Vietnamese refugees lived. As a result of the events the police arrested 370 and investigated 408 people linked to the attacks. Among those arrested were 110 citizens from western states and 37 from the east. Of the 2,050 police officers deployed in Rostock during the events, 204 were injured. Weeks later, an antifascist march took place on the streets of Rostock to denounce the pogrom. Hundreds of St. Pauli fans from Hamburg went to the 13,000-strong march. The Lichtenhagen events were repeated in other cities. In the following weeks there were attacks on around 40 sanctuaries and asylum centres in places such as Wismar, Lübz, Neubrandenburg, Güstow, Ueckermünde, Kröpelin, Schwerin, Retschow and Schwarzendorf.

tember 1995, St. Pauli played at Rostock again. The match had to be interrupted when the St. Pauli goalkeeper, Klaus Thomforde, and another player, Martin Driller, were stunned after home supporters threw a smoke canister that exploded near to them. Meanwhile, the police used tear gas to disperse the Hansa hooligans trying to get to the St. Pauli fans' stand. This all happened in the midst of fascist salutes, threats, the raising of scarves with the words 'Fucking St. Pauli' and chants such as 'We are building a tube line from St. Pauli to Auschwitz'. The attacks by local extremists continued until the Hamburgers left Rostock by train, escorted by hundreds of police.

The players affected by the gas canister suffered irritation to their eyes, forcing them to be taken off. Accordingly Hansa Rostock was fined 10,000 marks and made to play a match behind closed doors. All the same, the strong stance taken over the incidents by a section of supporters – linked to the autonomist and punk movements – was rejected by part of the St. Pauli's fan base that did not wish to politicise the club. This created an intense debate between those that wanted to take on the Nazis and those unhappy about turning the terraces into a front against far-right extremism.[24]

A year before the incident, the DFB had decided that the German team play England at Hamburg's Volksparkstadion on 20 April – a significant date in the Nazi imaginary because it was Hitler's birthdate. The day before, the German under-19 team was to play its English counterpart at the Millerntor. The idea that the stadium and city would be occupied by far-right *Mannschaft* hooligans led a section of St. Pauli fans to get mobilised. For many *Sankt Paulianers* playing the German national anthem at their stadium was a provocation in itself. The fanzines *Unhaltbar* and *Der Übersteiger*[25]

---

24. As well as fan groups and autonomists, other entities prepared to confront the neo-Nazi attacks. This was the case with members of the country's Turkish and Kurdish communities. In the Kreuzberg district in Berlin, dozens of Turkish-origin youth set up the Boys 36 self-defence group. The same happened in Bremen, where around 50 Turks armed with baseball bats smashed up a bar frequented by extreme-rightists. In the year 1992, as many as 398 anti-Nazi actions were carried out.
25. Self-funded publication, first appeared in 1993, that was a sort of successor to the *Millerntor Roar!* It had an editorial team made up of 20 club fans. It published five editions a year and had a circulation of 5,000. It dealt with current local, domestic

organised different actions against the federation's decision. On 3 December, during the match played at home against Wolfsburg, a protest was held in which 7,000 yellow cards were shown when the players went on to the pitch. A few days later, the DFB scrapped its plans, alleging that this was due to limited car park space at St. Pauli's ground, and moved the match to Berlin.[26] The wrangles over the match led the English Football Association to announce that its team would not play. At the beginning of April, in the midst of all these difficulties, the DFB definitively cancelled the friendly match.

Violence by HSV hooligans resurfaced in 1998. That summer the World Cup was held in France. On 21 June, Germany took on Yugoslavia at Lens. Hours before the game, extremist German fans assaulted police officer David Nivel, putting him in a six-week coma. Two Hamburg 'hools' were involved in the attack. A few months later, when FC St. Pauli and HSV played their respective matches at Stuttgart (against Kickers Stuttgart and VfB Stuttgart respectively), a group of extremist Hamburg fans attacked the *Sankt Paulianers* while they were waiting for a train at the city's main station.

In all, the 1990s were a socially turbulent time for the club. Because of the growth and consolidation of the 'St. Pauli myth', which made the club an international milestone for alternative football, its fans had to resist animosity from the most extremist fan groups in Germany. *Sanktpaulianers'* ideological stance made them a central target for extreme right-wing hooligans. But this did not intimidate St. Pauli. Instead, it fought back against the growing extremism, something that made the club unique in German football.

---

and international affairs, football-related issues, anti-racist and anti-homophobic struggles, the music scene and the local problems caused by gentrification. Among its many initiatives, it produced – in 1998 and in conjunction with Bitzcore Records – a compact disc (also produced as a double album). This was called *Der FC St. Pauli ist schuld daß ich so bin* and was a compilation of 30 characteristic *Sankt Paulianer* songs mixed with terrace chanting. Rondinelli, *Ribelli, Sociali e Romantici*, p. 187.

26.   Members of the *Der Übersteiger* editorial board came up with other initiatives, such as, in April 2001, denouncing supporters that had organised trips to games using the Lufthansa airline. This was in response to the company collaborating with 10,000 deportations of asylum seekers per year. Rondinelli, *Ribelli, Sociali e Romantici*, pp. 128 and 143.

PART IV

Stands with a Conscience

11

A Unique Mix of Football and Social Projects

The terrace culture developed around FC St. Pauli and the club's attainment of cult status were not mere side effects of the changes that much of the local social fabric was going through. They also came from the club having worked in unison with its fans and adopted its principles. It had understood the importance of fans, that their empowerment was a fundamental part of the club, and the need for FC St. Pauli to actively participate in the life and defence of its neighbourhood. This has enabled a series of organisations to be created that have determined the club's unique structure today.

As noted in Chapter 10, the late 1980s saw the growth of the far right in German stadiums. As neo-Nazism spread among football fans, the Pirates' supporters' organisations began to take shape. In October 1989, just a month before the opening of the Berlin Wall border crossings, the St. Pauli Fan Project was launched. This followed similar lines to the *Fanprojekt* set up by HSV six years earlier in the wake of Adrian Maleika's death. Its main premise was to teach young fans about the dangers of violence, racism and alcohol abuse. At the same time it created a support network that would allow these problems to be addressed successfully. The project, a precursor of today's *Fanladen*, had been approved by the club's manager, Peter Koch, and its vice president, lawyer Christian Hinzpeter, who recognised the potential benefits of working with the fan base. However, despite the explicit support and financial backing from the club, the *Fanladen* has always taken pains to maintain its independence from St. Pauli in order to avoid conflicts of interest between its activities and the running of the club.

Sven Brux,[1] current head of security at FC St. Pauli, was initially responsible for coordinating the *Fanladen*. Its team set up their headquarters in a shipping container behind the *Nordkurve* (North Stand). There they began doing the first coordinating of away trips for St. Pauli supporters, who were offered packages covering train fares and tickets to games. The first trip took fans to Leverkusen, North Rhine-Westphalia, to watch the match against Bayer (on 3 November 1989). On that occasion some 60 fans accompanied the St. Pauli team.

The *Fanladen* officially opened its doors on 15 February 1990, when it moved to a former hairdressing salon 25 square metres in size, located relatively near to the stadium. This key St. Pauli organisation was located on Beim Grünen Jäger Straße, after leaving its original premises in Brigittenstraße. Its main role was to coordinate ticket sales for St. Pauli matches played away from the Millerntor, and to organise travel for fans.[2] The trips were also intended to publicise the alternative fan model that had characterised St. Pauli since the Hafenstraße group had joined it. Moreover, travelling together encouraged fans to share experiences and to spread ideological awareness to non-politicised fellow supporters.[3]

---

1. In Cologne, Brux initially became a football fan through his city's home team, 1. FC Cologne. When he discovered punk, he had to personally endure the presence of neo-Nazi fans at the Müngersdorfer Stadion. In 1986 he moved to Hamburg to do the *Zivildienst* (compulsory community service) and became acquainted with the local punk scene and the Hafenstraße community. He also associated with the group of fans who attend St. Pauli games and ended up actively participating in the founding of *Millerntor Roar!* See Davidson, *Pirates, Punks and Politics*, p. 123.
2. Two or three hours before games that were considered high-risk, the *Fanladen* members responsible for coordinating the trip would meet with the stadium's heads of security and the police to organise logistics. Davidson, *Pirates, Punks and Politics*, p. 178.
3. The arrival of fans associated with the autonomous movement and squats met with resistance from some veteran supporters, who did not welcome the politicisation of the club. These differences of opinion could be seen when flyers began to appear around the Millerntor with the words 'Politik in unserem Stadion? Nein Danke' ('Politics in our stadium? No thanks'). *Millerntor Roar!* immediately responded to the campaign, declaring that 'football is as apolitical as the production of an atomic bomb'. The arguments between the two sections of fans were intense. Those who were against politicisation argued that 'doing politics' from the stands discredited the organisation and the fans, while those in favour of the club and fans

Aside from organising these trips, the *Fanladen* became a meeting point for the brown-and-white faithful. It was a place where fans could watch matches on television, share a few beers and discuss new ways of supporting the club. The *Fanladen* headquarters also sold fan-produced materials.[4] These included the first T-shirts with the skull and crossbones logo above the name St. Pauli, which together became the club's official logo. As Sven Brux put it, this was 'the symbol that we the poor use against the rich clubs like Bayern and Madrid'. The *Fanladen* also sold the *Millerntor Roar!* fanzine and the famous stickers proclaiming 'St. Pauli Fans gegen Rechts' ('St. Pauli Fans against the Right') – showing a fist smashing a swastika.[5] Two years later, the *Fanladen* moved to bigger premises in Thadenstraße. The project soon became a hub for St. Pauli fan culture, coordinating, together with the supporters' club spokespeople (*Fanclubsprecherrat*), 597 official fan clubs around the world – that way becoming the official link between FC St. Pauli and its international followers.

The *Fanladen* has also organised awareness-raising campaigns around issues such as football violence and racism. For instance, during the 2002/3 season, when the club was playing in the *Bundesliga 2*, the *Fanladen* and FC St. Pauli launched the *KiezKick* project. This allowed local boys and girls from disadvantaged families to play football for free. As a result, 60 children at risk of marginalisation between the ages of seven and 18 participate in training sessions that focus on socialising and having fun. The idea is that sporting activities keep young people away from the dangers of exclusion, violence

positioning themselves said, 'Of course we do politics, because we don't want to leave room for the fascists and nationalists who have been ruining the fun of football for years.' Rondinelli, *Ribelli, Sociali e Romantici*, p. 125; Petroni, *St. Pauli siamo noi*, p. 135.

4. *Fanladen* manages its own merchandising, independently from the official material sold by the club, in another example of its desire to maintain its autonomy from the organisation. Petroni, *St. Pauli siamo noi*, p. 126.

5. An estimated 2.3 million of these stickers had been sold by 2001. It was undoubtedly the most popular design, and the one identified with the 'St. Pauli counterculture'. Profits from the sale of the stickers went toward financing the *Fanladen*, thus allowing it to maintain its independence from the club. Rondinelli, *Ribelli, Sociali e Romantici*, p. 125.

and drugs. In addition, players from the club's first team often attend the twice-weekly training sessions.[6] The initial funding was raised through a friendly between St. Pauli and a team of local celebrities in July 2002, which officially launched the project and helped to publicise it. *KiezKick* has received several awards, including the 2006 City of Hamburg Integration Prize. To ensure its continued viability, financial support is still provided by the *Fanladen* – alongside other organisations and anonymous donors – although its main role is to organise the project's logistical aspects.[7]

Other *Fanladen* projects include the *U18 Ragazzi* programme, which organises social activities such as football and skating for local teenagers. It also sets up meetings with first-team players and coordinates away trips for young fans, who travel together separately from adult supporters (but accompanied by supervisors and social workers). The motto for these trips is 'no nicotine, no alcohol', and the main aim is to spread values such as antiracism and respect among teenagers. Pre-match meetings with young fans from rival teams are also organised to allow participants to interact and share experiences in a positive atmosphere, supervised by adults from the respective Fan Projects. The *Fanladen* also hosts recreational activities for teenagers on weekdays. So it comes as no surprise that in 2011 an estimated 20 per cent of FC St. Pauli spectators were under 18. Ultimately, the set of measures is intended to strengthen ties with the community, and to offer alternatives to young people suffering from drug addiction and other problems. To this end, the *Fanladen* is also an active founding member of the Association of Active Football Fans (*Bündnis Aktiver Fußball-Fans*, BAFF) network.[8]

---

6. During the summer months, training sessions are held on outdoor gravel near the Millerntor Stadium. In winter the club makes a gym or other venue available to allow the children's activities to continue.
7. The *KiezKick in Brasilien* project was carried out in July 2014, in conjunction with the World Cup in Brazil. Organised in conjunction with several Latin American non-governmental organisations, it consisted of taking eight young people to São Paulo to spend time and share experiences with peers from a different social and cultural background. Rondinelli, *Ribelli, Sociali e Romantici*, p. 253.
8. Created in 1993 with the involvement of St. Pauli supporters. Fans from some

Many of these initiatives began under the guidance of the NKSS. This is a national organisation promoting diversity and anti-extremism among fans, and supporting almost 50 projects around the country. The NKSS, which the *Fanladen* belongs to, receives financial support from both the German Football Association and League (DFB and DFL). It also has institutional backing from Hamburg City Council. The preventative measures that it has introduced, together with football's gradual commercialisation, have led to a deproletarianisation of German football that has progressively transformed terrace culture.

Since spring 2004, the *Fanladen* has also organised the annual *Antira Turnier* (antiracist tournament) in Hamburg. This happened after members had attended several editions of the *Mondiali Anti-razziste*, organised by the Emilia Romagna region's *Progetto Ultrà UISP* (*Unione Italiana Sport Per Tutti*, or Italian Union of Sport for All) project and held in a series of Italian towns since 1997.[9] The *Antira Turnier* is backed by FC St. Pauli, which allows the tournament to be played on its training grounds. Now a landmark event for left-wing and antifascist football fans around Europe, it is not just a football gathering but one to exchange ideas and experiences. It includes a range of activities such as talks and exhibitions organised during match weekends. There have even been meetings with Holocaust survivors and, in the 2016 edition, visits to the Memorial at the Neuengamme Concentration Camp (an extension of the Sachsenhausen Camp situated around 15 kilometres south-east of Hamburg city centre).

Another joint initiative by fans and the club was the *Fanräume* (supporters' area) project, which was originally conceived in

15 clubs around Germany take part in the network, which organises nationwide campaigns to denounce and address football-related discrimination of any kind – from xenophobia to sexism. The BAFF has launched initiatives against the criminalisation of fans, in favour of standing areas in stadiums and in support of reasonable match times.

9.   The first editions were held at Montefiorino in the province of Modena. From 2000 the tournament was played in Montecchio, a small municipality in Terni. In 2007 it moved to Casalecchio di Reno, a town near Bologna. Since 2011 the Mondiali Antirazzisti has been held in Bosco Albergati, near Cavazzona.

ST. PAULI

2007 to create a multipurpose space for fans. Six years later, on 1 June 2013, the *Fanräume* officially opened in the lower part of the *Gegengerade-Stand*, which was still being redeveloped.[10] The project received 40,000 euros from the Active Support Members' Department (*Abteilung Fördernde Mitglieder*, AFM) and nearly 400,000 euros from fundraising by fans.

Due to the efforts of the AGIM the AFM had been created a few years earlier, in 1999, coinciding with the tenth anniversary of the *Fanladen*. The department's priority was to give fans the chance to become active FC St. Pauli members, gaining a say over the running of the club through voting in the annual general assembly.[11] The AFM thus created a space for members who do not participate in sporting activities but actively contribute to the promotion of the club's different social initiatives. It also played a key role in promoting democratic participation in the club.

The AFM's creation has allowed 50 per cent of the club's social base to be signed up as members. This is a significant figure, considering that the AFM has brought together over 18,000 fans.[12] Thus, many supporters who ended up in the stands in the previous decade because they had been inspired by the self-management approach of the Hafenstraße residents came together in the AFM to establish fan control over the running of the club.

10. The area is 500 metres square and includes a conference room, a space for foreign members and a larger area in which concerts and cultural events can be held. It has become a meeting point for supporters before and after games.

11. General assemblies are organised at least once a year, and all members are eligible to participate (although those who have not paid their quarterly subs forfeit their right to vote). To prevent fraud, voting can only be done in person, and postal and proxy votes are not allowed. An electoral committee set up in 2001 oversees the voting. The most important decisions made by the General Assembly are to approve the accounts – a prerequisite for the DFB to renew the club's license – and to elect the club's president. The Board of Directors, made up of seven members elected by the assembly every four years, is in charge of nominating five candidates. Its members meet every two weeks and they also represent the club at official events.

12. It grew surprisingly quickly, jumping from 4,500 members in 2008 to 10,000 in November 2012. By August 2014 there were 12,000 members, and a few months later the figure reached 18,000 – more than 60 per cent of St. Pauli members, making the AFM the club's largest section.

Among other milestones, pressure from fans managed to reduce the visibility of advertising in the stadium and to block ads that were invasive or contrary to the club's values. For example, no advertising is done through the stadium's public address system immediately before matches, to encourage a symbiosis between players and fans. For St. Pauli, 'Football and *tifo* [choreographies] are the life blood of the club, sponsors have to adapt.'

The desire of the club's fans to influence the day-to-day running of the club was given expression when an organisational model prioritising member involvement began to be implemented in Germany. Until 1998, all German clubs had been structured according to the *eingetragener Verein* (e.V., registered association) model, which meant that their boards of directors were supposed to be democratically chosen by their members. This changed, however, when the DFL allowed clubs to become limited liability companies, a measure implemented to accommodate teams who wanted to attract investors in order to increase their competitiveness.[13] In 1999, to prevent fans losing control of their clubs, the DFB introduced a regulation (popularly known as '50 + 1') by which at least 51 per cent of the shares of these limited liability companies[14] had to remain in the hands of registered members' associations.[15] Fans could thus continue to control the clubs by maintaining decision-making power over the club's administration. This was the model Germany chose to back. It guaranteed democratic ownership by fans to prevent clubs from falling into

13. In the 2011–12 season, seven of the 18 German first division clubs still followed the e.V. model (Freiburg, HSV, Kaiserslautern, Mainz, Nuremberg, Schalke 04 and Stuttgart). The rest were controlled by private investors.
14. Initially only two clubs – Bayer Leverkusen and Wolfsburg – were allowed to maintain their organisational specificity, because their business links predated the regulations. Both were founded by companies: the pharmaceutical chemical industry in the case of Bayer Leverkusen and leading German automobile manufacturer Volkswagen in the case of Wolfsburg.
15. Not everybody agreed with the federation's decision. In 2009, Hannover 96 president Martin Kind suggested modifying the 50+1 rule to allow the advent of new investors strengthening clubs' competitiveness. The proposal was ruled out when 32 first and second division clubs voted against it.

the hands of corporate investors and billionaires. The system managed to

confirm the Bundesliga as a model based on active economic development and affordable ticket prices through the licensing system. Top priority is given to maintaining the operation of all League members during the season in order to ensure the stability, integrity, and continuity of national and international competition. The licensing system also sets out guidelines for transparent corporate governance.

This forces clubs to be financially responsible if they want to renew their competition licences.

In order to receive a licence from the DFL, clubs in Germany must submit proof of their financial soundness. The DFL also reviews each club's annual business plan. Even so, an additional 'safety net' in the form of a trust account provides insurance of sorts to guard against clubs undergoing financial difficulties during the season. But no club has failed to implement its financial viability plan since the Bundesliga began in the 1960s. If we add to this an affordable ticket-pricing policy and a salary cap for players, we have the three keys to the success of German football.

For many years, until the refurbishment of the Millerntor stadium was completed, the AFM occupied one of the old shipping containers near the main entrance of the Millerntor Südkurve (South Stand) fitted out as offices and exhibition spaces. As well as encouraging fans' active participation, the AFM also set up and became involved in various community projects, focusing primarily on young people. First-team players, coaching staff and long-term members participate in the activities organised by the AFM, which are intended to introduce young people to FC St. Pauli's core principles and values. The AFM also funds other activities, such as a vocational training programme under the slogan 'You'll Never Work Alone', aimed at helping young players to get work in the future. The initiative (also carried out by clubs such as

Hoffenheim, Freiburg and HSV) enjoys the active collaboration of companies in the city.

Along the same lines, in 2001 the AFM, together with FC St. Pauli, launched Young Rebels,[16] a campaign aimed at spreading St. Pauli's values among young people and encouraging new talent. Two years later, the AFM secured a building near the training ground to accommodate five young players. At the same time, it worked on developing a youth training centre, which was one of the DFL requirements for the club to renew its federal licence. The idea was to 'expand the club's social and cultural role in the local community and promote the well-being of young players – both on and off the field'. Local companies would support the project by giving the players work experience. Under the motto 'You'll Never Work Alone', the programme gave young people the opportunity to develop alternative career paths in case they did not succeed in professional football.

The AFM (whose president is Alexander Gunkel) allocates 75 per cent of its annual budget to running and developing activities for young people in the neighbourhood. This also covers the cost of training community workers who supervise the AFM's interventions.[17] The remaining 25 per cent goes to the maintenance and

---

16. *Young Rebels* is also the name of the biannual magazine that informs members of its activities, in conjunction with an email newsletter. Another similar project is AFM Radio, which broadcasts the club's matches live, with commentary by supporters and former players. Rondinelli, *Ribelli, Sociali e Romantici*, p. 217.

17. AFM also works with the Julius-Leber-Schule, a college where around twenty of the club's players, between the ages of 13 and 16, can combine study and training. St. Pauli provides transport for the students from the training ground to the school. Through the project they receive an education that allows them to develop a sense of identity and belonging within the club's culture, a goal that it is hoped will extend to the club's younger fans. With this in mind, in 2008 the club launched FC St. Pauli Rabauken, for children aged 0 to 13. The initiative consists of a kind of community centre at the Millerntor Stadium, where children can organise birthday parties and participate in other activities. The FC St. Pauli Rabauken also works with more than 30 primary and secondary schools through the *Schulkooperationen* programme, in which children participate in 90 minutes of recreational activities each week, and offers discounts for children to attend first-team matches. Rondinelli, *Ribelli, Sociali e Romantici*, pp. 218 and 227.

purchase of the computer equipment required for the day-to-day running of the project, and to cover design and printing costs.

One of the most notable projects the AFM participated in was the refurbishment of the club's Kollaustraße training ground. The idea was to enlarge the space and accommodate the under-17 and under-19 teams[18] so that they could share the facilities with the first-team players. In 2003, the AFM also financed the *Jugendtalenthaus* (youth talent house), which opened in 2004. This provides a meeting place for about 40 young players in the club's junior, under-17 and under-18 teams.

All of the AFM's initiatives are based on a holistic idea of education that aims to provide young players with comprehensive education at the sporting, academic and personal levels. It prioritises human education over success in sport, and transmits values such as respect for rivals, antiracism and fair play. To this end, coaches use a training method that prioritises player development and not the team's results. 'Those who enjoy playing will find it easier to learn new things', is the explanation given by Rainer Zastrutzki, coordinator of one of the club's junior football teams.

In addition to these projects, the AFM has also collaborated in campaigns such as Action Against Homophobia and Sexism – issues of central importance at St. Pauli. This campaign began in October 2007, thanks to the work of several activists and fans backed by the *Fanladen*. It was part of the Football Against Racism in Europe (FARE) Action Week organised by the European FARE network. Actions included handing out 10,000 flyers to raise awareness among fans, and distributing 10,000 stickers with messages in support of tolerance and against homophobia. Banners were also displayed at the *Südkurve* to denounce homophobic and sexist dis-

---

18.   FC St. Pauli has several men's teams as well as the first team. The younger categories are made up of the under-23s, under-19s, under-17s, under-16s and under-15s teams. The club also has seven women's teams, as well as a blind football team. In 2006, St. Pauli organised the first five-a-side football championship for blind players recognised by the DFB. Lastly, it has a team of retired veteran players. In late 2013, St. Pauli had over 3,800 male members and 500 female members playing in its different teams.

crimination in the football world. Meanwhile, the club as a whole made a strong commitment to opposing homophobia and sexism, becoming the first football team in the world to adopt an official stance against these kinds of discrimination. As well as the AFM, the campaign had the support of the *Fanladen* and Queerpass St. Pauli – a fan club promoting tolerance and respect in football.[19] Indeed, the St. Pauli fan base is known for fighting LGBT discrimination of any kind, as demonstrated when St. Pauli played 1860 Munich at the Millerntor stadium on 29 April 2016. During the match, the *Gegengerade* raised a banner stating 'All colours are beautiful', while different flags made a rainbow mosaic – the gay and lesbian pride symbol designed in San Francisco in 1978 by Gilbert Baker.

The AFM also runs a support programme for migrants and refugees, providing free tickets throughout the season in order to introduce and connect them to the club. St. Pauli's fan crews have a similar project in which they donate a percentage of their income to pay for tickets for refugees. The club also collaborates by giving out sporting material and official merchandise.

One of the latest initiatives the AFM has been involved in is the project to create a FC St. Pauli museum at the new *Gegengerade*.[20] This became an aim of St. Pauli fans after the police failed to incorporate a new station inside the stadium.

---

19.   Thanks to these fans, in May 2008 St. Pauli signed the Leipzig Declaration against discrimination.
20.   In 2010, to mark the club's centenary, an exhibition was held in 31 shipping containers in the Millerntorplatz (located near the main entrance to the stadium). Through documents, photographs and other materials the exhibition offered an overview of FC St. Pauli's history from its earliest days. The following year, Michael Pahl, author of the book on the club's first hundred years, and Roger Hasenbein, a member of the Supervisory Board, suggested creating a permanent museum with a traditional museum display and an interactive space. The project also included linking the museum to stadium tours that go into the area surrounding the stadium. In the end, the 1910 e.V. association was set up to promote the idea of the museum and organise temporary exhibitions and cultural events. These included the Football and Love festival, which was held for the first time in September 2013 and attracted 2,500 visitors. Activities ranged from flag and banner workshops to children's entertainment and exhibitions on sex discrimination and homophobia in football. Rondinelli, *Ribelli, Sociali e Romantici*, pp. 247–8.

Through all these organisational structures and the initiatives they coordinate and collaborate in, St. Pauli supporters have managed to democratise the club. This empowerment of fans means that the club's management now has to take their opinion into account when making decisions.

12

The Rebel's Choice of St. Pauli-Celtic

Aside from these organisations, which make up the club's network of associations and empower its fans, FC St. Pauli is also defined by its approach to football. Not in the sense of sophisticated tactics or intrigues to put together the best team at any cost, but in its particular approach to sport, from the perspective of fans. Unconditional support, colour on the terraces, chants, communion between players and supporters – all this is St. Pauli too. Or St. Pauli is essentially this, especially considering that it is not a winning team. It never has been, but then its fans do not demand wins. At least that's how it has been so far.

This spirit is almost certainly what attracted some Glasgow Celtic fans to the Millerntor. Celtic is one of Scotland's leading clubs, with a long tradition in European competitions (as demonstrated by the success of their 'Lisbon Lions' in the 1967 European Cup final). Celtic's sporting record is clearly a world away from that of St. Pauli. Yet the Glasgow team has established a fraternal connection with FC St. Pauli. In fact, the relationship is so special that it is the only club friendship officially acknowledged by St. Pauli fans.[1]

It all started in the 1990s, when members of the Hafenstraße Bloc contacted the editors of *Not the View*, one of the fanzines published by Celtic supporters.[2] This was a natural move bearing in mind that

---

1.   Aside from this official friendship, Ultrà Sankt Pauli 2002 (USP) does have a good relationship with Schickeria München, one of the most important Bayern Munich *ultra* groups, and also with the Filmstadt Inferno 99 supporters group for Babelsberg 03 – a Potsdam club playing in the lower divisions of German football. The USP also has good relations with the Marseille Olympique Extreme Commando, the Fortuna Düsseldorf crew, the Sampdoria Rude Boys, the Ternana Calcio Freak Brothers and some members of the Atalanta Brigate Neroazzurre.
2.   In fact, Sven Brux, a former punk from Cologne who became part of the Hafenstraße community and then worked with FC St. Pauli, was invited to participate in a conference on football in London in the early 1990s. It was there that

the *Fanladen* always has tried to keep in touch with what is going on in the organised fan movement in Europe. As a result, some St. Pauli supporters started to accompany Glasgow fans when Celtic played in European competitions. In 1992, the fanzine editors travelled to Hamburg in a trip that strengthened the rapport between the two groups. The close friendship, expressed graphically in 'The Rebel's Choice' label, was demonstrated by frequent mutual visits. The ideological affinity between the two groups of fans obviously helped, even more so given the good relationship between the *Millerntor Roar!* team and the editors of *TAL fanzine*,[3] a left-wing publication linked to Irish Republicanism that was a touchstone for the most politically committed Celtic fans.

In the 1996–7 season, Celtic played HSV in the first round of the UEFA Cup. In sporting terms, the qualifying round was quite straightforward. The Hamburg team beat the Scots 2–0 in the first leg at Celtic Park. In the second-leg match, the scoreboard at the Volksparkstadion again showed a comfortable 2–0 win for the home team. But there were incidents in the stands at both matches. The friendship between the Scottish team and St. Pauli (HSV's local rivals) was enough for militant HSV supporters to want to take on the Celtic radicals on the day of the Glasgow match on 10 September 1996. And they did so joining forces with their counterparts from the 'Blues Brothers'[4] (Rangers, Chelsea and Linfield FC).[5] For

he came in contact with the Celtic supporters. Petroni, *St. Pauli siamo noi*, p. 148.

3.   TAL is an acronym of *Tiocfaidh Ár Lá*, Gaelic for 'our day will come' and a famous slogan of the Irish Republican movement. The idea of starting a political, non-sectarian, antifascist, anti-racist publication was raised in 1991, but the first issue was not published until late the following year – to coincide with an 'Old Firm' game. The fanzine was founded in response to an incident involving a group of Celtic fans during a derby against Rangers on 2 January 1988, when the Celtic *'Bhoys'* chants targeted midfielder Mark Walters, the Teddy Bears' first black player. In addition, at the end of the first half Celtic fans threw hundreds of bananas on to the pitch, leading to a delay to the start of the second half. Years after the print version was launched, TAL was published online. Its coordinators included several members of AFA/NO.

4.   Radical fans of these three teams call themselves the 'Blues Brothers'. They all share loyalist and far-right sympathies. Their members supported loyalist Northern Ireland armed groups such as the Ulster Defence Association.

5.   Before the game, Hamburg extremists gathered at the Louden Tavern, a

the second-leg match, more than 4,000 Scottish fans travelled to Hamburg. Most made their way to the St. Pauli neighbourhood, where they waited for the match to start. Predictably, given the incidents of the first round, rioting took place. The night before the match, HSV hooligans attacked the Zum Letzen Pfennig pub (later known as the Jolly Roger), attacking customers with glasses and bottles. The provocations continued on the Volksparkstadion terraces, where HSV extremists burned Irish flags while singing songs in support of Rangers and Ulster Defence Association (UDA, a Northern Irish unionist organisation) paramilitaries. That night a group of 200 Hamburg hooligans returned to storm the same pub.

Despite these experiences, Celtic fans have continued to travel to St. Pauli. Although for many of them Hamburg's main attractions are the beer and the Reeperbahn nightlife, others focus on more serious matters that have strengthened ties with St. Pauli supporters. Their connection is essentially based on sharing similar ideological positions (antifascism/antiracism) and attitudes to football. Unconditional support for your team, regardless of its results, is a philosophy shared by both groups of fans, along with an explicit rejection of racism, sexism and police repression.[6] In addition, Pirates' and *Bhoys'* fans also oppose the increasing commercialisation of football, which has been noticeable in both clubs for years.[7]

meeting place for loyalist Rangers fans. Once in the stands, they sang racist songs and gave fascist salutes. After the match, members of the Celtic Soccer Crew came across forty HSV radicals armed with sticks and brass knuckles. Fighting lasted all night and during it a German supporter was stabbed in the abdomen. Petroni, *St. Pauli siamo noi*, p. 150. For more on the Celtic Soccer crew, see J. O'Kane, *Celtic Soccer Crew: What the Hell Do We Care?* (London: Pennant Books, 2006).

6.   With regards to this, goalkeeper Volker Ippig says, 'the atmosphere at the Millerntor was unique. The public never booed or hissed, only positive stimulation came from the stands.' G. Joswig, 'Fußball hat mein Leben gerettet!', *11 Freunde*, 05 March 2013.

7.   Just as some St. Pauli supporters were unhappy about their club reducing the Jolly Roger to a 'brand', there were Celtic fans that didn't like their club doing the same with Irish identity after Fergus McCann arrived in 1994. Agitation at Celtic against this type of branding emerged in January 1996 in response to the '*Bhoys* Against Bigotry' campaign that aimed to suppress the Irish political tradition of many Celtic supporters. Rondinelli, *Ribelli, Sociali e Romantici* p. 149.

The fraternity keeps growing stronger, as can be seen at the annual Celtic-St. Pauli Party, which draws a flood of fans from the Scottish club to Hamburg each spring. The gathering usually ends with a series of concerts featuring punk rock and Irish folk music in local venues such as Knust club, one of the St. Pauli fans' regular haunts at 30 Neuer Kamp, where supporters gather to watch FC St. Pauli matches on TV. Groups that have played in the annual celebration include De Drangdüwels, Shebeen, Glasnevin, Adelante, The Porters, The Bible Code Sundays, Gary & the Exiles, Millerntor Brigade, The Wakes, In Search of a Rose, Nuthouse Flowers and Galician outfit Falperrys, to name just a few.

In addition, a delegation of Celtic supporters always attends the *Antira Turnier*, which has been organised by the *Fanladen* since 2004. The antiracist football tournament brings together left-wing and anti-fascist fans from clubs around Europe each year. Matches are usually played at the Waidmannstrassem grounds used by the St. Pauli amateur team and also for the first team's training sessions. Other activities are organised during the tournament, such as guided tours of the neigh-bourhood, visits to the Neuengamme concentration camp, debates on subjects such as fan culture and repression, DJ sessions and concerts.

This friendship between the two teams was also shown on the pitch in May 2010, when Celtic played at the Millerntor for the first time in a friendly to mark FC St. Pauli's centenary. Many locals still have fond memories of the match despite a 2–0 win by the visitors. These nostalgic fans include members of the St. Pauli fan crew Ultrà Sankt Pauli 2002 (USP), who have a good relationship with their Scottish counter-parts, the Green Brigade. Both have a shared understanding of stadium culture, which they combine with political and social activism.

The terrace culture in Hamburg is based on values such as solidarity and respect, which is the bedrock of St. Pauli fan culture. That is why it is common to see banners in the Millerntor stands with messages or slogans about current affairs – both local and international.[8] And

---

8.   Such as the banners expressing the fans' solidarity with Iranian citizens crossing half of Europe in their flight from the war, displayed in August 2015 with the slogan 'Refugees Welcome'.

this attitude is not limited to fans: coaching staff and players are also encouraged to get involved in political activities organised by fans. They are all part of the same team, and they do not want to limit their relationship solely to match days. Symbiosis, communion, unity of action in all spheres and on all fronts – related to both sport and society. All for one: players, coaches, managers and fans. That is the idea.

Aside from the USP friendship with Schickeria München and Film-Stadt Inferno 1999 (fan crews from Bayern Munich and Babelsberg 03, respectively), the comradeship St. Pauli fans have with Celtic supporters also spreads to fans of other clubs with an ideological affinity. These include teams such as Livorno, Atalanta and Ternana Calcio in Italy, Clapton FC in England, Standard Liège in Belgium, Athletic Club de Bilbao in the Basque Country and Rayo Vallecano in Madrid. Indeed, St. Pauli played one of their 2015/16 pre-season friendly games against Rayo Vallecano at the Millerntor Stadion on 18 July 2016. The match, which ended with a 4–2 win for the local team,[9] was attended by 9,839 spectators, including a considerable number of radical Rayo fans – known as *Bukaneros* (an adaptation of the Spanish for buccaneers) – who made their presence known by setting off flares and smoke bombs in the stands.

9.   '4-2. El St. Pauli golea al Rayo', *Mundo Deportivo*, 18 August 2015, and D. Martín, 'La fatiga mata al Rayo Vallecano', *As*, 18 July 2015.

13

From Hell to Centenary

Meanwhile, back on the pitch, the 2000–1 season (which marked the tenth anniversary of the *Fanladen*) was expected to be complicated for FC St. Pauli. The most pessimistic prediction was that the team would struggle to avoid relegation to a lower division. In the end, the opposite occurred. For the fourth time in its history, FC St. Pauli managed to go up to the *Bundesliga* after finishing third in the league behind 1. FC Nürnberg and Borussia Mönchengladbach. And it was all because the players pulled together under coach Dietmar Demuth. The team got off to a promising start, with three consecutive wins: 3–6 at the LR Ahlen ground, 5–0 against SV Waldhof Mannheim and 4–0 against the Stuttgart Kickers. For much of the season, St. Pauli was second behind Nuremberg, until Borussia Mönchengladbach took over second place. Nonetheless, St. Pauli reached the penultimate match with a chance at automatic promotion. It only needed to beat Hannover 96 on its home turf. Things got off to a bad start with excessive dribbling by Austrian goalkeeper Heinz Weber – on loan from FC Tirol Innsbruck – who handed 'The Reds' their first goal on a platter. A few minutes later, the local team extended its lead to 2–0. But St. Pauli came back in the second half. First Holger Stanislawski and then Ivan Klasnić managed to make the final result a draw. The final score of 2–2 left the matter of promotion up in the air until the last match. It was up to St. Pauli. Almost 5,000 fans travelled by train to Nuremberg to support the team, with around 30,000 more following the match on a giant screen in Heiligengeistfeld. Fifteen minutes before the end, Turkish midfielder Deniz Baris, who had come up through the lower levels of the club, headed a rebound from the crossbar to score the winning goal for St. Pauli: 1–2. The club was back in the first division.

Beyond the euphoria of the sporting win, and despite the financial difficulties it was going through, FC St. Pauli continued to lead social initiatives. Thus, in January 2001, St. Pauli became the first German football team to contribute to the national fund to compensate Jews who had been forced to work during the Nazi period. St. Pauli fans' anti-establishment spirit was demonstrated once again in May of that year, when a group of around a hundred who had travelled to Alemannia Aachen's home ground displayed a banner with the slogan 'Big Schilly is watching you'. The fans were expressing their opposition to a federal interior minister, Social Democrat Otto Schilly, who had approved measures to control fans: installation of CCTV systems, greater police presence and more searches at stadium entrances.

On the sporting level, the euphoria of having returned to the *Bundesliga* soon faded. In the 2001–2 season, St. Pauli only racked up four wins – and ten draws and 20 defeats. This obviously was not enough to keep them in the first division. FC St. Pauli ended the season in last place, with 70 goals scored against them (including four by HSV) and only 22 points – twelve short of salvation. The team was relegated to the *Bundesliga 2* along with Freiburg and 1. FC Cologne. But a single feat still made it a historic season for fans: St. Pauli's victory against Bayern Munich, which earned it the nickname *Weltpokalsiegerbesieger* (World Club Champion Beaters).[1] On 6 February 2002, the Munich team – ranked fifth in the *Bundesliga* – had played at the Millerntor. In a surprise win, the home side, ranked seventeenth, beat the visitors 2–1. Within the space of three minutes, both Thomas Meggle and Nico Patschin-

---

1. A play on words based on the fact that St. Pauli had beaten the winners of the last Intercontinental Cup (in other words, the world champions): Bayern Munich. In Tokyo on 29 November 2001, the Bavarian team had defeated Argentina's Boca Juniors with a goal by Ghanaian defender Samuel Kuffour. Taking advantage of the opportunity, the Pirates proclaimed themselves vanquishers of the team at the top of international football. T-shirts with the slogan 'Weltpokalsiegerbesieger' on the front and the St. Pauli eleven on the back were quickly printed and became a hit. The first run of 400 screen-printed T-shirts sold out in no time. The second batch of 25,000 sold out in three months. The next batch of 50,000 sold out in a year. By January 2013 more than 120,000 had been sold. The success surprised even the designers, who admitted that inspiration had struck in the wee hours of the morning at the Jolly Roger bar. L. Wöckener, 'Wie St. Pauli zum Weltpokalsiegerbesieger wurde', *Die Welt*, 12 January 2013.

ski put the ball past goalkeeper Oliver Khan. Willy Sagnol's goal in the 87th minute was to no avail. The referee's final whistle sealed Bayern's first ever defeat at the FC St. Pauli stadium. This milestone aside, this was a year to be forgotten for St. Pauli.

The following season was worse still. Despite occasional wins against Braunschweig, Mannheim and Duisburg, St. Pauli failed to find its footing and finished 17th with 31 points, six short of Rot-Weiß Oberhausen – the lowest team not relegated. Furthermore, as these two disastrous seasons unfolded, a serious financial crisis hit the club, while Reenald Koch resigned as club president, citing professional reasons for the decision.

Relegation to the second division after the 2001–2 season had naturally affected the club's finances. The big salaries of the players signed to take on the challenge of the *Bundesliga* became a burden. The club had already suffered a financial downturn two years earlier when its former commercial sponsor World of Internet collapsed. But this time FC St. Pauli could not rely on the help of one of its main patrons, the millionaire and former president of the club Heinz Weisner, who had donated some of his personal wealth to save the club during hard times in the late 1990s.[2] Indeed, when Weisner stepped down as St. Pauli president in October 2000, one of his final decisions was to sell 50 per cent of the club's merchandising and marketing rights, which he owned, to the firm Upsolut Merchandising. This, as we shall see, was a controversial move.

Despite this difficult economic situation, neither the club nor its fans stopped actively participating in social and political projects. In 2002, in the midst of the financial crisis, St. Pauli supporters began a series of protests against one of the Millerntor advertisers, the men's magazine *Maxim*, which featured a photograph of a woman in lingerie on its cover. According to these fans, the magazine presented a demeaning, sexist view of women that was contrary to the principles approved by the club. On that basis they rallied against its presence and St. Pauli eventually decided to remove all the magazine's advertising from the

---

2. This time, 'Papa Weisener', as he was popularly known, had financial problems of his own and was unable to help the club he had become president of in 1990, when he replaced Otto Paulick in the role.

stadium. It is no accident that St. Pauli is the club with most female fans in Germany.

Meanwhile in local politics, CDU member Ole von Beust became mayor of Hamburg as part of a coalition of Christian Democrats, liberals and the new populist-right Party for a Rule of Law Offensive (*Partei Rechtsstaatlicher Offensive*, PRO). The PRO had been founded two years earlier by former local judge Ronald Schill and emulated the Freedom Party of Austria (*Freiheitliche Partei Österreichs*, FPÖ) led by Jörg Haider between 1986 and 2000. The election campaign of the 'Schill Party', as it was commonly known, focused on law and order and included intense propaganda on safety and foreigners, which shocked Hamburg citizens.[3] On the other hand, the SPD lost one of its traditional stongholds – after four decades governing the city and despite being the party with the most votes.

Things were not improving for St. Pauli on the pitch. After coming 17th in the 2002–3 season it returned to the *Regionalliga* after 17 years in the national leagues. Playing in the third division obviously did not help the club's finances – quite the opposite. The financial situation was dire. The DFB required that the club's ledgers 'show a

---

3.   One of von Beust's first decisions was to evict the occupants of the '*Bambule*' Wagenplatz in Karolinenviertel, a self-managed site with caravans, old railway wagons and mobile homes. It had been established in the 1990s in a vacant green space adjoining St. Pauli's Alter Elbpark – known for its ecological market and techno-rave parties. The community largely consisted of punks who had resisted a first eviction attempt in 1994, clashing with state security forces (when 20 police officers were wounded). In September 2002 a new eviction date was announced. On 4 November that year nearly 2,000 agents from Berlin and Schleswig-Holstein managed to clear the 18 vehicles stationed there. An unauthorised demonstration in solidarity with the evicted inhabitants of the '*Bambule*' was quickly organised in St. Pauli, ending in more confrontations with the police. Further acts of protest took place in the days that followed, such as the spontaneous rallies around the Millerntor after FC St. Pauli games. Supporters would gather at the *Nordkurve*, near Feldstraße. Then they would hold an unauthorised street demonstration until they reached the Karolinenviertel. Police did not act due to the large number of fans. The then-president of FC St. Pauli, Corny Littman, asked demonstrators not to wear club badges, a request that exacerbated the conflict between the more politicised St. Pauli fans and the club's executive board. Finally, in 2003, mayor Ole van Beust called a press conference to announce that the city had decided to offer an alternative space to the '*Bambule*' Wagenplatz in the Altona area. Rondinelli, *Ribelli, Sociali e Romantici*, pp. 171–2.

reserve of 1,950,000 euros' before granting the club a licence to play in the *Regionalliga*. This condition had to be met by 11 June 2003 at the latest. In order to comply with the DFB requirement, St. Pauli had to sell key assets, such as its youth training facilities, which were purchased by Hamburg City Council. Despite this, there was still a huge hole in the accounts that had to be covered quickly.

In the midst of all this, FC St. Pauli unexpectedly chose theatre impresario Cornelius 'Corny' Littmann to replace Reenald Koch as club president. Littman had received 78 per cent support[4] in a vote at a general assembly on 25 February 2003. Leaving aside official formalities, it was an exemplary choice, making him the first openly homosexual president of a German football club. Littmann dressed in drag when accepting the role, and made a declaration that became a motto: 'I'm as faithful to my club as I am unfaithful to my lovers. My club proves that you can be gay and manly.'[5] His term, however, was not without controversy. After a series of disputes, in 2007 he announced his resignation. He later retracted and the assembly ratified his presidency until he unexpectedly quit in 2010, after the club's promotion to the *Bundesliga*.

The first problem that Littmann encountered as president was the club's critical financial situation. The DFB's demands and the club's relegation to the *Regionalliga* seemed like a death knell for

---

4. For years he had toured Germany with the Familie Schmidt theatre troupe, until he opened the Schmidt Theatre in the Sankt Pauli neighbourhood in August 1988. From then on, he combined his work at the club with managing various theatres and venues, such as Docks club, Mojo and the Golden Pudel. In 1999 he was named Hamburg Entrepreneur of the Year. He was also a member of the German Academy of Football Culture and a supporter of sporting initiatives such as the *Kein Platz für Rassismus* (No Place for Racism) campaign. Littmann had also been involved in grassroots politics. In 1980 he was a top candidate for the Greens in the federal election. He actively participated in the gay rights movement in the 1990s.
5. Supporters critical of Littmann thought that he exploited his homosexuality to project a 'cool' image of a gay activist at the helm of the antifascist club. Those fans believed that he was actually an ignorant, inflexible and authoritarian president. 'His presidency led fans to believe that either you form part of modern football or you die. Littmann is the symbol of modern football because he made a commitment to save St. Pauli, but he sold out its ideals.' Although he was well connected and a good communicator, Littmann had a strained relationship with the club's more active fans. Petroni, *St. Pauli siamo noi*, p. 198.

St. Pauli. One relegation after another had pushed it to the point of collapse. The club came up with a number of initiatives to raise funds to survive, such as bringing forward the selling of tickets for all the following season's matches. Fans responded to this cry for help by purchasing 11,700 season tickets during the summer. In addition, the club launched the *Retter* (Saviour) campaign, which aimed to raise capital to ensure the continuity of the club by selling brown T-shirts with the club badge and the words *Retter* and *Weltpokalsiegerbesieger* (World Club Champion Beaters).[6] However, the success of the initiative was dampened by criticism from some fans that were against the T-shirts being sold at around 40 outlets of the American fast-food chain McDonald's.[7]

There were other fundraising initiatives, such as the Drink for St. Pauli campaign. In this various pubs and bars donated 50 cents for each bottle of beer sold on 6 and 7 July 2003, thereby raising another 20,000 euros. Prostitutes and phone sex operators in the nearby red-light district did collections. The Astra brewery launched the initiative Drink Astra–Save St. Pauli, in which the club received one euro for each case of beer sold.

Finally, on 10 June 2003, one day before the DFB deadline for providing proof of sufficient funds to renew the licence, HSH Nordbank certified that St. Pauli had the 1,950,000 euros required for the 2003–4 season. The rescue operation had been a success. To round it off, Bayern Munich played a friendly match at the Millerntor stadium on 12 July. The game, dubbed the *Retter Finale* (final salvation) was possible thanks to Littman's personal connection with Ulrich 'Uli' Hoeneß, the Bavarian team's general and commercial manager.[8] After the match, the former player – wearing a *Retter*

---

6. T-shirts sold for 15 euros, ten of which went to the club. Over 25,000 units were sold in Germany and other European countries. A second batch of black T-shirts was printed with the word *'Retterin'*, targeting the team's female fans.

7. The company used it as an opportunity for a marketing campaign with the motto *'Hamburger helfen Hamburgern'* ('Hamburgers help Hamburgers').

8. A former player with Bayern Munich and 1. FC Nurnberg in the 1970s, he remained linked to the footballing world after he hung up his boots. In 1979 he was named general and commercial director of the Bavarian team, a position he held until 2009 when he replaced Franz Beckenbauer as president of Bayern Munich. In 2014 he resigned as a result of personal tax debts.

T-shirt – accompanied Littmann on a lap of honour with the team.[9] Almost 200,000 euros were raised that day, although it was not the last fundraising initiative. Before the start of the championship, FC St. Pauli still managed to organise a music festival to increase its financial reserves.

Having overcome the difficulties that had almost destroyed it, St. Pauli turned its attention to the 2003–4 season in the *Regionalliga*. That year, the team had an uneventful championship after Andreas Bergmann, the youth team coach, took over the senior squad. It racked up five wins and three draws in the last ten games, leading St. Pauli to end up in 8th position but way too low for promotion. On the social level, the tensions between a section of fans and the presidency continued. A few hours before the derby against HSV's second team at the Volksparkstadion, the police confiscated materials that fans were planning to use to do a *tifo*. The move inflamed tensions. At the end of the match, which ended with a 1–0 win for the home team, some of St. Pauli fans' seating was set on fire. A few days later, on Littmann's orders, sanctions were issued against six members of the St. Pauli fan crew (*ultras*) in an arbitrary process that did not allow the accused to defend themselves. This sparked another protest at the stadium, consisting of a 30-minute strike in the stands during the match against Holstein Kiel on 20 March 2004. From then on, banners with the words 'Diffidati con noi'

---

9. The president of FC St. Pauli was widely criticised by sections of the club's supporters who disagreed with the rampant marketing of the *Retter* campaign. A supporter-driven mobilisation had been turned into a marketing strategy. The sale of the T-shirts in some commercial chains, like the Budnikowsky supermarket and McDonald's hamburger chains, was unacceptable to these fans. The money generated by placing advertising in erotic phone services was also troubling for a club whose supporters claimed to be anti-sexist. In the first games of the next season, banners were displayed with slogans such as '*1 Kilo Kult: 1.99 euros*', 'FC Mainstream 1910?' and 'Who will save our supporters?' To top it off, the then mayor of Hamburg, the conservative Ole von Beust, a friend of Littmann's, was photographed at the St. Pauli Fan Shop as a club 'saviour' during the *Retter* campaign organised by fans. This prompted fans of Altona 93, a modest Hamburg club, to make fun of the Pirate team's values through spreading the slogan 'St. Pauli, CDU, and McDonald's'.

('Locked out with us') in support of the banned *ultras* were displayed along with anti-Littmann slogans.

Things did not improve the following year, and St. Pauli ended up 18 points short of what it needed to go up to the second division.[10] The team finished seventh, with 52 points. On the community level, organisations like the *Fanladen*[11] and the *Fanclub-Sprecherrat* collaborated with FARE to pay tribute to club members who had been persecuted and killed during the Nazi period, an act that reaffirmed the club's opposition to any manifestations of racism and fascism.[12]

But, this gesture aside, relations between the presidency and part of the fan base remained strained. Indeed, as the season progressed banners criticising the club's increasingly commercial direction continued to be displayed in the stands, particularly in the part of the stadium used by the fan crews. The fact was that Littmann's policies while at the helm of the club showed the metamorphosis the club was going through. More and more supporters were only interested in the football on the pitch, with no concern for the repercussions of the growing commercialisation.[13] On the other hand, another section of fans realised that losing the battle over commercialisation would make St. Pauli a soulless club, with no distinctive features to make it stand out from the other German

10. The 2004–5 season was launched with the slogan '*Viva* St. Pauli Third-Class Struggle' as a tribute to Fidel Castro's Cuba. In the official team photo, the players appear wearing military caps and shirts and saluting with closed fists, against a background of Cuban flags in the brown and white team colours. Petroni, *St. Pauli siamo noi*, p. 186.

11. That year, it marked its 15th anniversary by publishing a book entitled *15 Jahre Fanladen St. Pauli, 20 Jahre Politik im Stadion*.

12. A plaque was placed in front of the *Südtribune* at the Millerntor Stadium with the words: 'In memory of FC St. Pauli members and fans who were persecuted or murdered by the Nazi dictatorship from 1933 to 1945.' Davidson, *Pirates, Punks and Politics*, p. 154.

13. In July 2003, the club's president cancelled St. Pauli's leasing agreement with Brigitte Meyer, who had managed the Millerntor Stadium's bar-restaurant Clubheim for almost two decades. Fans and players had gathered and socialised there during that time. Protests against her expulsion intensified when St. Pauli chose to lease the space to an outside catering company. Many disillusioned veteran fans decided to stop going to the Millerntor in favour of the stands of more modest clubs such as Altona 93. Petroni, *St. Pauli siamo noi*, pp. 167–8.

teams. All of this was taking place against the backdrop of genera-
tional renewal in the stands, with Hafenstraße veterans making way
for young fans devoid of the militant, fighting background of their
predecessors. Passivity was gradually gaining ground. To make
matters worse, St. Pauli again suffered financial solvency problems
that were resolved after bargaining with the Inland Revenue.

Despite the financial difficulties and the team's lacklustre performance on the pitch, the club's civic activities continued. In 2004, for
instance, the 'Laut gegen Nazis' ('Loud Against Nazis') campaign
was launched by a group of fans alongside local music producer
Jörn Menge. The aim was to encourage fan's active opposition to the
rise of far-right activism in Germany.[14] The scope of the campaign
expanded thanks to the participation of various artists and well-
known figures from the music world.[15]

The team's stretch in the wilderness of the Regionalliga did not
end that season as St. Pauli finished sixth. Coinciding with the
winter break, the first team travelled to Cuba to play several friendly
matches in the run-up to the championship.[16] It was a trip that had

14.   In the Saxony state elections on 19 September 2004, the NPD led by Holger
Apfel won 9.2 per cent of the vote (190,909 votes), giving this neo-Nazi party twelve
seats. That year, the NPD had 5,300 members. In the Brandenburg elections, the
DVU, another far-right group, won 6.1 per cent of the vote and also made it into
the regional parliament – unsurprisingly considering it had already won five seats in
1999. As such, it became the first far-right party to be re-elected in regional elections
in Germany. The rise of these two parties was due to opposition to the proposed
labour market reform by the federal government of Chancellor Gerhard Schröder
(SPD). In other words, the far-right parties benefitted from the protest votes of the
citizens who objected to the reform. See S. von Mering and T. Wyman McCarty
(eds.), Right-Wing Radicalism Today: Perspectives from Europe and the US (New York:
Routledge, 2013).
15.   One of the highlights of the campaign was a series of around 80 concerts held
in March 2013 under the slogan Rock gegen Rechts (Rock Against the Right), with
groups that played a range of different styles. Campaign organisers visited schools
and youth centres in areas with high rates of support for neo-Nazi groups and parties,
particularly in East German cities. St. Pauli was one of the sponsors of the project,
and its fans supported it by making personal donations and participating in its local
educational activities. Rondinelli, Ribelli, Sociali e Romantici, p. 252.
16.   The plane carrying the St. Pauli expedition landed in Havana on 10 January
2005. The team played various friendly matches with the Cuban national team
and FC Villa Clara. Aside from the sporting aspect, the delegation went on several
cultural expeditions to get to know the country and its people. On January 18,

an enormous impact on one player: midfielder 'Benny' Adrion. Making the most of a build-up of injuries that prevented him from playing regularly, he decided to end his professional football career and devote himself body and soul to a St. Pauli social project: *Viva con Agua*.[17] Adrion's visit to Cuba was key in making him aware of deficiencies in that country, particularly after he discovered that training grounds there lacked running water in winter. In September 2006, he launched a programme in collaboration with the German non-governmental organisation *Welthungerhilfe* (World Hunger Aid),[18] which aimed to provide safe drinking water and sustainable health services through 21 international projects. These were performed in 15 countries, including Cuba, Benin, Ethiopia, Madagascar, Rwanda, Nicaragua, Tajikistan and Cambodia. The main purpose of *Viva con Agua* was to provide the means with which to get safe drinking water to schools and nurseries in these countries. The first project was carried out in Havana, where pumps were installed to supply around 150 schools.[19] Thanks to this work, safe drinking water reached over 300,000 people. Aside from the club itself, various fan organisations, such as *18 auf 12*, became involved in the project.

Also in 2005, FC St. Pauli launched a new initiative to make its fans feel part of the club, inviting them to paint the inside walls of the stadium. Since then, the Millerntor walls have been decorated with images and phrases like 'no one is illegal' and 'only love

St. Pauli drew 1–1 with Villa Clara, dubbed 'Cuba's clockwork orange' because of the colours of its kit. In the hours before the match, St. Pauli players took the opportunity to visit the mausoleum where Ernesto Che Guevara is buried in Santa Clara. In Havana some players even ventured to play beach volleyball. Petroni, *St. Pauli siamo noi*, p. 186.

17. The sports clothing brand Do You Football – the official FC St. Pauli brand from 2005 – has participated in this project since 2008. www.doyoufootball-shop.com/wir/ueberuns/ (accessed 15 June 2015).
18. This non-government aid agency working in the field of development cooperation was founded in 1962 and has participated in and supervised more than 7,000 projects in over 70 countries in Africa, Latin America and Asia. All together it has provided 2.52 billion euros worth of funding.
19. In 2009, Adrion was awarded the Federal Republic of Germany's Order of Merit, by the then President Horst Köhler, in recognition of his work at the helm of *Viva con Agua*.

counts', in support of refugees, gender equality and the fight against homophobia.[20]

Back in the sporting arena, the team did not have a memorable 2005–6 season, finishing sixth after its third consecutive year in the *Regionalliga*. The exception to this was its performance in the cup. That year, FC St. Pauli reached the semi-finals after eliminating Wacker Burghausen in the first round, VfL Bochum in the second, and doing the same with prestigious rivals Hertha BSC in a nail-biting game at the Millerntor that ended 4–3 after extra time. St. Pauli also defeated Thomas Schaaf's Werder Bremen 3–1 in the quarter-finals thanks to goals by Michél Mazingu-Dinzey, Fabian Boll and Timo Schultz. St. Pauli's cup dreams ended in the semi-finals, however, against Bayern Munich, the team that ended up winning the league and cup double that year. St. Pauli had no chance against the Bavarians, as reflected in the 0–4 final score. It was all over for FC St. Pauli in the 'Bokal' – as fans dubbed that year's DFB-Pokal (cup) due to the first letters of its rival's names (Burghausen, Bochum, Berlin, Bremen and Bayern). Despite being knocked out, the matches were profitable enough to allow work to start on the renovation of the Millerntor stadium[21] in December 2006.[22]

However, the situation changed dramatically the following season (2006–7). Despite an unsteady start leading to the replacement of trainer Andreas Bergmann in mid-November,[23] FC St.

20. 'Sankt Pauli, fútbol y política en el barrio', *El País*, 3 July 2014.
21. The demolition of the *Südkurve* began in December 2006, to make room for the new stand that was to be built to comply with the requirements of the federation and allow the club to keep the professional licence issued by the DFB. The following year, the *Haupttribüne* (Main Stand) was also expanded. The new South Stand opened on 18 July 2008, coinciding with a friendly match between FC St. Pauli and the Cuban national team, which ended with a clear 7–0 win for the home team. Petroni, *St. Pauli siamo noi*, pp. 161 and 229.
22. That year, the Millerntor Stadium hosted the FIFI Wild Cup – an alternative FIFA World Cup – which was held in Germany in 2006. It included teams that are not officially recognised, such as Greenland, Northern Cyprus, Zanzibar, Gibraltar, Tibet, and the Republic of St. Pauli, with players from non-professional sections of the FC St. Pauli, as negotiated by the club with the DFB. Rondinelli, *Ribelli, Sociali e Romantici*, pp. 233–4.
23. After playing in several teams, Bergmann hung up his boots in 1989. In 2001 he became the coach of the FC St. Pauli second team. He continued there until

Pauli managed to get its act together and fight for the title with the help of a team of two coaches: former St. Pauli player Holger Stanislawski – who did not yet have a coaching qualification – and his assistant André Trulsen. The duo managed to rally the squad and turn it into a winning team. In the end, St. Pauli was proclaimed *Regionalliga Nord* champion with 63 points – only three more than third-place FC Magdeburg which missed out on promotion to the second division. After three seasons in the third division, St. Pauli was back in *Bundesliga 2*. In the midst of celebrating, the players wore shirts with a slogan that said it all: 'Back from Hell'.

The return to the German second division was smoother than expected. During the 2007–8 season in *Bundesliga 2*, St. Pauli did not have to suffer much to stay up. They finished ninth, four points above the relegation zone. That championship helped to consolidate St. Pauli's place in the second division. The trend continued the following season, when St. Pauli came eighth, taking it into a less turbulent area of the league table.

In July 2009, Hamburg hosted a new edition of the popular *Schanzenfest* street festival, organised by alternative left-wing groups since 1988. The event attracted over 10,000 visitors that year, but in the evening almost a thousand people clashed with police. According to several witnesses, the rioters fled in the direction of the Jolly Roger pub on Budapester Straße, a meeting point for radical St. Pauli fans. Although nobody had taken refuge in the pub, the police stormed the premises armed with pepper spray and batons, surprising the hundred-odd patrons celebrating a birthday party inside.[24] That night, the rioting resulted in 67 arrests. The

---

March 2004, when he was named first-team coach. After two years at the helm of St. Pauli, unsatisfactory results led him to be replaced by Holger Stanislawski (on 20 November 2006).

24. The disproportionate police response drew widespread criticism, even from the club itself. Tay Eich, a Supervisory Board member, said, 'The police operation in and around the Jolly Roger is completely unacceptable and needs accounting for.' According to some sources, the attack was related to incidents that took place in front of the pub in March 2009, at the end of the match against Hansa Rostock. In these a police officer was seriously injured. Davidson, *Pirates, Punks and Politics*, pp. 202–3.

incidents disrupted the festival, which had to be cancelled. A second part was organised in September, and also ended in turmoil after an assault on a police station.

During that busy summer the 2009–10 season began, which would coincide with FC St. Pauli's centenary. Under Stanislawski, the team played an almost perfect championship. In the second-to-last match of the league, St. Pauli won 1–4 at the Fürth ground and was automatically promoted to the *Bundesliga*. At the end of the match, St. Pauli fans who had travelled to support the team peacefully invaded the pitch to celebrate the victory. St. Pauli finished runner up, only three points behind the top team 1. FC Kaisers-lautern. What mattered even more than winning second place was that the club had won promotion to the first division on the hundredth anniversary of its founding. One of the championship's stars was Marius Ebbers, whose 20 goals and nine assists were crucial to helping the team reach its most cherished objective in that special year. The promotion and the centenary were not the only reasons to celebrate. There was also the relegation to the third division of Hansa Rostock, St. Pauli's greatest rival, after losing the relegation playoff against FC Ingolstadt. Without a doubt, that was a perfect season for St. Pauli fans. A triple celebration.

The centenary celebrations officially kicked off on 15 May with a match at the Millerntor (where building works were still in progress). The local team were the St. Pauli All Stars – including the former players Volker Ippig, Klaus Thomforde, Dirk Zander, Michael Dahms, Ivan Klasnić, Holger Stanislawski and André Trulsen. Their opponent was FC United of Manchester – the team created by disaffected Manchester United supporters that opposed American billionaire Malcolm Glazer's takeover of the club. The match, attended by 300 English fans who had travelled from Manchester, ended in a 3–3 draw. Three days later, the 'boys in brown' faced the '*Bhoys* in green', that is, St. Pauli played Glasgow's Celtic, before 27,000 spectators in the second game celebrating St. Pauli's 100-year anniversary. This time the Scots won 0–2, thanks to goals by midfielder Patrick McCourt and forward Morten Duncan Rasmussen.²⁵ To commemorate the day, the Hamburg team wore a strip similar to the one worn by the club's founders a hundred years earlier.

Over the next few days, FC St. Pauli organised a number of sporting activities for its fans, including a street football tournament. At the same time the Millerntor stadium hosted a women's football tournament. One of the most eagerly awaited events was the centenary concert organised by the club at the Millerntor on 29 May. The line-up included punk rock bands such as Slime and Die Ärzte, Italian ska-punk group Talco, Scottish folk-rock outfit The Wakes, Canadian Celtic-punk band The Real McKenzies and Mexican fusion band Panteón Rococó. Local participants included the groups Fettes Brot, Kettcar and Phantastix, and musicians Paul Sheridan and Günter Peine. It also featured 500 singers from the Seemanns-Chor Hannover. This choir, founded in 1993, sang versions of St. Pauli chants for the occasion. All the concert's proceeds – over 100,000 euros – went to social programmes the club is involved in. To round off the centenary celebrations, an exhibition (*Das St. Pauli Jahr 100*) on the club's history since its founding was opened in June 2010.

In addition to these events, that season the first team played in a commemorative jersey designed by Do You Football. The special jersey was reversible: the bronze-coloured side displayed the new sponsor Ein Platz an der Sonne (replacing the Romanian car manufacturer Dacia), while the brown side featured a collage of prominent places, moments and characters from the club's history. The second jersey was white and mimicked a vintage-style collar with laces.

Aside from FC St. Pauli fans and supporters, local residents and hundreds of shops and brands joined the centenary celebrations. One of the companies that got into the spirit of the celebrations was Orion, an erotic products manufacturer that produced 20,000 condoms for the occasion featuring the club badge.

25. A. Lomax, 'St. Pauli 0 Celtic 2: Match Report', *The Telegraph*, 19 May 2010.

14

Social Romantics Try
to Reclaim the Club

After the giddiness of the anniversary celebrations, things slowed down. The next season, 2010–11, FC St. Pauli finished last in the Bundesliga table with only 29 points, nine short of salvation. The team did not work together as expected and lacked focus in several matches. It often conceded goals in a match's final minutes. One of the most painful defeats took place at the Millerntor on 7 May 2011, the second-to-last day of the league, when the almighty Bayern crushed St. Pauli 1–8 – with striker Mario Gómez getting a hat trick. The score was hardly surprising considering that St. Pauli was the team that conceded most goals in the league that year – with 68 goals against and only 35 for. The only joy that season, which caused quite a stir, came three months before the end of the championship (on 16 February 2011), when Ghanaian striker Gerald Asamoah scored a great winning header for St. Pauli at its eternal rival HSV's home ground.[1] When the final whistle blew, the visiting St. Pauli fans in a corner of the Volksparkstadion could not hide their euphoria, with shouts of 'Hamburg is brown and white!' The goalkeeper Benedikt Pliquett, who had played the game of his life, ran over to the area where fans were celebrating wearing a T-shirt with the words 'Derby Winner!!!' He kicked the corner

---

1. The game was originally scheduled for 6 February but it was postponed due to heavy rains. That did not stop hundreds of HSV extremists, accompanied by far-right Rangers hooligans and others who had travelled from Belgrade, Berlin, Bielefeld and Karlsruhe, from gathering in downtown Hamburg on the evening of the 5th and heading to St. Pauli together. Once there, they raided the Jolly Roger pub and smashed shop and restaurant windows in the area. Around 1,500 police officers were deployed and 45 hooligans were arrested. Petroni, *St. Pauli siamo noi*, p. 193.

flag with the HSV logo, shouting 'We are St. Pauli!'[2] 'It was the best day of my life', Pliquett said the next day. After 34 years, the Pirates had once again beaten the almighty HSV at home.[3] But contrary to expectations, that win was the start of a downwards spiral.[4] The euphoria of the victory quickly faded. The season finished with St. Pauli back in the second division, just a year after its promotion to the *Bundesliga*.

At the same time, the progressive redevelopment of the Millerntor, started in 2010, began to show results. The *Haupttribüne*, the main stand, was completed around this time. It included 4,800 'business' seats and executive boxes – almost half of its overall capacity. One of the boxes was leased by the local striptease joint Susis Show Bar, which incorporated a pole-dancing bar for 'scantily dressed' young women to entertain guests during matches. Fans who had been fighting sexism for years described this as 'a punch in the guts – a blow against the club's values and ethics'. Meanwhile, the redevelopment of the *Südkurve* – required in order to keep the

---

2. Interestingly, Hamburg-born Pliquett had started his career as a player with HSV, where he debuted with the amateur squad in the 2002–3 season. The following year he joined the VFB Lübeck second team. In 2004 he arrived at FC St. Pauli as a reserve goalkeeper and played with the Pirates until he signed for Sturm Graz in the summer of 2013. In the 2015–16 season he left the Austrian team for CD Atlético Baleares, whose president is the German businessman Ingo Volckmann and which plays in the Spanish Second Division. Before joining the St. Pauli first team, Pliquett had participated in USP activities. He was a *Südkurve* regular and sometimes attended away games. Before the derby, coach Stanislawski informed him that he was first-choice goalkeeper, thinking he would be more motivated after having been attacked at Altona station by HSV radicals a few months earlier while returning from a St. Pauli away game. Petroni, *St. Pauli siamo noi*, p. 194.

3. St. Pauli's previous victory against HSV had been on 3 September 1977, when the Pirates defeated their greatest rival in a league match at home 2–0. On that occasion Franz Gerder and Wolfgang Kulka scored the goals that took St. Pauli to victory.

4. As former St. Pauli player and coach Thomas Meggle said, 'Our problems began with the derby.' Oke Göttlich, president of the club since November 2014, agreed: 'A lot of things went wrong. There was no structure. There were no proper – and I know this is a term not many at this club like to hear – control mechanisms.' 'There was no sustainable scouting system', he added, 'no professional video analysis.' Hesse, 'St. Pauli: The Club that Stands for All the Right Things ... Except Winning', *The Guardian*, 6 September 2015.

club's DFB licence – was to include space at affordable prices for 3,000 spectators.

All of this once again demonstrated what some fans saw as the club's shift towards commercialisation and sexism. The team's return to the *Bundesliga*, they said, had led management to accept juicy sponsorships without considering ethical criteria. This process threatened the values enshrined over the previous decade, and corrupted the club's alternative nature. Among the most critical followers were the *Sozialromantiker* (Social Romantics): a kind of lobby group that sought to preserve the club's values and prevent its growing commercialisation.[5] These fans obviously did not welcome the presence in the stadium of the Susis Show Bar, or the choice of Kalte Muschi as the club's official drink.[6] 'That is just macho bullshit […] the club has mortified us', said a female fan. The fanzine *Der Übersteiger* also joined the criticism with a provocative illustration on the cover of issue 101, published on 3 December 2010, showing a topless pole dancer and the headline '*Tittchen oder Schnittchen?*' ('Breasts or Canapés?'). The stadium upgrade also included installing several LED screens in the stands, allowing fans to read the SMS text messages sent during matches. The devices debuted in the last game before the winter break, when St. Pauli faced FSV Mainz 05 in a match that ended with the *sankt-paulianers* losing 2–4.

Disappointed at the series of marketing measures implemented by management, St. Pauli fans began organising protests to protect the club from extreme commercialisation. On 22 December 2010,

---

5. These ideals were listed at the previous year's fan conference: close social and political ties between the neighbourhood and the team, the refusal to sell the name of the stadium to a corporation, rejection of sponsorship agreements with companies suspected of fascist, racist or homophobic sympathies and the desire to keep the 90 minutes of football free from excessive marketing. Accordingly, the club's management was forced to turn down a tempting sponsorship offer by German electricity company RWE, which was not approved by fans. See 'Sankt Pauli, fútbol y política en el barrio', *El País*, 3 July 2014 and Davidson, *Pirates, Punks and Politics*, p. 179.
6. The phrase literally translates as 'cold pussy', which is why many fans believed that adopting the brand would violate the anti-sexist message from the stands.

just six days after the LED screens were launched, the group going by the name Social Romantics posted an explicit statement on its website:[7] 'Enough is enough. We cannot go on like this. Now, after all this time, we say: enough!' The group's demands included not allowing advertising in the minutes before the start of matches, no ads in the new stands, terminating the Susis Show Bar lease, getting rid of the LED screens and audio-visual announcements during matches, turning VIP sections into affordable seating areas, not selling the name of the stadium, not doing business with sponsors either suspected of collusion with fascism, racism or homophobia or linked with the war industry and painting the walls of the club's crèche.[8] The Social Romantics warned the club that if its demands were not met they would start a campaign against the stadium's catering service, bombard the email servers of sponsors with spam, call for an extraordinary general assembly and even boycott matches. 'The time for meetings and talking is over. Enough!' insisted the manifesto. By the end of the year, over 3,000 people had signed the petition.

To make themselves visible in the stadium, the Social Romantics chose to use one of the club's symbols[9] – the skull and crossbones (Jolly Roger), which had itself already suffered commercialisation and exploitation by the company that owned the club's merchandising rights.[10] From then on, the Social Romantics have used the

---

7.   Ironically, this group founded in 2008 took its name from the derogatory term used by Corny Littmann to refer to fans who opposed the introduction of a St. Pauli currency – the 'Millerntaler' – to pay for merchandising and food and drinks inside the stadium. The idea was to swap cash for poker chips that would in turn be sponsored by an online poker website. The former president called detractors of the plan 'social romantics'. The fanzine *Der Übersteiger* designed an alternative currency featuring the face of fourteenth-century pirate Klaus Störtebeker. See Davidson, *Pirates, Punks and Politics*, p. 178, Rondinelli, *Ribelli, Sociali e Romantici*, p. 295 and Petroni, *St. Pauli siamo noi*, p. 195.

8.   The centre, called Piraten-Nest (The Pirate's Nest), is run by the Pestalozzi foundation. The 1,385 square metre space spread over three levels is located between the *Südkurve* and the main stand and can accommodate a hundred children. Rondinelli, *Ribelli, Sociali e Romantici*, pp. 254–5.

9.   In general the main clashes between fans and management have to do with matters relating to the commercialisation of St. Pauli, security issues and the degree to which fans have the freedom to act. Rondinelli, *Ribelli, Sociali e Romantici*, p. 172.

10.   The successful Jolly Roger design was originally created for a batch of T-shirts

logo of a black skull and crossbones on a red background, which is similar to the Jolly Roger displayed at the *Gegengerade* in the 1980s. It also has symbolic undertones, as red was the colour used by pirates when they intended to attack giving no quarter and taking no prisoners. By adopting it as their own, the Social Romantics wanted to revive what had been the Hafenstraße fans' symbol of rebellion before the image was subverted for merchandising and turned into a successful logo.

In 2011, the protests continued. On 15 January, for a match between St. Pauli and SC Freiburg, the Social Romantics called for all fans to take red Jolly Rogers to protest against the management's decision to ignore their demands. That day, the whole stadium turned red,[11] from the back reaches to the *Haupttribüne*, where the veteran *Oldtras* crews displayed a sign with the words 'Bring back St. Pauli to me'. In the *Nordkurve*, the Nord Support fan club

---

produced by the *Fanladen*. In 1998 the club decided to produce a similar image, sparking a clash between fans and management that ended up in the courts. The judges eventually ruled in favour of the fans, who then decided to allow the club to use the design for free. The famous logo was the work of Steph Braun from the firm Texman. Due to its popularity, it was acquired (in October 2000) by the company FC St. Pauli Vermarktungs GmbH & Co. KG. The skull and crossbones first appeared on the players' strips in the 2000–1 season. The company outsourced the merchandising distribution to Upsolut Merchandising, which has since been responsible for the sale and use of the logo. This led many fans to decide to create and produce their own St. Pauli clothing rather than buy it at the official club store, in what was in fact an undeclared impromptu boycott. The Jolly Roger pattern is currently used in more than 350 merchandising items of all kinds, from T-shirts to toasters and dummies. An estimated 250,000 products featuring the skull are sold each year, generating a turnover of 13 million euros (of which only 350,000 go to the club). It is therefore clear that poor results on the field do not affect sales. Indeed, the club and the company have been in litigation for years over the merchandising licencing contract, which expires in 2034. See Rondinelli, *Ribelli, Sociali e Romantici*, pp. 214–15, P. Daniel and Ch. Kassimeris, 'The Politics and Culture of FC St. Pauli: From Leftism, through Anti-Establishment, to Commercialization', *Soccer & Society*, no. 2, vol. 14, 2013, p. 11 and 'Sankt Pauli, fútbol y política en el barrio', *El País*, 3 July 2014.

11. The choice of colour was no accident. As one fan critical of the club's management put it: 'Red is the colour of danger, as in traffic lights, with which we are asking management to stop before it's too late. But red is also the colour of political protest, of socialism. And red is the colour of love for a kind of football and a club that still entertains you and allows you to dream.' Rondinelli, *Ribelli, Sociali e Romantici*, p. 296.

also displayed banners with the black skull and crossbones on a red background, or vice versa, rather than the usual brown-and-white flag. Posters, scarves, T-shirts and flags: all helped to bring the chosen colours to the Millerntor. The high point came when the players entered the pitch and the fans started singing 'Bring back St. Pauli to me' to the traditional Scottish folk tune of 'My Bonnie Lies Over the Ocean'. At the end of the match a thousand fans marched through the neighbourhood's streets to spread their demands among the local residents. They walked in the rain behind a banner with the words 'Bring Back St. Pauli – Reclaim Your District'.

The supporters, along with dozens of residents, also protested against urban interventions and the gentrification that was taking place in the district.[12] A symbol of these changes, beyond the construction of new buildings, apartments, office blocks, restaurants and stores, was the construction of the Elbe Philharmonic Hall – popularly known as the 'Elphi'. The hall building was designed by the Swiss architecture firm Herzog & de Meuron. It was to be started in 2007 above an old warehouse (Kaispeicher A) on the banks of the Elbe in the HafenCity (Port of Hamburg) district. The cost, originally budgeted at 100 million euros, would end up swelling to almost 800 million. The Elphi was one of the flagship projects of a docklands regeneration plan that included luxury penthouse apartments and a hotel – the Westin Hamburg. The façade was clad with more than 2,000 glass panels giving the building a futuristic look.

Added to this, several multinationals had decided to set up in Hamburg. This prompted Dutch and Swedish property agents to acquire numerous properties in St. Pauli and Altona to be able to charge extremely high rents to freelance workers in the telecommunications, architecture, engineering and graphic design fields. In the face of this flood of foreign investors who were convincing the local authorities to build hotels, lofts and luxury apartments, St. Pauli fans and local residents came together to defend 'the St. Pauli way of life'. The protest underlined that the number of 'Social Romantics' was much greater than the 4,000 or so fans that had

---

12. Petroni, *St. Pauli siamo noi*, p. 169.

signed the online manifesto.[13] After this show of strength, a meeting was organised between the representatives of the different fan clubs and the board of directors to examine all the advertising campaigns and guarantee that sponsors complied with the existing ethical criteria. The pressure from the protests succeeded in re-establishing a constructive dialogue between the club and fans.

The club's management decided to cancel the pole-dancing shows featuring scantily clad women but the Social Romantics continued to demand that Susis Show Bar give up its box in the stadium. They also continued lobbying to change VIP areas into affordable seating. In the end, the biggest success of the protests was getting the club's management to negotiate certain issues with fans. It was clear that any commercial activity that the club embarked on required the approval of fans. To keep executives on their toes, the campaign launched by the Social Romantics continued throughout the 2010–11 championship. At the start of the next season the club announced that the Susis Show Bar lease would not be renewed. It was another win for St. Pauli fans, probably one of the most resounding since the *Retter* campaign that had saved St. Pauli when on the brink of disappearing years earlier.

The 2011–12 season is partly remembered for the match against 1. FC Union Berlin, in which Marius Ebbers scored a goal with his hand, unnoticed by the referee. He immediately owned up to the fault, leading to the goal being annulled.[14] But two other episodes that season illustrate what makes St. Pauli different. In November 2011, the club decided to issue bonds in order to raise money for the redevelopment of the stadium and the upgrading

13. Despite the impact of this action, few fans attended subsequent assemblies to vote against the commercialisation of the club. This can be explained by the gradual depoliticisation and demobilisation of St. Pauli supporters, which was another aspect that the *Sozialromantiker* wanted to change. In reality, protest actions are usually organised by USP members and people associated with the fanzine *Der Überstiger*. Petroni, *St. Pauli siamo noi*, p. 197.
14. Ebbers tried to head the ball, but in a reflex action he pushed it away with his hand. At that moment the score was tied at 1–1. In the end, St. Pauli claimed victory with a second goal in the 92nd minute. For his gesture the striker received a Fair Play Medal from the DFB in 2012. P. Sagioglou, 'Das Sagt Fair-Play Ikone Marius Ebbers zum Andreasen-Tor', *Kölner Stadt Anzeiger*, 19 October 2015.

of the training facilities. As part of the club's economic strategy, the 'Bonus Sankt Pauli 2011/2018' provided an interest rate of 6 per cent per annum until the bonds' expiry date: 30 June 2018. The decision to use crowdfunding and encourage the participation of fans was a success. The bonds sold out in just over four weeks, with more than 5,000 investors putting in almost six million euros.[15] The second significant episode that season had to do with the actions that allowed the club to prove to the DFB, the DFL and the Federal Interior Ministry that the club had implemented a code of conduct (which we will return to later). The measures were demanded following the pitch invasion by Fortuna Düsseldorf fans in the return leg of the relegation playoff against Hertha Berlin on 15 May 2012. St. Pauli was sanctioned twice that season for objects thrown from the stands. A partial or total closure of the stadium was not enforced but the club had to pay several fines and install a tunnel leading to the pitch to protect referees and rival teams.

After a period of calm lasting 18 months, the black-and-red Jolly Roger returned to the stands at a match against VfR Aalen on 25 September 2012. On that occasion, fans were protesting against plans to build a police station in the lower part of the new

---

15. 'El St. Pauli se financia con seis millones de euros de sus aficionados', *El Mundo*, 9 December 2011. Originally built in 1961, the *Gegengerade* entered St. Pauli mythology when it accommodated the bloc of fans from the Hafenstraße that burst into the Millerntor in the 1980s. The last match before the old stand was demolished was St. Pauli against Paderborn on 6 May 2012. A little over a year later, the reconstruction was complete. The new *Gegengerade*, with a capacity of 11,000, officially opened on 3 February 2013 at a match between St. Pauli and Energie Cottbus. The *Gegengerade* has more standing spaces (9,000) than any other stand in Europe, a measure intended to prevent fans from being passive when supporting the team. To take advantage of the reconstruction, the upper part of the stand was decorated with a large mural with the words '*Kein Fußball den Faschisten*' ('No Football for Fascists'). Curiously, this mural was the subject of controversy in 2014 when the German national team trained at the Millerntor Stadium before playing Poland. The DFB, following its own guidelines to keep sporting events free of any kind of political expression, decided to cover part of the antifascist mural with a large canvas, which left only the words '*Kein Fußball*' visible. This provision outraged militant St. Pauli fans. The fan club's spokespeople sent an open letter strongly criticising the federation's decision: 'This is an offence against all football fans who work every day to promote antifascist and antiracist behaviour, and to advance the marginalisation of the right in stadiums.'

Gegengerade.[16] The idea of police quarters in the space that had once been home to the Hafenstraße-Bloc was galling. Many fans considered it a provocation. What's more, the design included cells for fans arrested in riots. The whole plan was intended to meet the demands of the DFB for the renewal of club licences. However, what really angered fans was the management's decision to build the police premises next to the supporters' area: the *Fanräume*. A decision that fans 'did not know whether to describe as madness or insult'. In response to the proposal, fans lobbied for the space that had been allocated to the police to house the future St. Pauli museum. On 14 September, an emergency meeting was called to prepare a campaign to demand the construction of the museum instead of the police station.

The animosity of the more radical FC St. Pauli supporters towards the security forces is indisputable. Several episodes of repression have fanned the hostility of fans towards police. This aversion was ironically subverted when a banner with the acronym ACABAB ('All Cops Are Bastards Apart from Boll') was displayed in the stadium, in reference to former St. Pauli captain Fabian Boll, who combined his football career with his job as a police inspector. The St. Pauli fans' affection for Boll, however, also had to do with his past as a young player training with the HSV youth team. After attending games with friends behind the north goal line at the Millerntor stadium, Boll became a St. Pauli fan. From then on, he regularly attended HSV training sessions wearing St. Pauli jerseys, a gesture for which he was reprimanded by HSV.

---

16. In 2010, coinciding with the FC St. Pauli centenary, more than 30 interconnected shipping containers were placed near the Millerntor Stadium to host a temporary exhibition on the club's history. The project attracted the attention of hundreds of fans interested in creating a museum. In October 2010 the temporary exhibition ended and the containers were removed. The 1910 e.V. platform working to create the FC St. Pauli museum started organising events to make itself known. These included Football and Love in September 2013. A year later, on 11 October 2014, a match played in honour of former St. Pauli captain Fabian Boll raised 75,000 euros, of which 25,000 went to the Kiezhelden platform, 17,017 was allocated to the 1910 e.V. project and a further 5,000 funded St. Pauli's blind football department. See Davidson, *Pirates, Punks and Politics*, p. 226 and Rondinelli, *Ribelli, Sociali e Romantici*, p. 256.

At the match against Aalen, red flags and Jolly Roger banners could be seen all over the stadium, even in executive boxes. The entire ground came together to demand 'Fans want a museum, not a police station!' In the midst of protests, the team continued its losing streak. The 0–1 defeat against VfR Aalen led to the dismissal of coach André Schubert. His departure was officially confirmed on 26 September after very poor results on the pitch, with only one win in seven matches. Schubert was replaced (in the interim) by the then-athletics director, Helmut Schulte. Against this background of changes to the team's coaching staff, St. Pauli president Stefan Orth announced the start of conversations with fans to decide on the best way to resolve the issue of the police HQ location.

In the 2012–13 season, FC St. Pauli settled into the second division, finishing 10th: well clear of relegation but not high enough to dream of returning to the Bundesliga. With Daniel Ginczek, a German striker of Polish descent, as the team's highest scorer, netting 18, St. Pauli got through the championship without major upheavals other than another change of coach. Former Borussia Mönchengladbach player Michael Frontzeck had taken over as coach in October 2012 and remained at the helm until November 2013, when he was replaced by the former 1. FC Lokomotive Leipzig coach Roland Vrabec. Marius Ebbers, who had worn the brown-and-white shirt since 2008, also left the team at the end of the season. His professional attitude, sportsmanship and scoring prowess made him a favourite with the St. Pauli faithful. On the day of his farewell game against Eintracht Braunschweig,[17] Ebbers called for fans to take toys to the stadium and donate them to an organisation working with underprivileged pre-schoolers. At the end of the match, the pitch was full of stuffed toys thrown by fans from the stands.

The uniqueness of St. Pauli and its fans, and its association with antifascism and the far left, earned the club enemies everywhere.

---

17. The midfielder Florian Bruns, who had played for the Pirates since 2006, also left the club that same day. The under-21 international joined Werder Bermen's 'B' team, where he remained until he hung up his boots in the 2014/15 season. Curiously enough, in that farewell game Bruns and Ebbers were able to bid goodbye to the Millerntor by scoring a goal each.

The Pirates' club became an international symbol of rebellion, and for decades this made it the target of far-right crews. Unsurprisingly, trips by St. Pauli fans to away matches have often been an odyssey. This was the case in February 2012, when FC St. Pauli visited Aachen, a city in North Rhine-Westphalia, near the Belgian and Dutch borders. On the afternoon of the match between St. Pauli and Alemannia Aachen, various neo-Nazi groups, including the *Kameradschaft Alsdorf-Eupen*,[18] organised a march through the city streets. However, the problems did not end there. A bomb threat was received at the stadium where the match was to be played. According to the message, the bomb had been placed in the part of the stands set aside for the St. Pauli fans. In the hours leading up to the match, several left-wing organisations and businesses had received similar warnings.

Aside from these peculiar welcomes from rival team's fans and the first team's sporting performance, in December 2013 the St. Pauli neighbourhood was rocked by protests in defence of the Rote Flora,[19] a cultural centre that had been squatted for three decades.

18. Members of both organisations form part of the Karlsbande Ultras (KBU), which split from the Aachen Ultras in 2010 when it decided to implement an antidiscrimination and antiracist policy in the stands. Although they claim to be apolitical, the KBU has various members from fascist groups.

19. The building that houses the social centre, located at Achidi-John-Platz 1, Schanzenviertel, was built in 1888 as the Tivoli Theatre (also known as the Concerthaus Flora and Flora Theatre). As it was not damaged in the aerial bombings during the Second World War, it continued programming plays and operas until 1943. It was then used as a warehouse before reopening as a theatre in 1949. Later it was a movie theatre from 1953 to 1964, and then the 100 Töpfe warehouse chain occupied in the building until 1987. The theatre producer Friedrich Kurz submitted a project to turn it into a musical theatre, leading to the building being partly demolished in 1988. This was met by growing protests from local residents, which eventually led investors to pull out of the development project. The building then remained empty until August 1989, when the City Council decided to lease it to various activist groups, who turned it into a cultural centre. The new occupiers have been served with a series of eviction notices. However, negotiations with the authorities meant their removal has not been enforced. In 2001, the occupants refused to continue negotiating with the Hamburg Senate, which decided to sell the property to businessman Klausmartin Kretschmer for a sum of 370,000 marks. When the lease contract expired in 2011, Kretschmer was free to sell to any buyer. In view of this possibility, demonstrations were held to prevent eviction and ensure that the centre were not demolished.

Since 1989, the Rote Flora had been an icon of Hamburg's alternative scene and autonomous movement. On 21 December 2013, 7,300 protesters attended a demonstration to stop its eviction and the redevelopment of its land. The defence of the Rote Flora was also palpable in the Millerntor stands. During the last match before the winter break, in which St. Pauli played SC Karlsruher, local fans displayed banners in support of the Rote Flora. The 21 December protest was the start of a struggle that was burned into the heart of Hamburg. The demonstration was not just in defence of the Rote Flora but also against the eviction of several families from the apartment blocks known as the Esso Houses – named after the petrol station opposite, and against the European Union's treatment of the refugees expelled from Italy (some of whom were resettled in Hamburg, where they became known as the *Lampedusa-Gruppe*). Immediately after the start of the march, when protesters had barely advanced 20 metres, they was blocked by police, even though it was an authorised demonstration. This led to a series of riots that ended with 500 demonstrators and 117 police officers being injured (with 16 hospitalisations), as a result of protesters throwing rocks and bottles and police using water cannons and pepper spray. As well as the clashes with police, after the rally there were attacks on luxury hotels, banks and two attacks on the St. Pauli's Davidwache police station. In the end, 16 people were arrested. Police spokesman Mirko Streiber described them as the worst riots Hamburg had seen in years.[20]

Some days later, on 28 December, taking advantage of the media impact of these incidents police claimed that 40 masked protesters wearing St. Pauli scarves had attacked the police station near the Reeperbahn and seriously injured an officer. This served to justify a state of emergency (*Gefahrengebiet* or 'danger zone'), for the first time since the measure had been introduced. The order affected three areas (St. Pauli, Altona and Sternschanze, with a combined population of almost 80,000). The order, issued by mayor Olaf

20. 'Hieren a 117 policias en disturbios en Hamburgo, Alemania', *La Jornada*, 21 December 2013.

Scholz, extended police powers in the period between 4 and 13 January. Officers were permitted to stop and search arbitrarily, even without reason for suspicion, and to remove people from the designated danger zone. A total of 62 people were expelled from the area during the nine-day period and a further 800 were stopped and identified. In addition, 2,000 vehicles were searched and there were traffic and public transport disruptions. It was the first time an effective 'danger zone' had been declared indefinitely or in an urban area.

The rebellious nature of the neighbourhood was once again evident in the many demonstrations organised. Protesters carried very curious flags with an adaptation of the Jolly Roger in which the usual crossbones were replaced by toilet brushes, which is what demonstrators used as shields and wielded as a satirical symbol of disobedience.[21] It all began with a video broadcast on the news that Tuesday, showing a police officer confiscating a toilet brush while searching a hooded man. The images immediately went viral and led to the widespread use of the Jolly Roger with the crossed toilet brushes to mock the police. In the end the protests stopped the sale of the building that housed the Rote Flora.

That season, FC St. Pauli kept its place in the second division without too much difficulty. In spite of a good start to the league, with a 1–0 home win against 1860 München, St. Pauli went on to finish eighth. The 48 points gained were enough to prevent headaches, but they were nonetheless insufficient to aspire to promotion.

The following season fans were full of hope. The football played under Roland Vrabec the previous year had fanned expectations. Many St. Pauli supporters caught a whiff of the promise of a successful season and a return to top-flight football, but an erratic start leading to Vrabec's dismissal on 3 September 2014 dashed the hopes of the St. Pauli faithful. Vrabec was replaced by another familiar face, Thomas Meggle – a former club player over three separte periods. The team's poor results prompted another change of coach

---

21.   L. Hernández, 'Entendiendo Hamburgo: St. Pauli FC y un cepillo de baño', *Diagonal*, 10 January 2014.

that same season. The man chosen to pull St. Pauli back from the abyss was Ewald Lienen, a former player with a strong personality who had coached CD Tenerife.[22] The new coach instilled his values of hard work and sacrifice in the team. And that was how, despite having been bottom of the table for many weeks, St. Pauli bounced back to avoid relegation in a nail-biting final match of the season. The outcome, and Lienen's tireless efforts, earned him recognition among St. Pauli fans and management, who renewed his contract as head coach for the 2015–16 season. Lienen became a character beloved by fans for his guts and passion towards the team and the stands. What's more, he fully identified with the club's values, as can be seen from an interview he gave shortly before a match between St. Pauli and Red Bull Leipzig. In a very critical tone, he said, 'if the alternative is to leave football in the hands of fascism and commerce, I do not accept these choices'.

The changes that affected FC St. Pauli went beyond the bench. On 16 November 2014, as part of the renewal of the board (whose members include two fan reps), a new president was elected. As a result, Oke Göttlich replaced Stefan Orth, who had been in the post since 2010. Göttlich's appointment was well received by fans.[23] The new president's past as a supporter of the club seemed like a good opportunity to improve the team's sporting performance while also keeping the values associated with St. Pauli intact. Göttlich is sometimes referred to as the 'fan president' because he had actively participated in the protests organised by the Social Romantics. It seemed as though the years of tension between the presidency and

22. From 1995 to 1997, Lienen was a member of the coaching staff under Jupp Heynckes at CD Tenerife. In the summer of 1997, when the former Athletic Club coach left the Canary Islands to sign for Real Madrid, Lienen returned to Germany to coach Hansa Rostock. He then signed for 1. FC Cologne, where he remained as coach until he returned to Tenerife in 2002, now as head coach. However, poor results led to his dismissal six months later, in January 2003.
23. Before taking up the presidency, Göttlich had contributed to various fanzines edited by St. Pauli fans. When he took over as president, he was the owner of a small music label that published offbeat electronic music and neo-folk. His past as a member of the active fan scene strengthened his synergy with the more active section of St. Pauli fans.

fans would finally end. Reconciliation was helped further by the fact that the team avoided relegation to the third division. The club's good financial situation was another good omen, with a turnover of 30.74 million euros in the 2013–14 season, resulting in FC St. Pauli earning a net profit of 730,000 million euros.

Meanwhile, renovation work on the Millerntor's *Nordkurve* had been underway since 2014. Demolition of the old stand had begun after the match against SC Karlsruher on 25 October 2014. The last three conventional floodlight towers that remained were removed the following month, completing the redevelopment of that part of the stadium. The new *Nordkurve* officially opened on 25 July 2015, the first match day of the 2015–16 season, in which FC St. Pauli played against Arminia Bielefeld. At the end of the refurbishment the Millerntor ended up with a capacity of 29,546 spectators overall, including 17,000 standing places. The stadium reached capacity when spectators crowded in to watch the first game of the season, setting a new attendance record at the Millerntor.

In the midst of these encouraging developments came the tragic news of the death of former St. Pauli player Andreas Biermann. At the age of 33 the former defender committed suicide as a result of the depression he had suffered for five years. Despite making his illness public and receiving months of treatment after a failed suicide attempt on 19 November 2009,[24] he finally took his own life on 18 July 2014. Biermann had worn the St. Pauli jersey from 2008 to 2010. He had joined the St. Pauli youth squad after leaving the club Tennis Borussia Berlin, but his good performances soon saw him reach the first team, for which he would play 33 matches. Shortly after Biermann's death, in August 2014, a group of around

---

24. Biermann unsuccessfully tried to commit suicide in November 2009. He decided to quit professional football, joined an amateur team – the Spandauer Kickers – and made his condition public. He started studying psychology and wrote his autobiography *Rote Karte Depression* (Depression: Red Card). However, he tried to take his life again during a trip to Majorca with his teammates in the summer of 2012. Finally, on 18 July 2014, he threw himself in front of a train. See M. Beltran, 'La rendición de Biermann', *Panenka* 28 July 2014 and A. Biermann, *Rote Karte Depression* (Munich: Gütersloher Verlagshaus, 2011).

15 relatives, friends, doctors and therapists who had treated him decided to launch the *St. Depri* project to provide support and education for people with depression. A donations system was put in place to raise money for the initiative with collaboration from the *Fanladen* and Jolly Roger pub.

Adding to the tragedy of losing Biermann, the 2015–16 season coincided with the drama of the refugees fleeing the Syrian conflict. Thousands of people were forced to leave their homes and set out in search of an uncertain future away from the bombings and civil war ravaging their country. Others came from Iraq, Eritrea, Lebanon and Afghanistan. Many of these refugees were hoping to reach central Europe, which they pictured as a land of opportunity. After a journey full of hardship across much of Europe, they reached Germany. According to the International Organisation for Migration, 800,000 refugees were expected to arrive in Germany in 2015. More than 50 per cent of Germans said they were concerned about the high number of refugees coming into the country. This discontent had a negative impact on Chancellor Angela Merkel's approval rating, which dropped to 46 per cent – the lowest level since the crisis in the eurozone.

Far from the warm reception they had expected, many refugees were greeted with harassment from neo-Nazi groups and German citizens who felt threatened by their arrival. Several shelters equipped to house refugees were burned down. Racism and xenophobia resurfaced and spread virulently as a result of the country's economic stagnation. In 2011 there were 18 attacks against buildings occupied by refugees. The following year there were 24, and by 2013 the number reached 50. In addition, 18 far-right demonstrations were held in front of refugee shelters in 2013. The following year there were 256 rallies to protest against the presence of migrants and refugees. Also in 2014 there were 150 attacks on refugee shelters, a figure that reached 199 for just the first half of 2015.

Organisations such as Pegida[25] and HoGeSa,[26] together with
political groups like the NPD and Alternative for Germany (*Alter-*

25. Acronym for *Patriotische Europäer gegen die Islamisierung des Abendlandes*
(Patriotic Europeans against the Islamisation of the West). The organisation was
created in Dresden in 2014 by Lutz Bachmann, a public relations executive given
a three-year prison sentence in 1997 for drug dealing and burglaries in the Saxony
capital. Pegida initially operated as a Facebook group and YouTube channel with
a moderate public image. Its motto is '*Wir sind das Volk*' ('We Are the People').
On 20 October 2014 18,000 people marched through Dresden's city centre. On
every Monday since Pegida has organised demonstrations against the German
government's refugee policy and the supposed threat of the West becoming
Islamised. The organisation is also ultranationalist and against the two-party system
(conservative-social democrats). Following the attacks on French magazine *Charlie
Hebdo*, Pegida's protests attracted almost 30,000 demonstrators. This success,
achieved by presenting itself as a civil-society group independent from the political
parties, led to its spread to other German cities, such as Dusseldorf, Kassel, Leipzig and
Frankfurt. Its model was also exported to places such as Denmark, Sweden, Austria,
the Czech Republic, Switzerland, Catalonia and Canada. In November 2015, after
the Paris bombings, the following demonstration drew less than 8,000 protesters.
Months earlier, in January, Bachmann was forced to resign following the publication
of photographs showing him dressed up as Adolf Hitler. Without Bachmann at the
helm, Pegida went into decline, as reflected by the dwindling numbers responding
to its protest calls. For this reason, in April 2015 Bachmann resumed a leadership
role with the idea of turning Pegida into a political party. The group has several
offshoots, including Bärgida in Berlin and Legida in Leipzig. According to a German
public broadcaster, racist attacks on refugee shelters and houses has doubled since
Pegida emerged. Nonetheless, a survey conducted in December 2014 found that 34
per cent of German citizens publicly supported Pegida.
26. A movement that began in North Rhine-Westphalia in 2012 in the form
of an internet forum known as GnuHoonters, with almost 300 members from
17 German hooligan groups. Its most visible leaders include Andreas Kraul (aka
Kalle Grabowski) and Dominik Roeseler, a Mönchengladbach city councillor and
member of the populist-right Pro NRW party. Other notable figures are Siegfried
Borchardt, former leader of the Borussenfront linked to Die Rechte, and HSV
hooligan Torsten de Vries. In 2014, the Facebook group (of up to 40,000 followers)
became known as HoGeSa, short for *Hooligans gegen Salafisten* (Hooligans
Against Salafists). Its organisational model follows that of the European Defence
League, an offshoot of the English Defence League, an Islamophobic organisation
created in 2009 that uses football stadiums to spread its message. HoGeSa's main
focus is to organise protests 'against Salafism' in Germany, such as the one held
in Breslauer Platz, Cologne, on 26 October 2014, which drew between 3,000 and
5,000 demonstrators and ended in clashes with the police. The event was attended
by illegal neo-Nazi brotherhoods and members of Die Rechte, the NPD, and the
German Identitarian Movement. HoGeSa includes members of far-right and neo-
Nazi groups such as the NPD and Pro NRW. Unsuccessful rallies as well as disputes
over the control of its finances have led to internal struggles in the organisation.

native für Deutschland, AfD),[27] stirred up old ghosts by means of a populist anti-immigrant discourse. This gained roots among the 'proles' and ended up influencing the political agenda of the major parties. Added to the mood was Germany's win at the 2014 World Cup in Brazil, a victory that inspired unprecedented patriotic fervour.

Hamburg also received this human exodus. Five hundred refugees reached the city each day. In response to this, and in view of the low temperatures forecast, the city council passed a bill allowing asylum seekers to be housed in empty commercial buildings, so that they would not have to sleep outdoors or in tents. The measure was temporary and included the provision of financial compensation for the owners of the buildings. The council also fitted out shipping containers as housing for refugee families. However, conditions worsened with the arrival of winter in October 2015. By then, Hamburg was home to 35,000 refugees, 4,200 of whom lived in tents – mostly without heating.[28]

---

27. A political party with an anti-immigration and Eurosceptic ideology, founded in February 2013. One of its main proposals is to get rid of the euro and return to the German mark). Its 20 founders include Bernd Lucke, the University of Hamburg economics professor who led the party until he was ousted by Frauke Petry in July 2015 in response to the rise of Pegida. They also include former *Frankfurter Allgemeine* journalist Konrad Adam, economics professor and former SPD member Jörn Kruse (head of the Hamburg chapter) and former CDU members Alexander Gauland and Gerd Robanus. AfD describes itself as liberal conservative, which makes sense given that most of its members are from the ranks of the CDU and Free Democratic Party (of liberal ideology). Its core programme is based on the defence of Christianity and the traditional family, rejection of same-sex marriage, climate change scepticism, toughening of conditions for asylum and opposition to the energy transition, as well as a return to the German mark. The AfD also opposes bailing out peripheral European Union states and the construction of mosques. Its populist, xenophobic discourse has gained roots among the middle and working classes and in university and business elites. Its first electoral success came during the 2014 European elections, when it won 7 per cent of votes and seven seats in the Strasbourg parliament.
28. In the municipal elections held in February 2015, the CDU candidate, economist David Erkalp, tried to exploit the presence of refugees. His campaign posters blamed the SPD and refugees for 'all Hamburg's evils: crime, burglaries, and its bad reputation'. Ironically, Erkalp's family comes from a Syrian minority living in south-eastern Turkey. Suso, *La claveguera marró*, p. 287.

The arrival of hundreds of impoverished people in Hamburg created a growing demand for basic necessities. Accordingly, many individuals and associations worked to provide clothes, shoes, toothbrushes, personal hygiene products and children's toys. Many St. Pauli fans were among the quickest to respond. Some of them joined the Refugees Welcome assembly that soon sprang up in the neighbourhood.

It was not only individuals who came together to support the newcomers. On 26 August 2015, the second session of the St. Pauli district assembly took place at the Millerntor's *Ballsaal Südtribüne*. At the meeting, attended by almost a thousand people, the assembly decided to coordinate the actions and campaigns in support of refugees coming to Hamburg. By allowing the use of its premises, FC St. Pauli became directly involved in initiatives aimed at welcoming people fleeing their countries due to armed conflict and Islamic State's actions.[29] Once again, St. Pauli was one of the first football clubs to get involved in the campaign.

This was the background to the friendly that St. Pauli had agreed to play against Borussia Dortmund on 9 September 2015. The match, taking place during a break in the league – to allow the qualifying games for the 2016 UEFA European Championship – became a match in support of the refugees. On that day, 25,731 spectators filled the Millerntor. A thousand of them were political exiles, attending as guests of the Pirate club. At the end of the match, players from both teams displayed banners with the club badges and the words 'Refugees Welcome'. In the stands, the fans expressed their support by displaying signs with slogans such as 'Say it loud, say it clear: refugees are welcome here!', 'No Border, No Nation' and 'Solidarity with undocumented immigrants'. That day, the club raised 45,000 euros in donations. 'That's why I love this club', said a proud fan.

Soon afterwards, controversy arose when FC St. Pauli announced its refusal to participate in a campaign in solidarity with refugees

---

29. In this same spirit, the St. Pauli official online store sold orange and black scarves including the words 'Refugees Welcome' and the club badge. All proceeds from sales of the scarf went to help refugees.

launched by the DFL, with the support of the *Bild* newspaper. The initiative, whose slogan was 'Refugees Welcome – Wir Helfen [we help]', was made up of the 36 teams in the top two divisions of German football. St. Pauli argued that it had been helping refugees for weeks and did not consider it appropriate to join the action proposed by the DFL. The team's refusal upset the director of *Bild*, Kai Diekmann. He tweeted from his personal account, 'No heart for refuges. Shame on FC St. Pauli #refugeesnotwelcome', and 'That will make the AfD's day'. These tweets immediately upset a large number of St. Pauli fans. Rather than making the club reconsider its position, Diekmann's comments unleashed a wave of support for its refusal to participate in the campaign. Pirate fans flooded twitter with the hashtag #Bildnotwelcome and questioned the sincerity of the tabloid's initiative.[30] Some pointed out that it had a 'xenophobic editorial line', often close to conservative nationalism.[31] Little wonder then that many fans considered the campaign to be 'nothing but empty words'.

That was not the club's only socially oriented activity that season. To mark International Holocaust Remembrance Day, held on 27 January each year, the *Fanladen* proposed that the players of the first team wear a jersey in which the sponsor's logo (which was Congstar that season) was replaced by the special slogan: '*Kein Fußball den Faschisten*'[32] ('No Football for Fascists').[33] The manage-

---

30. Although no *Bundesliga* team joined St. Pauli's protest, the supporters of some teams, such as Borussia Dortmund, did express their disagreement in the stands, displaying banners with the words 'Bild not welcome' as a sign of solidarity with St. Pauli fans.
31. On 4 April 2006, shop assistant Mehmet Kubasik, a German citizen of Turkish origin, was murdered in Dortmund by members of the National Socialist Underground, an armed neo-Nazi organisation that committed various murders throughout Germany between 2000 and 2011. Shortly after Kubasik's death, *Bild* published information linking him to an organized crime network. It was this type of stigmatisation, associating foreigners with organised mafias, which led St. Pauli to reject the newspaper's campaign. 'Football Club Rejects Bild's Pro-refugee Campaign', *The Local*, 16 September 2015. See also Suso, *La claveguera marró*, p. 63.
32. A football version of the motto *Kein Fußbreit den Faschisten* (Don't give an inch to the fascists), historically used by the alternative left and the German autonomous movement.
33. 'Trikot-Schriftzung "Kein Fußball den Faschisten": St. Pauli setzt Zeichen

ment of both FC St. Pauli and the Telekom Deutschland subsidiary endorsed the idea. There were no objections from the DFL either. So on 12 February 2016, at a match against RB Leipzig,[34] St. Pauli players took to the Millerntor pitch with the antifascist slogan on their shirts.[35] Meanwhile, through the stadium's speakers the presidents of both clubs read a manifesto that called for respect and tolerance, and openly denounced any manifestation of fascism or racism. In this way, St. Pauli once more reaffirmed its explicit rejection of any form of discrimination.

In April 2016, FC St. Pauli launched a new community initiative based on local engagement and aimed at strengthening ties between club and neighbourhood: honey production. St. Pauli's commercial director Andreas Rettig announced that the club had decided to help the repopulation of bees, which are a threatened species, by installing two beehives at the Millerntor. The results came in the form of honey. In addition to helping to improve the environment, the club announced its intention to sell the honey on a self-managed basis, under its own brand *Ewaldbienenhonig*, which is a play on words between '*bienen*' (German for honey) and the name of the head coach, Ewald Lienen. At a press conference to launch the

---

gegen Rassismus', *Zeit*, 10 February 2016 and 'FC St. Pauli spielt mit Sondertrikot gegen RB Leipzig', *Der Tagesspiegel*, 10 February 2016.

34.   The choice of rival was also significant. Just a month earlier there had been serious incidents involving around 250 neo-Nazis in the traditionally left-wing district of Connewitz (Leipzig). This followed a rally organised by Legida (the local chapter of the Pegida movement), which drew 2,000 people. Demonstrators displayed banners with slogans and chants such as 'Merkel: get lost and take the Muslims with you' and 'Merkel out now'. During the riots on Wolfgang-Heinze street, protesters erected barricades and smashed shop windows, as well as setting fire to cars and rubbish containers. The attack had been announced on social media as 'Storm on Leipzig'. Five police officers were injured and 211 far-right extremists were arrested as a result. Historian Sascha Lange described it as 'the biggest attack by right-wing extremists on shops and houses in Leipzig since the November Pogrom of 1938'. The previous day, a group of about 20 neo-Nazis had attacked several foreigners – six Pakistanis and a Syrian – on Cologne's streets.

35.   It was the first time these words had been displayed at the Millerntor. That same season, at the start of a match, St. Pauli players came on to the pitch wearing tracksuits with the motto printed on the back. Three years earlier, the club's management had allowed fans to decorate the upper section of the *Gegengerade* with the same message – visible from one end of the stand to the other.

campaign, the club's spokesperson asked residents within a three kilometre radius from the stadium to put flowers on their balconies to help grow the native bee colony. 'Others have balconies to celebrate championships; we have them for bees', said Rettig.[36] In this St. Pauli also proved to be a 'different' club.

Once the 2015–16 season was over, with the players on holiday, the club decided to reaffirm its commitment to refugees. Thus, the middle of Millerntor stadium's *Nordkurve* was decorated with a mural with the words '*Kein Mensch ist illegal*' ('No one is illegal'), in the style of the antifascist slogan painted on the *Gegengerade*.[37]

---

36.   'St. Pauli: German Club Makes Honey to Help Declining Bee Population', BBC, 5 April 2016.
37.   The mural was painted by various fan clubs based in the *Nordkurve*, including Nord-Support, Pröppers Vendetta, Sankt Pauli Mafia, Egons Horde, Die Spinner and FC Tortuga.

15

Stadium *Ultras'* Antifascism in 2002

Another element making St. Pauli unique is its fans. The arrival of the Hafenstraße squatters in the 1980s transformed the experience of watching matches in the stands. Their active, transgressive support for the club developed over the years, culminating in the creation of USP (the *Ultrà Sankt Pauli* fan crew) in 2002.

Years earlier, groups such as the *Passanten* had started imitating the Italian football crew model.[1] Founded in 1995–6, *Passanten* was the first group to adapt the chants of other European fans, mainly Italian and French *ultras*, such as '*Aux armes*', '*Forza St. Pauli*'[2] and '*Äppel wolln wir klaun*'. The actions designed to enliven the atmosphere in the stadium gradually expanded with the first cardboard choreographies. Megaphones also appeared at that time to coordi-

---

1.   *St. Pauli Passanten* was founded in the 1995–6 season to improve the atmosphere in the stadium and accommodate anybody who wanted to actively support the team. Although it was still influenced by the English model, the *Passenten* broke new ground by adopting elements from the Italian crews in the Millerntor stands. It was originally based at the *Meckerecke* corner terrace, on the southern part of the stadium between the *Gegengerade* and the *Südkurve*. The following season it moved to the *Gegengerade*, where it lobbied to maintain the standing section and created Block 1 with the support of the *Fanladen*. Together with groups such as the *Supportblock* (founded in 1997), it created the 'singing area' to lead the chants of supporters in the stadium. This debuted at a match between St. Pauli and FC Carl Zeiss Jena on 7 November 1997. Until then, older fans had been more influenced by British terrace culture, while the new generations adopted the Italian *ultra* model (based on the use of banners and other elements, complex choreographies and permanent organisational structures). The model had also been adopted in countries such as Portugal, the former Yugoslavia, Spain, southern France and the Netherlands. It was around this time that fans first chanted the famous '*Aux armes*', which went on to become one of the St. Pauli faithful's favourite war cries.
2.   For more on this, see the article 'Das Herz von St. Pauli (el cor de St. Pauli)', published on the *FC St. Pauli Fanclub Catalunya* blog, 13 May 2013: www.stpaulicatalunya.cat/b/2013/05/das-herz-von-st-pauli-el-cor-de-st-pauli/ (accessed 7 March 2020).

nate chanting in the stands. Until then, most fans would cheer their teams on by singing spontaneously for a few minutes of the match, without organisation or continuity.

In 1996, another notable *sanktpaulianer* fan group was founded: the St. Pauli Skinheads. This was created by young skinhead fans, including cofounder Jan Walli. The group, which still exists and currently has around 70 members, is unambiguously antifascist and antiracist. It has brought together all the skinheads who regularly attend St. Pauli matches. The group frequented the Ballkult, a bar located near the stadium that was renamed the Jolly Roger in 1997. In this mainstay of Pirate club's supporters, located on Budapester Straße, the St. Pauli Skinheads organised their first concerts and all-night parties.[3] Its members have also performed campaigns to raise awareness of skinhead subculture among other St. Pauli fans. Since 2006, the group publishes its own fanzine, *In the Streets of Hamburg.*

Another group that followed in the footsteps of the *Passanten* was Carpe Diem, which was made up of former members of the Klaus Thomforde Fan Club. The group was named in honour of St. Pauli's goalkeeper in the late 1980s and early 1990s, and changed its name when its idol retired in 1999. Carpe Diem took up the southeast end of the *Gegengerade*. From there they tried to coordinate the first choreographies ('*tifos*'), copying the Italian *ultras*. They travelled to Italy to watch a match between Ternana Calcio and AS Livorno, in the first of a series of trips that contributed to the politicisation of the St. Pauli fan crews. The first contact between St. Pauli fans and Italian crews, however, had been in 1989, when Juventus drew HSV in the UEFA Cup and St. Pauli fans went to the Volksparkstadion to support the Italian team.

Three years later under its new name, due to an increase in members, Carpe Diem decided to join forces with other small,

---

3. Music and skins have been inseparably intertwined since young men with shaved heads first appeared in Hamburg in the early 1980s, making it one of the hallmarks of followers of the style. It comes as no surprise that St. Pauli Skinheads released a CD (10,000 copies) of football-themed songs by various groups.

active fan clubs to create the USP.[4] The USP was an organisation of about 80 active members whose purpose has been to coordinate supporters in the stadium. During the 2002–3 season, the USP displayed its banner in the southernmost end of the Gegengerade for the first time, before moving to the southern end of the stadium, the Südkurve, in 2007. The USP has maintained strong links with the left-wing and antifascist tradition that has characterised St. Pauli fans since the 1980s. Its leaders come from local activist circles in Hamburg, and they do not stop being crews when leaving the stands. Being an *ultra* means going to demonstrations, protesting against neo-Nazis and strengthening the club's political commitment.

The creation of the USP was bound up with the desire to reverse the growing tendency of St. Pauli fans to prioritise sporting success over everything else. However, the convergence of the various fan clubs that made up the USP was not easy, given the explicitly antifascist and leftist nature that was sought for the new body from the outset. The group was also criticised by fans who saw it as incompatible with the tradition of what had until then been spontaneous support by St. Pauli fans.

Currently there are about 70 people in USP's active inner core, which meets at the *Fanladen* every Wednesday to coordinate the day-to-day running of the group. Yet the number of fans in the USP stands is much greater. At the organisational level, the group reproduces certain aspects of the Italian crew model. However, it has a democratic, non-hierarchical structure that respects the club's countercultural principles and values. Thus, there are '*capos*' (leaders, although the name *Vorsänger*, 'leader of chants', is preferred). These stand – megaphone in hand – behind the fence bordering the pitch, coordinating the fans.[5] The organisational structure of the USP

---

4. The name of the group came up for discussion at preliminary meetings. Not everybody agreed with the idea of calling themselves *ultras* because of the negative connotations of the term in the media, where it was linked to German groups that did not share the ideals of St. Pauli fans. Despite this debate, they agreed to keep *ultra* in reference to the Italian model.

5. To encourage fans to support the team, USP negotiated with the club to stop playing ads and music on the stadium loudspeakers ten minutes before the start

includes various subgroups, such as the *Choreogruppe*, in charge of devising and planning the *tifos*, and the editors of the current USP fanzine, *Bash!* Many young fans participate in these groups and therefore play a role in the USP.

During Corny Littmann's presidency, the USP were among the harshest critics of the club's marketisation strategy. Indeed, banners with the words 'Littmann Out!' were regularly displayed in the stand used by the St. Pauli *ultras*. Despite acknowledging the USP's work in creating atmosphere in the stadium, actions like these generated misgivings among other fans.

In the 2009–10 season, the St. Pauli crews displayed an unusual degree of maturity in supporting the fans of Hansa Rostock, one of their arch rivals. The reason for this was that FC St. Pauli had reduced the number of seats allocated to visiting fans for the match to be held at the Millerntor on 28 March 2010. Instead of the usual 1,900 seats, only 500 were made available. The club's decision was prompted by a brawl that had taken place during the previous season. This ended in controversy on the turf over a gesture by Deniz Naki, and in serious clashes with law enforcement officers at the train station and around the stadium.[6] To prevent a similar situation recurring, the St. Pauli management, with the approval of the police, decided to allocate fewer seats to visitors. The decision angered St. Pauli fans, who expressed their discontent by displaying a large banner with the words: 'Today Rostock, tomorrow us?' The USP believed that limiting away fans' presence in matches that the authorities arbitrarily considered high risk was a direct attack on the rights of all fans – not just those supporting Hansa. The official website of the USP railed against what the organisation saw as a 'dangerous precedent'. Many fans expressed disappointment with

---

of matches in order to create a festive, colourful atmosphere and rally around the players. Rondinelli, *Ribelli, Sociali e Romantici!*, p. 155.

6.   The incidents began the day before the match, when police arrested one of the Hansa Rostock hooligans as a preventative measure. This led his companions to attack a police station with stones and bottles. On the day of the match, police were deployed to escort St. Pauli fans that had travelled to Rostock.

the club's stance. It was the first time that St. Pauli had banned or reduced the number of rival fans at Millerntor.

In the end, Hansa Rostock rejected the 500 tickets offered by St. Pauli. That day, the match was played without any visiting fans in the stands. The protests by St. Pauli fans, however, did not stop. Several fan clubs worked together through the *Ständiger Fanausschuss* (the Permanent Fans Committee created in 2008) to coordinate actions such as remaining silent during the first five minutes of matches and not cheering or performing choreographies. The boycott was intended to send a clear message to St. Pauli management, the police and the federation: fans have rights. A banner displayed in the *Südkurve* read, 'Imagine there is football, and nobody is allowed to go.'[7] The aim was to emphasise the importance of spectators as a legitimising force in football. But the protests were not understood by everyone. Some St. Pauli fans that did not agree with the actions of the *ultras* shouted insults against the organisers, such as '*Scheiß* USP' (Fucking USP).[8] The controversy over the protests lasted several weeks, and even 'threatened to cause a split among St. Pauli fans'.

The match against Hansa Rostock ended in a 3–2 win for the home team. However, the game was interrupted several times by flares and fireworks. In the 2011–12 season, the two teams met once more, this time in the second division championship. Expecting more commotion, police declared St. Pauli a 'special zone',[9] where they had the power to arrest anybody who could not provide proof of identity or was suspected of being a political activist or belonging to a fan group. In the meantime, visiting fans marched through neighbouring Altona without incident. This time, however, FC St.

---

7. An image that was captured in the 2011 documentary *Das Ganze Stadion*, directed by Felix Grimm.
8. Most of the fans that objected to the USP measure were in the more expensive seats on the upper tier of the *Südkurve*. The *ultras*, on the other hand, use the lower section of the stands, which is cheaper and provides standing room. During the match a banner was displayed with the words 'Even idiots have rights.' Petroni, *St. Pauli siamo noi*, p. 193.
9. This covered the St. Pauli districts and those of the *Landungsbrücken* (docks), *Fischmarkt* (Altona fish market), and *Sternschanze* (Altona district).

Pauli decided to appeal the authorities' decision. Meanwhile, its *ultras* organised a series of actions, including a funeral procession behind a coffin with the word '*Fankultur*' on it, in reference to the death of fan culture as a result of a series of travel bans.

At the start of the match, around 2,000 fans stood outside the stands, near the AFM container adjacent to the *Südkurve*. This action drew attention to the protest in the stadium. Meanwhile, on the pitch the home team sent Hansa Rostock into relegation, with a resounding 3–0 win. At the end of the match, incidents near the Jolly Roger pub ended in the police being involved. During the rioting, a small group of fans took the opportunity to break the windows of a pub frequented by HSV fans. This action was used by certain media outlets to criminalise the St. Pauli crew, even though it had nothing to do with the USP and was censured by the *Fanladen*.

The USP did not evade sanctions either, such as those imposed by the DFB for 'unsporting behaviour'. (This was especially for displaying banners with slogans like 'ACAB' – All Cops Are Bastards.) However, as well as criticism the USP also received recognition. For example, in October 2011 it was one of three recipients of the Hans Frankenthal Prize[10] awarded by the Auschwitz Foundation Committee. This was for its work in fighting fascism, racism and homophobia through the Alerta Network.[11] In addition to the cash prize, which was used to buy choreographic materials, the USP also was given a bunch of flowers. The following morning, a delegation

---

10. Hans Frankenthal and his brother Emil were two young German Jews who managed to survive the Auschwitz death camp. After his captivity, Hans, then 19, wrote a book about his experience entitled *The Unwelcome One: Returning Home from Auschwitz*.

11. A European network of fan associations founded in November 2007 to fight fascism, xenophobia, homophobia and discrimination of any kind on the terraces. The network currently organises Action Days to draw attention to different specific issues. Topics addressed have included anti-fascism (with campaigns such as Remember History, Support Resistance), antiracism (Refugees Welcome) and the fight against discrimination (Fight Homophobia). As its name suggests, Alerta Network is coordinated through the internet via its website. Activities organised through USP include an anti-racist football tournament held in Hamburg each year with the involvement of dozens of fan groups from across Europe.

from the group left the bouquet near the grave of Fritz Bringmann – a member of the Communist Party who had died that April. Bringmann had been a member of the anti-Nazi resistance and was arrested and tortured by the Gestapo in 1935 for having painted, with a brother of his, the slogan 'Down with Hitler' on a city roof.[12]

In July 2012, the DFB, together with the DFL and the German Ministry of the Interior, held a 'security summit' to address an increase in violent acts at football stadiums. This was despite such levels being way below those in the late 1980s and early 1990s, when 'hooliganism' emerged in Germany.[13] The measures they agreed on included the implementation of a 'code of conduct' based on a zero-tolerance policy towards violence, with penalties for infringement including bans from stadiums for a period of three to five years. Other decisions included confirming prohibition of setting off fireworks in stadiums, which had been announced at the start of the 2011–12 season. The ministry and federations invited the 54 clubs from the three German football divisions to sign this package: one that did not take into account the opinions of fans. Only one team, Union Berlin, refused to sign the agreement. But St. Pauli fans sprang into action. At a meeting between several club executives and reps from the *Ständiger Fanausschuss*, the *Fanclub-sprecherrat*, the *Fanladen* and the AFM, it was agreed to reject most of the proposals in the report. Furthermore, the vice president of St. Pauli, Gernot Stenger, resigned from the committee that was to draft the 'Safe Stadium Experience' report.

---

12. Lübeck-born Fritz Bringmann worked as a plumber until 1935, when, aged 18, he was arrested and tortured by the Gestapo over anti-Nazi graffiti. He was sentenced to two years in prison and sent to the Sachsenhausen death camp, then transferred to the Neuengamme camp in 1940. In 1944 he escaped but was then captured by the SS. He was then sent back to Neuengamme, where he remained until the liberation of the camp by the Allied forces. A communist, Bringmann participated in founding the Free German Youth movement. From 1970 to 1995 he was general secretary of the Amicale Internationale KZ Neuengamme (international association of Neuengamme survivors). He died in Aukrug on 31 March 2011 and is buried in the Ohlsdorf cemetery in Hamburg.

13. In fact, statistics show that more people are arrested during Oktoberfest (the annual beer festival held in Munich) each year than as a result of football-related violence. Davidson, *Pirates, Punks and Politics*, p. 238.

The DFB and authorities' desire to eradicate violent behaviour in stadiums revealed their ignorance of fan culture. Their strategy prompted various groups of fans around the country to work together to oppose the proposed rules. One of these joint protest actions was the *12:12 Ohne Stimme Keine Stimmung* (No Voice, No Atmosphere) campaign, consisting of remaining silent in the stands, without cheering on the team, until twelve minutes and twelve seconds into each match. The action was repeated in several stadiums on different days until 12 December (12/12/12), the day on which the 'Safe Stadium' document was to be signed (hence the numerical symbolism of the campaign). Finally, five clubs, including St. Pauli and Union Berlin, voted to postpone the agreement, citing the need to consult their fans before signing.

Excessive zeal in applying this set of measures led to comical episodes. For instance, St. Pauli was fined 20,000 euros because, according to the federation, its fans shouted 'Nazi!' every time the name of a player from the home team was announced over the speakers at the Hansa Rostock stadium. Actually the St. Pauli fans were calling out the name 'Naki' in homage to their team's Kurdish-German player Deniz Naki, who wore the St. Pauli shirt from 2009 to 2012, and specifically to a match played at Rostock on 2 November 2009. That day, with St. Pauli ahead thanks to a goal by Matthias Lehmann, the referee momentarily suspended the match because a flare was let off in the visiting fans' section. Once the match resumed, six minutes from the end, Naki scored – clinching the game 0–2. He celebrated by making a threatening cut-throat gesture to Hansa Rostock fans. Then, as St. Pauli players celebrated the win in front of their supporters, Naki planted a St. Pauli flag on the pitch. When he made his way down the tunnel to the dressing room, two Hansa players were waiting for him, away from the camera, to reproach him for planting the flag.[14] 'He is a hot-blooded young player, he didn't realise the implications of his action. He was very foolish. He needs to realise he made a big mistake', said Christian Bönig, the FC St. Pauli team manager. Although Naki

---

14. T. Padilla, 'La voz no está en venta', *Panenka*, no. 50, March 2016, pp. 92–5.

apologised for what he described as an 'unsportsmanlike, disrespectful, and inappropriate' attitude, his actions made him a hero in the eyes of the Pirate fans. This is why they shouted his name at the Hansa Rostock match three years later.[15] The extreme rivalry between St. Pauli and Hansa Rostock went beyond the stadiums and match days. So much so that in May 2011 a young man was beaten up by a group of Hansa Rostock extremists simply for wearing a St. Pauli jacket.

Leaving aside these episodes of enmity with the East German team, in 2013 the USP launched a new campaign in support of refugees.[16] 'Refugees Welcome' was, after all, one of the most popular slogans printed on the club's merchandise. In the campaign, St. Pauli *ultras* approached refugee reception centres on the city outskirts to arrange transport and tickets for migrants who wanted to attend FC St. Pauli matches. 'I was very scared. I didn't know who I was with, or what St. Pauli was. I had no idea where these guys were taking me, but at the stadium I was greeted by a very positive atmosphere. I felt at home', said Megd Abo Amsh, a young Syrian refugee invited to one of the St. Pauli matches.

The club implemented other similar initiatives. These included offering the chance to attend training sessions and get tickets to the Millerntor stadium, through the *Kiezhelden* social platform,[17]

---

15. For more information on his career at St. Pauli, see C. Viñas, 'Un jugador kurd al futbol turc', *Ara*, 12 February 2016, p. 48.

16. In 2004, two years after the USP was founded, the USP Antirazzista taskforce was set up. It has taken care of various political refugees who arrived in Hamburg, visiting them at reception centres and accompanying them to watch St. Pauli matches at the Millerntor and other stadiums. Petroni, *St. Pauli siamo noi*, p. 189.

17. Organised by the club and by fan associations such as the AFM and the *Fanladen*, the *Kiezhelden* was set up in the 2013–14 season to carry out non-profitmaking social and cultural projects. It receives much of its funding from donations managed through the Better Place platform. In 2013, for example, it devoted 10,000 euros from the sale of merchandising to financing local community activities. In the run-up to the 2013–14 season the *Kiezhelden* logo was displayed on the official first-team shirt. But it was replaced from the first match of the season as the club had reached a agreement with the Relentless energy drinks brand (created by the Coca-Cola Company in 2006) for it to become the official sponsor of the team kit. In addition to FC St. Pauli, Relentless also sponsors punk music festivals and skate competitions, and even funds social projects in Hamburg. This is

for the 350 Africans who arrived in Hamburg from the island of Lampedusa (Sicily) in spring 2013.[18] This was how football became a 'catalyst for attention and awareness [...] to promote the integration and aggregation' of these newcomers.

The joining of the USP by a crop of young supporters reflected a new state of affairs. Attracted to fads rather than activism, these new fans have adopted dynamics that were unusual among St. Pauli fans, such as participating in fights with rival fans, thus ruining the awareness-raising efforts of older *ultras*. But despite this minority fascination with hooliganism, most St. Pauli fans continue to espouse a political position that is 'avowedly libertarian, left-wing, and profoundly antifascist [...] arising from the radical political history established since the mid-1980s'.

---

something it has in common with previous team sponsors, such as Fernsehlotterie, which sponsored FC St. Pauli for three years while donating 5 per cent of its revenue to social projects. In 2014, the *Kiezhelden* launched 20 projects thanks to various donors providing it with 45,000 euros. Its areas of interest and action are interventions against social injustice and inequality in the local area and to promote youth education and welfare, the fight against social exclusion and discrimination of various groups and the development of creativity in the areas of culture and diversity in Hamburg. Its campaigns include *Ein Rucksack Voll Hoffnung* (A Backpack Full of Hope), which collects clothes for Hamburg's homeless. It has also participated in the DFB's *Anstoß für ein neues Leben* (Kicking Off a New Life) campaign to rehabilitate juvenile offenders through football.

18. On 25 October 2013, the Jolly Roger pub financed tickets for a group of refugees to watch St. Pauli play Sandhausen at the Millerntor. Fans in the *Gegengerade* displayed banners with messages of solidarity and support for the refugees. After the match around 5,000 people participated in a demonstration in solidarity with the migrants who had arrived from Lampedusa. During the rally, which started near the stadium, there were moments of tension with the police. In response to the presence of these African migrants, St. Pauli fans resumed the *Kein Mensch ist illegal* (No One is Illegal) campaign and carried out actions such as writing a manifesto, printing stickers and painting murals with the words: 'We are here to stay'.

PART V

St. Pauli: Passion without Borders

16

Global Expansion and the Fan Clubs in England, Scotland and Ireland

According to various estimates, FC St. Pauli currently has about 20 million fans and supporters worldwide, 11 million of whom are in Germany. An exorbitant amount considering the team's modest (if not negligible) sporting success, the fact that it usually is in the second division, and that it coexists alongside HSV – a team with a history of major wins that naturally receives more media coverage.

The reason is simple: FC St. Pauli is different. To sum up its singularity, fans use the slogan 'St. Pauli is the only option' ('*St. Pauli ist die einzige Möglichkeit*'). The fact that some of its members and supporters describe themselves as activists is also key to understanding the club's popularity around the globe. St. Pauli is a team that inspires affection: the eternal loser that everyone likes and many feel sorry for. The small team that has never won a major trophy but which has something special that attracts fans. The team with the skull and crossbones logo printed on black T-shirts that so many people wear without knowing that it is a German football team. Because, as it happens, St. Pauli is also an aesthetic associated with punk, nonconformist skater hip-hop, and even Black Bloc activism. St. Pauli is image, politics and football. It is all of these things and more. However, it has perhaps become a commercial fad due to the exploitation of the St. Pauli 'brand', or at least it may be heading in that direction. Be that as it may, in spite of everything St. Pauli is still different. A *rara avis*[1] in professional football. And this is why most of the supporters who were part of the group that changed the club's image still maintain that 'St. Pauli is not a fad, it's

---

1. [Translator's note]: Latin for rare bird.

the only option'. For many St. Pauli supporters, the club is unquestionably a different way of understanding life, society and sport.

However, many voices are now speaking up against the club's growing popularity. These are the voices that are calling for a return to the origins, to the essence of a humble local club. If we take a stroll around the Millerntor on a match day it is impossible to miss the tourists and supporters who come from all over Europe to see St. Pauli play. It would seem inconceivable to travel to Hamburg without visiting the stadium in the St. Pauli area. This is the dilemma facing the club: on the one side are those that believe it is possible to invest in the club's professionalisation and go up to the *Bundesliga* without St. Pauli losing its rebellious spirit; on the other, there are those who see this kind of investment as a step towards FC St. Pauli's greater commercialisation and thus loss of the values that have defined it since the 1980s.

In any case, it is clear that St. Pauli is not like other teams. 'We are a cool, sexy club. We're not like all of the other clubs in the world. We're not normal', says one of the club's executives in the documentary *Paulinen Platz*. And this connotation explains how a small club without sporting success has so many supporters and fan clubs around the world. According to various surveys, St. Pauli is the most popular club in Germany, the one that most fans of other teams identify or sympathise with, and the one with most female fans. Many supporters have got together and set up fan clubs, which have become central pillars of St. Pauli's social world. They currently number around 600 worldwide.

Some of these associations are based in the British Isles, where almost a dozen fan clubs follow the progress of FC St. Pauli: in Yorkshire, Glasgow, London, Manchester, Belfast, Derby, Southampton, Kent, Winchester, Brighton and Salford. All of them were founded in the last ten years, coinciding with the gradual commodification of the 'modern' game. The historical connection between modern football and the working class – the neighbourhoods or cities that often give the clubs their names – has been disrupted by several factors. These include the exponential increase in ticket prices and season passes (which has seriously affected English, Scottish and Irish clubs); the acquisition of clubs by tycoons and investment groups (which sometimes have links to dictatorships wanting to do business and at the same time whitewash their authoritarian regimes); the clubs' lack of involvement in local life; the gradual loss of identity that had traditionally shaped these clubs; the increasingly noticeable presence of tourists in stadiums; and the constant introduction of rules intended to silence the noisiest supporters in the stands. All of this led to the birth of St. Pauli fan clubs in Britain, as it did in other places such as Catalonia, Athens and Brittany. Members of these had begun feeling alienated from the sporting sphere they were emotionally and geographically linked to as this has gradually been emptied of content. They watched as club executives prioritised the financial exploitation of football over the interests of fans. They saw their clubs purchased by investors without roots in their cities, who only saw business opportunities and a symbol of status among Western capitalist elites. If we add the antifascist ideology and transformative activism that characterise the noisiest St. Pauli supporters, we have the ingredients that led these British fans to take notice of a 'loser' club from Hamburg's docks. Naturally, the fact that St. Pauli was the first and only team to officially declare itself against any form of fascism, racism and sexism didn't do any harm either.

Accordingly, groups of Scottish, Irish and English fans set up their various fan clubs, which always revolve around meeting in a pub to watch St. Pauli matches together. As a member of York-shire St. Pauli says, 'on a forum, we realised that there were several local fans of the German club. So we decided to meet at The Well, near Leeds station, where they show all the matches, and create a kind of fan club: 'disorganised since Friday the 13th'.[2] Something similar happened with groups of fans in London, Southampton and Glasgow, who initially came together without any particular aim other than the desire to support the Pirates. Nonetheless, as these supporters went about their business they also tried to raise

---

2. [Translator's note]: the name echoes the club motto 'non-established since 1910'.

awareness about the existence and feasibility of a different model of professional football clubs: one that is more cooperative and embedded in the life of the local neighbourhood and the city's associative fabric.

Naturally, one of the main activities of these groups is organising trips to Hamburg, which allow their members to meet and share experiences with other similar groups and with the club itself. Every trip to St. Pauli entails staying at the Backpackers Hostel, located on the edge of St. Pauli. The establishment is run by Volkerm, a veteran FC St. Pauli fan who was part of the first group of squatters and anarchists that started attending matches at the Millerntor in the 1980s. Time permitting, other unmissable highlights include watching the St. Pauli women's football and handball teams play, and having a few beers at the Jolly Roger pub, where the most ardent fans gather after every match. You can also have a *Mexikaner* (a famous St. Pauli vodka-based drink mixed with tomato juice, tabasco, pepper, salt and powdered chilli) at St. Pauli Eck, another legendary local bar located at 87 Simon-von-Utrecht Straße, on the corner of Hein-Hoyer straße. If the visit coincides with the annual festival in the Port of Hamburg (one of Europe's largest ports), it is the perfect trip.

Every year in May, Hamburg celebrates the *Hafengeburtstag*. This commemorates the charter issued by Emperor Frederick Barbarossa on 7 May 1189 to the people of Hamburg, granting freedom from shipping duties if they sailed from the River Elbe to the North Sea. The celebration, which reached its 830th anniversary in 2019, is attended by 1.5 million people and includes a parade of over 300 boats, a fish auction and a multitude of fair booths and stages hosting everything from concerts to cooking workshops.

As well as the regular match watching, spreading the word about St. Pauli and trips to the Millerntor, the St. Pauli fan clubs also have a political and social substratum. Activism by members of the different supporters' association has taken the form of organising awareness-raising campaigns around issues like the plight of refugees. The Yorkshire St. Pauli fan club, for example, is part of Football for All, a project that started out organising football matches with PAFRAS (Positive Action for Refugees and Asylum Seekers) – a charity based in West Yorkshire. The project allows refugees and exiles to play weekly football matches against members of the fan club itself. The Southampton St. Pauli fan club also channels its activism towards refugees and helping their integration into the community through football, by organising an event called Southampton Transformed. Meanwhile, St. Pauli London manages a food bank and is involved in collecting donations of non-perishable products.

One of the most socially active fan clubs (along with Yorkshire) is the Glasgow St. Pauli Supporters Club. This comes as no surprise considering that St. Pauli's sister club Celtic is Glaswegian. The city has a group of St. Pauli fans who engage in activism in the community. Glasgow St. Pauli organises activities such as film screenings, fundraising nights, Christmas dinners for the disadvantaged, concerts and football matches. Its members also accompany young refugees living in Hamburg to the Millerntor to watch St. Pauli matches. In fact, they estimate that they have raised over £10,000 for organisations that work with unprotected children, refugees, the homeless and victims of domestic violence (much of which has been raised through online donations).[3]

As mentioned earlier, these fan clubs (which have memberships ranging from around 30 members in London to 48 in Glasgow, and almost a hundred in Yorkshire) have largely emerged as an alternative to the current model of football. English, Scottish and Irish St. Pauli fans have been left without local football clubs they can identify with (aside from a few exceptions: Glasgow Celtic, United Glasgow, Clapton Community FC, Dulwich Hamlet FC and FC United of Manchester). Therefore, they are quick to declare that supporting the Hamburg team is not a fad. They explain this by appealing to the singularity of St. Pauli, which they say is illustrated by 30,000 antifascists still filling the stands of the Millerntor every fortnight. An undeniably unusual occurrence in today's football.

---

3.   www.sports.vice.com/en_ca/article/4xz4dg/meet-the-st-pauli-fan-clubs-springing-up-across-the-globe (accessed 11 April 2020).

17

The Unfinished Business
of Women's Football

St. Pauli's uniqueness is also demonstrated by the fact that it is the European football club with the most notable presence of women in its stadium. Nearly 30 per cent of spectators who attend matches at the Millerntor are women – a record-breaking figure in Europe. This can be explained by the club's commitment to supporting equality and fighting sexism (an attitude clearly shared and often encouraged by fans). The many actions organised over the years against certain decisions or campaigns that denigrated women have been crucial to achieving this proportion of female support. Examples include the opposition to *Maxim* magazine being advertised at the stadium in 2002, and the battles against leasing VIP boxes to Susis Show Bar and against the sports drink Kalte Muschi in 2010. These campaigns, organised by St. Pauli's 'Social Romantics', were high points in the feminist struggle within the traditionally male and non-inclusive world of football.

Despite the large number of women who attend FC St. Pauli matches, there is only one women-only fan club. Logically there is some tension between supporters who think it is important to have visible women-only spaces, and those who believe that women should merely be welcomed in the club and present in all of its spheres. One fan stated, 'Having women-only groups in the stadium would create ghettos and undermine the idea of the big FC St. Pauli family, which is all-embracing and respectful of any kind of difference.' The amateur status of the women's team and the lack of widespread support from the club's fans are issues that still need to be resolved. The club has a duty to encourage the women's teams' professionalisation, and to give it the standing it deserves. In such a massively male-oriented sport,[1] it is imperative to place more importance on the women's team. This is particularly so in a club whose priorities include upholding equality and supporting all kinds of social initiatives.

Through their activities, the *FC St. Pauli Fanclub Catalunya* got to learn of the existence of the St. Pauli women's football team. They were thrilled to find out that one of its players was Catalan, a discovery that filled them with pride. They quickly tried to contact her to request an interview so they could find out more about her experiences at the club. A Catalan playing with St. Pauli is not something that happens every day. The search finally bore fruit and they managed to talk to Guida Maymó Camps, an architect from St. Just Desvern who had gone to Hamburg to look for a job.

Maymó explained how one of the first things she did when she got to Hamburg was ask her acquaintances whether they knew of any women's football team. She played the sport and wanted to combine doing so with her professional work. Everybody she talked to immediately suggested St. Pauli, a club that Maymó had not heard of until then. Soon after trying out and joining the team she realised that it was not an ordinary club. From the start, the pre-requisites for joining the team surprised her: 'sporting and human education'. At the time, she was the only non-German in the FC St. Pauli women's first team.[2] She began as a centre back and then, after two new player signings, she played as a right-winger.

---

1. An example is the discriminatory language used in the footballing world. For instance, the term *Mannschaft* (team), which is also used to refer to women's teams, derives from the German word for man (*Mann*).
2. At the same time, a Basque player, Romina Garcia Hinsch, was playing in the women's second team at St. Pauli. She had joined the club in summer 2005, at the age of 21. She started playing in defence, but later played as a forward and having a free role. As well as going to training sessions and matches, she collaborated and became involved in various projects, such as the AntiRa Festival, an international women's football tournament that was held to celebrate the 20th anniversary of the St. Pauli women's section, and a project with a Kenyan club. After eleven seasons with the team, Garcia Hinsch says: 'What I've always loved about FC St. Pauli is the club's ideology, and being able to experience it by playing in the league. For me, playing with the St. Pauli women's team means making lifelong friends and

In Germany, women began playing football almost as soon as it arrived in the country. As in Britain, where Victorian-era puritanism deemed having women on football pitches as 'inappropriate and dangerous', German girls who played were also admonished.[3] Even doctors did their bit and warned that playing football could harm their fertility. Ignoring these irrational theories, in the 1920s German women began creating their own clubs. Three decades later, in 1955, the DFB banned women. According to the top brass of German football, women were 'too fragile, and unable to practice the sport without injuring themselves'. The association remained firm in its decision in the 1960s, and it was not until 30 October 1970 that the German Football Association officially allowed women to play. Nonetheless, there were still certain conditions: no studs on their boots, a smaller and lighter ball, and 70-minute matches.

Despite these conditions, the first German women's football league finally began in 1971. A year later, St. Pauli tried to organise a women's team, but unfortunately the attempt was doomed to failure. The club would have to wait until the 1980s for a group of young women to get together and form a team. These members of St. Pauli's first women's team were fans who regularly watched matches at the Millerntor and had links to the autonomous movement and the Hafenstraße. As Hagar Groeteke – one of the activists of that first core group and current coach of FC Lampedusa St. Pauli – explains, a group of people living in these squatted buildings had been playing in a mixed team, the FC Hafenstraße, which used a local school as its home ground. Then they

---

feeling comfortable, as if I were at home.' Interview with Romina Garcia Hinsch (31 October 2016).

3. The practice of women's football in Britain developed in the second half of the nineteenth century, almost parallel to the emergence of modern football. Despite some earlier sporadic, unsuccessful attempts, the first women's clubs were not created until the late 1890s. The country's first official women's competition was held in 1895. Among the pioneers were the women in the British Ladies' Football Club, which had Scottish feminist aristocrat and activist Florence Dixie as its president and Nettie Honeyball – a pseudonym for Mary Hutson – as its first captain. See J. Williams, *A Game for Rough Girls? A History of Women's Football in Britain* (London: Routledge, 2003) and T. Tate, *Girls with Balls: The Secret History of Women's Football* (London: John Blake Publishing, 2013).

decided to organise a women's team as a form of 'empowerment and emancipation', to show that women's involvement in football was not limited to simply attending male matches as spectators. Nonetheless, the idea did not make much of an impact on the club at the time. Management declared that there was no room for a women's team, citing the lack of appropriately equipped facilities (with separate dressing rooms and showers). Despite this lack of encouragement, the women persevered. To achieve their aim they requested official support from the Hamburger Fußball-Verband (the regional federation of the DFB, created on 1 February 1947, which covers Hamburg clubs). While doing so they targeted Hannelore Ratzeburg (current vice president of the women's section of the DFB, then head of the Women's Committee of the Hamburg Regional Football Federation). They also organised protest actions to put pressure on St. Pauli executives, such as breaking the lighting box at the winter training ground on several occasions. This was in protest at the club not providing them with a key to be able to turn on the electric lighting.

In addition to the help they received from various quarters, one of the male St. Pauli teams allowed them to use their training facilities, 'in recognition of the young women's right to play in the club and to address the discrimination and exclusion they were subject to'. Eventually FC St. Pauli's management agreed to the creation of a women's team. It was initially incorporated in the club's youth section and was finally set up as a self-managed section within St. Pauli in the 1990s. Resources were, of course, limited. This explains some oddities, such as the fact that the female players had to play in the shirts used by the men's teams in the previous season.[4]

That first team, which was described as 'responsible, feminist, supportive, and without prejudice', laid the foundation stone for St. Pauli women's football. Since then its key principle has been self-management. All of the women in the various teams are expected to feel part of the club and contribute something to it.

---

4. The shirts worn by the women's first team were often reused in subsequent seasons. After several attempts, the women's section of the club managed to get Kiez Curry – a Hamburg store specialising in sausages – to sponsor the team's kit.

The players in the first team train twice a week. At first they shared a dressing room with VfL Hammonia von 1922, another women's team from Hamburg. Later they got their own dressing room and a common room used by all St. Pauli women's teams, on the ground floor of the *Nordkurve* stand. The twice-weekly training sessions prepare the players for the matches they play each weekend. There is a spirit of comradeship among the players, which extends to the tradition of travelling together, which they have done to places such as the north coast of Germany and Finland, along with coaching staff. These journeys strengthen the bonds of friendship among the teammates.[5]

The women's section has gradually seen its status regularised within the club. It holds an annual general assembly and it has its own governing board, which is responsible for overseeing and coordinating the section's social interventions. Starting in 2005, one of these was to provide financial support (to cover bus travel) to the Old is Gold Slum Youth women's team in Amhara, a suburb of the Kenyan capital Nairobi.[6] However, the club's support was questioned when the African team's managers expelled two of its players for being lesbians.[7] This was not the only social initiative launched by the St. Pauli's women's section, which had previously supported a project in Nicaragua.

Even though St. Pauli is a unique club, it did not give its women's section as much recognition as other clubs. (Union Berlin, for example, organises a Women's Football Day every year). Also,

---

5. This is not the only non-competitive activity that the female players undertake. They also hold a yearly gathering including all of the other women football players at the club, in which, for example, they play a table football tournament or matches in which physically disabled kids are included. The women also organise Christmas dinners and trips to the theatre – a sponsor for the team.

6. James Waithaka founded the Old is Gold Slum Youth Ladies Football Team in 2003 after he quit the Mahare Youth Sports Association. That same year, the team debuted in the Nairobi Women's League, becoming runner up.

7. The controversy generated and FC St. Pauli's complaints led to the reinstatement of both players. Bizarrely, the African team thought the German club wanted all of the players to be lesbian. In any case, St. Pauli decided to abandon the project and support a similar initiative geographically closer to home. A Norwegian club took over from St. Pauli as sponsor of the Old is Gold Slum Youth team.

despite the anti-discrimination values espoused by *Sankt Pauli* supporters, this has not meant that the women's team enjoys a large following. This means that St. Pauli women's matches are often watched by a handful of family and friends. It was not until 2015–16 that a group was created to support the women's team, which took the name *Ey, die Hunde* (Hey, the Dogs). The team's sporting success led to an increase in followers, and at the end of the season the club decided to build a stand at the Feldarena – where the women's team play, and which is located next to the Millerntor. Naturally this boosted the team's performance. After winning the regular Hamburg league[8] (thanks to goals from players such as Nina Philipp, Londa Malika Sellami and Ann-Sophie Greifenberg),[9] the FC St. Pauli women faced TuRa Meldorf[10] and TuS Schwachhausen in the *Regionalliga* promotion playoffs. In the end, the team was promoted to the third tier of German women's football.

In recent years, FC St. Pauli has restructured its lower-level teams, which has allowed it to increase the number of women's teams. Now, aside from the first team, the *St. Pauli Frauen and Mädchenfußball* section now has a second team (2. Frauen) and teams in the under-21, under-17, under-15, under-13 and under-11 categories, as well as an under-30 team made up of more seasoned players. In all, around 80 girls and 90 women are part of the section.

The priorities of the women's section were hotly debated. In the end, the club decided to create a first team to prioritise sporting performance in the highest possible tier, and a second team in the spirit of 'grassroots sport' ('*Breitensport*'), open to any woman who

---

8.   The St. Pauli team won the championship with 60 points – six more than runner up Union Tornesch 1. FC. The statistics were excellent: 103 goals scored and only nine conceded, remaining unbeaten throughout the season, with no defeats and only three draws. A 1–9 win at Eibek 1. Fr.'s home ground in the last match rounded off a historic season for the St. Pauli women's team. To celebrate the league title its players took a ride on a barge to the breakwater at Hamburg port. A few days later, a party was held at the Fanräume to thank fans for their support during the championship.
9.   The three St. Pauli players were the top-three goal scorers in the championship. Philipp was first with 41 goals, while her teammates Sellami and Greinfenberg scored 19 and 14 goals respectively.
10.   In that match the St. Pauli team drew 1–1 and almost a thousand spectators attended the match.

wants to play football. The choice for the first team's targets created some misgivings, since, in principle, St. Pauli does not pursue sporting success. As former St. Pauli player Guida Maymó explains, 'In reality, the first team tries to win but without stressing, giving priority to building a strong team spirit. But the more radical wing of the women's section sometimes complains that the first team doesn't really understand what it means to be part of St. Pauli.'

As we have seen, there are a number of weak points that undermine the growth of women's football at St. Pauli, which the club will surely try and address in the years to come. To make the necessary changes, it will be necessary to encourage and promote support for the women's game among fans. Although efforts in this direction have already produced an increase in the number of fans attending the women's team's matches in recent seasons (as demonstrated by the creation of *Ey, die Hunde*), there is still a long way to go.

Women's football is not, however, the only specific sports section at FC St. Pauli. The club has more than a dozen different sections, ranging from American football to boxing, cycling, marathon, rugby (men's and women's), chess, table tennis, gymnastics, boules, triathlon, blind football and handball.[11] All of them are made up of amateur sportspeople but this has not prevented them from achieving success. The women's rugby team, for example, has won eight German titles, including five in the last decade.

St. Pauli is thus an eminently multi-sports club with many branches taking sport into the neighbourhood, shaped by different perspectives – from fans to players. That said, it is men's football that absorbs almost all of the club's financial resources, and a greater commitment to the other sections is required. Handball, for example, is an extremely popular sport in Germany; so much so that

---

11.   Each year, players from the first handball team – like other St. Pauli teams – go on a trip without their coaches to strengthen their fraternal bonds. In 2015 the team chose to go to Barcelona. Months before the trip they contacted the Catalan St. Pauli fan club to organise activities during their stay in the city. As well as going on cultural tours with a historical focus to learn about the reality of the Catalan capital beyond the usual tourist landmarks, the team played a handball match at the Nova Icaria pavilion against Handbol Poblenou, on 14 May 2015, and watched one of the FC Barcelona handball team's training sessions.

the 'Final Four' of the top European handball tournament is played in Cologne each year. The country has very strong teams, including THW Kiel, Felnsburg, Magdeburg and HSV Hamburg, which tend to contest these championship playoffs. As for the FC St. Pauli handball team, it plays its matches at the Budapesterstraße sports centre, next to the Millerntor. Although it is an amateur team, its matches attract about a hundred supporters every weekend. This indicates that there is interest in the sport. There is no doubt that a firm commitment to its non-professional sections would boost participation in and support for FC St. Pauli.

The cases of handball and women's football can be extrapolated to other sections of the club, which has, at the same time, implemented measures to promote sport among disadvantaged groups. A particularly noteworthy example is that St. Pauli organised the first official (DFB-recognised) five-a-side championship for the visually impaired, in which its own blind football section participated. Also of note is the work carried out by the FC St. Pauli marathon section, which is among the most politicised in the club. Although it was formed less than five years ago, it has over 800 practising members. In 2012, it launched the Run Against the Right marathon to denounce neo-Nazism. There have been several editions of this race, which is organised in collaboration with local antifascist organisations and groups.

However, FC St. Pauli does not just promote sport through its official sections. It also supports and promotes traditionally minor disciplines such as beach volleyball. Indeed, the duo Mischa Urbatzka and Markus Böckermann claimed top honours in the 2013 German championship while representing FC St. Pauli.

18

Music, Democracy and Solidarity in the District and Stadium

The first conclusion that can be drawn from St. Pauli's success as a cult club has to do with a phenomenon that cannot be understood by simply watching the team play or going to the stadium. Belonging to the Pirate club, even if only as a fan or supporter, is about more than this. It is a political stance and a commitment to a different approach to sport, to an idea of clubs as more than just professional organisations related to sporting activity. What makes St. Pauli attractive is what it represents, its distance from other professional clubs, its clear and direct response to any social problem. It is attractive because it is a different and approachable football club.

Any attempt to understand the phenomenon today must consider the club's relationship with the city and the neighbourhood in which it emerged and grew. And it must also take into account the rise of autonomist politics and related new forms of organisation and self-organisation from the 1980s onwards. In fact, the club's current structure is directly influenced by the empowerment people gained through activity in new movements such as squatting, environmentalism and autonomy and mutual support (both among workers and local residents). These movements took hold in an area decimated by high unemployment rates, with many families suffering social exclusion, and where access to housing was a major problem, all of which triggered a seemingly unstoppable process of gentrification. St. Pauli's anomaly in this sense can be seen in three crucial spheres: its links with culture and music, its relationship with the St. Pauli district, and its fierce defence of minorities. All of these are moulded by the particular political stances that FC St. Pauli has constantly maintained: from fighting racism and discrimination of any kind to defending refugees.

The connection between St. Pauli and music has always been strong. An example is the team running on to the Millerntor pitch to the strains of 'Hells Bells' by Australian hard rock band AC/DC. And that is not the only instance: whenever St. Pauli scores a goal at the Millerntor, Blur's 'Song 2' is triumphantly played on the stadium speakers. However, these are not the only bands close to the club's heart. In order to understand this interaction, we must once again look to the city and neighbourhood home of FC. St. Pauli. As previously mentioned, St. Pauli is Hamburg's port and red-light district. It is famous for Herbertstraße, the only street on which prostitution was allowed during the Nazi regime. It is also the heart of Hamburg's music scene. St. Pauli prides itself on hosting and promoting unknown bands, as it once did with the Beatles, who played at the Indra Club, the Top Ten and the Star-Club – near the Reeperbahn. When recalling this period, John Lennon said, 'I was born in Liverpool, but I grew up in Hamburg.'

The club's promotion of music and the arts in general, its uniqueness and its links to 1980s countercultural movements such as punk have led many bands to identify with FC St. Pauli over the last 30 years. One of the first artists to notice St. Pauli and be drawn to it was English punk poet and folk singer John Baine (better known by his stage name Attila the Stockbroker). After participating in the Festival of Political Songs in East Berlin in 1989[1] and visiting the Millerntor for the first time, Baine became a St. Pauli fan, returning to the stadium year after year. Indeed, he per-

---

1. The Festival of Political Songs was created in 1970. It was one of the biggest cultural events in the GDR. Artists who played over the years included Silvio Rodriguez, Mercedes Sosa, Oskorri and Milis Theodorakis [Translator's note]: these are Cuban, Argentinian, Basque and Greek folk musicians, respectively. The festival was organised by German Free Youth, which was founded in 1936 as the antifascist youth movement of the German Communist Party. Several editions of the festival were held until 1990, when it lost both its purpose and the cultural infrastructure as a result of German reunification.

formed in the *Fanladen*'s 10th anniversary celebrations during the 2000–1 season.

It should also be noted that the club allowed the Millerntor to be used as the venue for the Viva St. Pauli Festival in 1991, which featured the famous German punk bands Slime and Die Toten Hosen. The event's success helped further strengthen ties between the club, the music community and the counterculture scene. As a result of this connection, a number of well-known German bands and musicians, including Sascha Konietzko (frontman of KMFDM), Fettes Brot, Die Ärzte, Bela B., Kettcar, Tomte, Le Fly[2] and Slime became FC St. Pauli fans.

St. Pauli's influence on the musical community is not just limited to Germany. Many bands beyond the country's borders have an affinity with the Hamburg club. For instance, it is not unusual to see Asian Dub Foundation's group members or The Sisters of Mercy[3] singer Andrew Eldritch[4] wearing St. Pauli T-shirts. In recent years, a number of bands have been particularly significant for FC St. Pauli. These include Californian punk rock group Bad Religion,[5] whose members even played against the club's third team. On 31 August 2000, the band, along with some of the club's former players, played in a charity match that ended with a 4–2 victory to the home team.

Other bands that have expressed their fondness for St. Pauli include Norwegian band Turbonegro, which recorded a version of their song 'I Got Erection' including adapted lyrics in German

2. Le Fly is a Hamburg-based hip-hop band that played its song 'We Love St. Pauli' at the club's centenary celebrations in 2010, which coincided with the St. Pauli first-team's rise to the *Bundesliga*. The concert was recorded and the group made a video clip with images from that performance.
3. British post-punk band founded in 1980, which has released three studio albums and three compilation LPs.
4. In 2006, during the *Sisters Bite the Silver Bullet* album tour, Eldricht wore a T-shirt with the St. Pauli skull and crossbones flag.
5. Punk-rock band founded in Los Angeles in 1979 and still active today, making it one of the longest running bands in the punk scene. The band's lyrics usually have a strong social component, such as the song 'American Jesus' – a satire against the United States' role in the international community, and 'Kyoto now!' which criticises the countries including America that refused to sign the Kyoto Protocol.

dedicated to St. Pauli. Glasgow band The Wakes wrote the song 'The Pirates of the League', performed at the FC St. Pauli centenary festival, and then also played a match at the Millerntor. And the Italian group Talco's LP *Mazel Tov* (Destiny Records, 2008) included the song 'St. Pauli' – dedicated to the club – which struck a chord with the European youth scene.[6] Other groups that have paid tribute to the Pirates include the indie band Art Brut, with its track 'St. Pauli', and Canadian punk rock band The Pagans of Northumberland, who also recorded a song titled 'St. Pauli' – proclaiming the band's love for the club and its fans.

However, culture and music are not the only spheres in which St. Pauli has shown its uniqueness. From a club policy perspective, its statutory provisions are key: in terms of shaping internal democracy and decision making, and in relation to the local and wider geographical areas. St. Pauli's official stance against racism and any form of discrimination is laid down in its official statues, as is its organisational structure (in which fans have a major say in decisions affecting the club by means of the power of the general assembly) and the building of a community around the club and neighbourhood.

FC St. Pauli's associative structure is centred on its 30,000 members. The most fundamental and important element is the general assembly (*Mitgliederversammlung*), which is the club's legislative body and governed according to the principle of 'one person, one vote' (proxy and postal voting are not permitted). Meeting at least once a year, it is the platform that gives fans a say in the club's administration. Any FC St. Pauli member can participate in the general assembly but voting is restricted to those who are up to date with their quarterly membership payments. Aside from discussing specific or one-off issues, the assembly can vote on

---

6. During the Silent Town tour in 2016, which took them to Catalonia, the Italian group played at Sala Razzamatazz in Barcelona, along with Dr Calypso and Ebri Knight. During the concert, held on 20 February that year, several members of the Fanclub Catalunya went on stage with a St. Pauli flag while the musicians played a song dedicated to the club.

the club's annual accounts. As such, it has the power to reject these if members detect omissions or incorrect or unclear figures.

Together with the general assembly, the electoral committee (*Wahlausschuss*) and the supervisory board (*Aufsichtsrat*) also play a key role in the club. The electoral team was created in 2011 to monitor election processes and prevent fraud or undue pressure by fans to approve a particular decision or candidate. The supervisory board – renewed every five years – is responsible for guaranteeing that all FC St. Pauli organisations abide by club statutes as well as meet the objectives set out by the assembly. With five members chosen from among former players or people with experience in administering and managing the club, the board resolves any disputes between members and monitors the implementation of regulations during assemblies and in activities organised by the club.

FC St. Pauli's organisational structure draws on the principles laid out in the club's statutes, which govern all of the club's activities and are binding on all members. The official text, approved in 2001, contains 36 articles that explain the main purpose of the club: to encourage involvement in sport, both directly (through amateur participation in the club's sporting activities) and indirectly (by attending matches). It also incorporates other basic objectives, such as promoting the idea of sport as an element of social cohesion and incorporation in society, regardless of ethnicity, culture and religion; respecting and defending antifascist and antiracist values, and fighting any kind of discrimination; and ensuring that the name of the stadium is not sold to any commercial concern.

As well as the articles of association reflecting St. Pauli's essence and spirit, the 2009 assembly passed a series of additional general guidelines that were intended to guarantee the club's sporting authenticity, as well as its ethical values in the way the club is organised and acts. These guiding principles were based on democracy, respect, engagement with the neighbourhood and the club's responsibility to its members, community and society. They form the corpus that defines why FC St. Pauli is more than just a simple sporting entity, and the links between sport, politics and society. For instance, the principles allow St. Pauli to refuse to collaborate with any company that produces or supplies military equipment,[7] nor with firms of a Nazi or fascist orientation. In addition, they require that the team's sponsors and the businesses using the club's corporate image conform to St. Pauli's social and political sensibilities.

The basic principles guiding the actions of the club, approved by the club's members, are as follows:

- FC St. Pauli, encompassing the totality of its members, employees, supporters and volunteers, is part of the local community. As such it should be influenced directly and indirectly by political, cultural and social changes.
- FC St. Pauli acknowledges its responsibility to society and acts in the sporting sphere in the interests of its members, employees, supporters and volunteers.
- FC St. Pauli is a club rooted in a district. The neighbourhood provides the club with its identity and requires the club to be socially and politically responsible towards its people.
- FC St. Pauli is a symbol of sporting authenticity and conveys a way of life. This allows people to identify with the club regardless of its sporting success.
- Tolerance and respect in our interactions are important pillars of the St. Pauli philosophy.
- While FC St. Pauli now consists of many sections, it has always been defined by football.

---

7. The club's deal with the American firm Under Armour, which replaced Danish company Hummer as the official supplier of sports equipment from the 2016–17 season onwards, sparked controversy among St. Pauli fans. The first reason was the link between the Baltimore-based company and the United States army (specifically the Wounded Warrior Project, a charity that raises funds for war veterans who are injured or suffering mental illness or post-war trauma). Under Armour also sells clothes designed for hunting and carrying weapons. All of this led to a first protest by active FC St. Pauli fans, which used social media to call on people to boycott the company's products. To reduce the pressure on it, the company embarked on a series of investments in Hamburg social initiatives to clean up its image. St. Pauli also announced that part of the proceeds of the club's merchandising would go to social and humanitarian activities.

- In addition to the general statutory provisions, the stadium regulations and code of conduct for the *Fanladen* form the basis by which FC St. Pauli members, employees, supporters and volunteers conduct themselves.
- Individuals and groups should act responsibly. The St. Pauli code of conduct should be positively passed on to younger generations.
- FC St. Pauli believes it is essential to invest in sporting activities for young people, and to implement a coherent educational programme to instil in young people the values of solidarity and respect.
- There are no fans that are 'better' or 'worse' than others. Everyone can express their support for the club as they see fit, provided that their behaviour does not conflict with the above provisions.
- FC St. Pauli will continue to be a good host. The club grants its guests extensive rights and honours them accordingly.
- Sponsors and commercial partners of FC St. Pauli, as well as their products, should be consistent with the club's commitment to social and political responsibility.
- The essence of sport is that it is a team game, and this should be its main focus. The atmosphere at matches should be based on interaction between fans and players.
- The sale of goods and services at FC St. Pauli should fit the principles of social and economic sustainability, and care and respect for the environment.

Clearly, the club's regulations and general guidelines reflect the very close relationship between FC St. Pauli and its neighbourhood. Since the 1980s, the club has endeavoured to be in tune with the St. Pauli district, addressing problems that affect local residents and becoming part of the social fabric. As a result, activities by the club's fans have strengthened the community, and awareness has been raised over 'acting locally and thinking globally' – this approach characterises all the club's social, cultural and political actions. The

'St. Pauli culture' is alive and well, and is summed up by educator Niccolò Rondinelli according to five basic features: space (the district's physical characteristics have shaped the character of its residents: densely populated streets, squats that are still holding out, the Reeperbahn nightlife and the fight against gentrification); experience (in recent decades the feeling of belonging to the FC St. Pauli family has been reflected in strong participation in both sporting events and a variety of social and political initiatives); interest (supporters cheering on the team cannot be separated from left-wing libertarian ideals); imagination (a symbolic universe has developed from participation in the sporting activities and the political initiatives organised by the club and neighbourhood organisations); and process (in the sense of serious activism strengthened through the networks created).

In short, the special nature of FC St. Pauli results in strong ties between club and district, the involvement in social and political activism that being a St. Pauli fan entails and the club being run democratically. The club cannot be understood without its neighbourhood, just as the district cannot be understood without the club. Belonging to FC St. Pauli goes hand in hand with a love of its district, with the pride at being part of it, with fighting shoulder to shoulder with residents, collectively suffering the gentrification of its streets and creating networks of solidarity and mutual support.

An inherent part of the strong club–district relationship (and the third element that makes FC St. Pauli exceptional) has to do with the club's strong defence of minorities. Since the campaign in solidarity with the Turkish community in the 1980s, FC St. Pauli has carried out many similar initiatives in recent years. A notable example was the 2006 'Wild Cup' organised by the Federation of International Football Independents (FIFI), which was inspired by the World Social Forum – the left's counterweight to the annual World Economic Forum in Davos. The idea behind the World Social Forum was to develop a socially minded critique of the capitalist model and a space through which to build economic, political and social alternatives based on solidarity and community. In the same spirit, the FIFI Wild Cup sought to offer an alternative to the business-based model of football imposed by FIFA and the other international bodies governing the sport. St. Pauli organised the 2006 edition, coinciding in time and place with the FIFA World Cup in Germany. The FIFI Wild Cup was an alternative tournament involving the squads that FIFA and UEFA exclude from their competitions because their states do not have international recognition. The idea was to have a cup based on a radically contrasting idea of football and the values of solidarity and mutual respect between peoples.

The first and only edition of the Wild Cup, held from 29 May to 3 June 2006, included national teams from Gibraltar (not admitted as a member by UEFA and FIFA until 2013 and 2016 respectively), Greenland, the Turkish Republic of Northern Cyprus, Tibet, Zanzibar and the Republic of St. Pauli – made up of amateur players from the district. There were, however, organisational hurdles to overcome. According to FIFI Wild Cup coordinator Jorg Pommeranz, both FIFA and the Chinese embassy in Germany opposed the tournament. Chinese diplomats even demanded the withdrawal of the invitation to the Tibetan team.[8]

The FIFI Cup began with the cry of 'This is a Sepp Blatter-free zone!' (in reference to the FIFA president who was dogged by allegations of corruption). Two groups of three teams were formed, playing a total of ten matches. Tibet and Greenland were eliminated first, after both lost twice in the first stage. In the semi-finals, Northern Cyprus played Gibraltar (winning 2–0) and Zanzibar played the Republic of St. Pauli (with the African team winning 2–1). Northern Cyprus ended up winning the tournament after beating Zanzibar 4–1 in a penalty shootout (after the match ended in a 0–0 draw). The Republic of St. Pauli lost the match for third or fourth place after Gibraltar beat them 2–1 at the Millerntor. The 2006 FIFI World Cup was a success from the organisers' point of view and initially there was a desire for continuity. But due to

---

8. The Tibetan team was made up of exiles, most of whom lived in India. See: www.spherasports.com/sankt-pauli-y-la-fifi-wild-cup-68587 (accessed 7 July 2016).

external pressures and its modest international impact, there has so far been only one edition of this alternative to the world championship organised by the global footballing bodies.

By holding this event, FC St. Pauli expressed its stance of defending minorities and their rights. The precedent is in keeping with St. Pauli's response to the successive waves of refugees arriving in Hamburg since 2012. In Part IV we saw how the club reacted to the human tragedy of 35,000 refugees seeking asylum in the city after fleeing the Syrian war, and the club's active participation in the local meetings of the Refugees Welcome campaign.

The rise in the number of refugees is probably one of the clearest consequences of the internationalisation of capitalism. The economic and geopolitical interests of certain Western states in Middle Eastern and North African countries laid the groundwork for dictatorships that devastated local societies following the decolonisation process (in the aftermath of the Second World War). They also paved the way for the emergence of terrorist groups. The combination of these factors became the foundation for what Zygmunt Bauman described as the only thriving industry in so-called developing countries: mass production of refugees.[9] Wars and armed conflicts bring about the displacement of hundreds of thousands of people who, from the outset, lack adequate support from any state authority. This entails the loss of any identity beyond that of refugee, and disenfranchisement in the land they arrive in seeking refuge (where they remain on an inexorably temporal basis). Faced with this situation, Western governments with the power and opportunity to act respond by building walls and fences, and by deploying guards. As a result, effectively refugees do not move to a different place but lose their place in the world. While it is impossible for them to return to their homeland, the governments of the recipient countries try to prevent them from settling. Fortunately, the solidarity of the people who live in these countries is sometimes diametrically opposed to the attitude of their governments.

---

9. Z. Bauman, *Tiempos líquidos: Vivir en una época de incertidumbre* (Barcelona: Tusquets, 2007), p. 52.

To a great extent, fear of the other, of the poor, and of newcomers is entrenched in our societies, fed by a sense of helplessness and insecurity. But faced with such a big and serious problem solidarity and fraternity can overcome fear of the other and newcomer and guide people's actions.

This was the case with the refugees who began arriving in Hamburg from the Italian island of Lampedusa in 2012. Traditionally, Germany has been a country that has taken in large refugee communities. The constitutional guarantees of due process for asylum seekers are probably the most robust in Europe, along with those in Nordic countries. In Germany the right to political asylum is real. It is embodied in the obligation of public authorities to provide food, shelter and health services to asylum seekers, and in active policies regarding employment, schooling and a basic income once asylum status has been granted. Among other things, this has led to the creation of significant communities of minorities that have been decimated and persecuted, such as the Kurds and Yazidis.[10]

From 2012 onwards, waves of refugees began arriving in Hamburg from different African countries through Libya, where they endured the consequences of the war that ended with the fall of the Gaddafi regime. The escalating violence that the country suffered (and still suffers) led them to flee to Europe, crossing the Mediterranean to the island of Lampedusa, located off the coast of Tunisia. There they joined 7,000 other refugees grouped together

---

10. Yazidis are a pre-Islamic Kurdish religious minority from the Middle East, who are influenced by Zoroastrianism. The central figure of Yazidism is Melek Taus, a peacock angel that the Islamic State and some Muslims identify as the devil in the Islamic faith. Based in the Kurdish autonomous region of Iraq, in the Sinjar Mountains near Mosul (northern Iraq), Yazidis have regrettably been in the news as a result of the attempted genocide by Islamic State troops during the offensive in the region in the summer of 2014. After razing towns and sexually enslaving Yazidi women and girls, the Kurdistan Workers' Party and People's Protection Units/ Women's Protection Units managed to open a humanitarian corridor allowing them to reach Turkey. Most Yazidis are now living in refugee camps run by the Turkish government, except for one run by Kurdish forces on the outskirts of Diyarbakir. See D. Forniès, 'Deu claus sobre la irrupció de l'Estat Islàmic i els kurds de l'Iraq i Síria', Crític, 21 August 2014.

in a camp where they received assistance through the Emergency North African programme. Then, in winter 2012, the Italian government recognised their refugee status and gave them 500 euros each to leave Italy and travel to another country in the European Union. This is how some of them ended up in Hamburg, where they were eligible for the city's winter emergency programme. However, in April 2013, once the social benefits had run out, many of these refugees found themselves on the streets. Then they joined camps in public parks to pressurise the German authorities not to send them back to Italy. To make themselves heard, they formed the group 'Lampedusa in Hamburg'. From the outset, the group received support from St. Pauli fans as well as public figures like the filmmaker Rasmus Gerlach (director of the documentary *Lampedusa auf St. Pauli*) and Lutheran pastor Sieghard Wilm, from St. Pauli church, who housed 20 of these refugees in his parish. Their main demand was for the German government to recognise the people concerned as having a right to political asylum. And this is what they expressed during a rally that ended in front of the City Hall building, in which they carried a banner with the words, 'We did not survive the NATO war in Libya to die on the streets of Hamburg.'

FC St. Pauli and its fans began to support the group and participate in their activities. For example, on 25 October 2013, when St. Pauli played Sandhausen at the Millerntor, the Jolly Roger pub bought several tickets so that some of the refugees could watch the match from the Gegengerade. At the stadium many banners were displayed in support of their plight. After the match there was a demonstration in solidarity with the Lampedusa migrants, which started near the stadium and was attended by almost 5,000 people. In view of the presence of these African migrants, St. Pauli fans resumed the No One Is Illegal (*Kein Mensch ist illegal*) campaign. The club's supporters also took part in a number of charity events, such as writing a manifesto in support of the refugees, producing stickers and painting murals including the words 'We are here to stay'.

Because FC St. Pauli is a football club that focuses on sociali-
sation through sport, probably the action most strongly linked
to the club was the creation of a football team made up of 30 of
these migrants. The team, formed by players from countries such
as Ghana, Nigeria and Togo, was called FC Lampedusa Hamburg.
Coached by three former players from the St. Pauli's women's team –
Hagar, Barbara and Nico – FC Lampedusa Hamburg began playing
friendly matches and competitions against teams made up of fans.
It also played against a team of Glasgow Celtic fans, and even the
FC St. Pauli first team. For the time being, FC Lampedusa Hamburg
cannot compete in the German league, and its activity is limited
to playing friendlies. Its members participate in all of the political
events organised by the Lampedusa in Hamburg movement, and in
initiatives by groups of refugees in Berlin, Potsdam and other parts
of Germany.

As FC Lampedusa Hamburg were unable to access munici-
pal training facilities, its coaches contacted FC St. Pauli to find a
solution, and in July 2016 the team was incorporated into the club's
structure under the name FC Lampedusa St. Pauli. As such, the
team made up of refugees could train one hour a week at the Pirate
club's training facilities.

FC St. Pauli also continues its ongoing campaign to raise awareness about the plight of refugees. Actions range from producing
'FC Lampedusa Supporter' T-shirts and stickers to denouncing
the refugees' situation in the media. The FC Lampedusa St. Pauli
experience, which has allowed players to get to know others and be
accepted by the community, is another example of the principles
that guide FC St. Pauli as an integral part of its surroundings. It
is also an example of the political, social, cultural and educational
side of football when it is understood as a potentially transformative human activity.

The stance taken by the club in recent decades regarding the
defence of minorities has also been adopted by some of its players.
As we saw in an earlier chapter, goalkeeper Volker Ippig took time
out to support the Sandinista Revolution in Nicaragua, and also

became involved in the squatters' movement. Another notable example is Deniz Naki, the Kurdish-German player who signed a three-year contract with St. Pauli in 2009. Naki is especially remembered in conjunction with the away match against Hansa Rostock on 2 November 2009. That day, after scoring one of the two goals that earned St. Pauli the victory that secured his team's promotion that season, Naki celebrated by making a cut-throat gesture in front of Hansa fans – who are known for their right-wing tendencies – and planting a Jolly Roger flag on the pitch. After leaving St. Pauli, Naki signed for FC Paderborn 07. In 2013 he went to Ankara, Turkey, to play for Gençlerbirliği Spor Kulübü. However, he left the club after a few months following a racially motivated attack for his explicit support of the Kurds' fight against Islamic State. Describing the incident, he said, 'It happened on Sunday. I was going out for a bite to eat when three men attacked me on the street. They threatened me and said it was the first warning, that the club doesn't need a player like me, and that I'll have to leave.'

After leaving Gençlerbirliği, Naki signed with Amed SK, a club based in the city of Amed, the Turkish name for Diyarbakir, the historical capital of Kurdistan located on the banks of the Tigris River in south-eastern Turkey. Amed SK has become a touchstone in the Kurdish people's national liberation struggle.[11] Similarly, Naki is something of a symbol for the Kurdish nationalist movement against the Turkish regime under President Erdoğan. This became clear when the Turkish Football Association decided to ban Naki for twelve matches for engaging in 'ideological propaganda', in 2015, at the height of an offensive by the Turkish government and army against the Kurds in Bakur.[12] After the match between Amed SK and Bursaspor, Naki dedicated the team's win to the Kurdish people in a Facebook post in which he wrote:

Today was an important victory for us. We have come through a dirty game with our heads held high and a clear conscience. In

11. In 2014 the team changed its name from Diyarbakir Belediye Spor to Amedspor – in Kurdish – in order to assert its national and linguistic identity.
12. The name given to the part of Kurdistan within Turkish borders.

such tough times, we are honoured to bring a glimmer of hope to our people. We have not surrender[ed] and we never will. Tonight we went on the pitch thinking about freedom because we have planted hopeful seeds for this. We thank all the politicians, artists, thinkers, and our people. We dedicate this win as a gift to all those who have suffered or died in 50 years of oppression in our land. *Her biji azadi* (long live freedom).

The Turkish government's attack on Naki did not end with this suspension. In October 2016, as part of the Turkish government's crackdown in response to the failed coup on 15 July that year, the state prosecutor charged Naki with spreading terrorist propaganda. His alleged crime, punishable with up to five years in prison, involved posting images on social media of the Turkish attacks on the Kurdish people, and calling for solidarity with Cizre and Dersim (in Bakur). The accusations against him triggered a wave of solidarity across Europe, particularly in St. Pauli. During a friendly match against Werder Bremen, most St. Pauli players went on to the pitch wearing jerseys with the name Naki and the number 23, which the Kurdish player wore during his time with the Pirate team. Finally, after a hearing in November 2016, Naki was acquitted of all charges.

As we have seen, belonging to and following FC St. Pauli goes beyond sport. Being St. Paulian extends into activism, fighting for the neighbourhood and minorities, and supporting social, political and economic alternatives. Yet since the 1980s, St. Pauli supporters also have been dealing and coexisting with a complex dualism. FC St. Pauli is a football club, part of a competitive sporting entity, and that obviously needs some success on the field in order to guarantee its survival. In this regard, St. Pauli's fans (like those of any club) are not homogenous, and there are conflicting opinions. As already mentioned, in the 1980s some fans were against the aforementioned politicisation of the club, preferring to focus on the sporting side. Others, however, considered that its social and political commitment was an integral part of the club. Without it, St.

Pauli would be just another football club. As one fan put it: 'I'm not interested in the club playing in the *Bundesliga*, I prefer to maintain the political and cultural principles we have managed to bring in, against commercialisation and gentrification.' Fortunately, despite the tensions that sometimes arise, it appears that this option prevails in the conscience and spirit of the club and its fans: the option against allowing advertising on the stadium's giant screens, against selling T-shirts with player's names that promote individualism and against changing the name of the Millerntor to that of a sponsor. The option of supporting a different, alternative model engaged with the local district. A model with which residents can identify, which sees itself as a club at the service of the people, which defends political and social commitment and believes that sport, as a human activity, is inseparable from politics. A model that advocates taking action to change the system (and football) to one that is fairer and more supportive.

19

St. Pauli is the Only Option

In our exploration of the history of FC St. Pauli, we have shown its bourgeois origins and its beginnings as a club linked to local elites with an interest in sport. In other words, it was a club without a social or alternative background. Its current identity did not emerge until the mid-1980s, when the arrival of social movement activists triggered the changes that turned St. Pauli into a cult phenomenon.

Between these two periods, St. Pauli survived two world wars – which precipitated the disbanding and demise of numerous teams – and a decade of Nazism. Despite the links (of little consequence, as we have seen) between some of its executives and the Third Reich and NSDAP apparatuses, FC St. Pauli made it through the disasters of National Socialism and the bombing raids on Hamburg. Ironically, the postwar period of hardship and scarcity was when the club was most successful in sporting terms thanks to the dream team known as the Magical Eleven. The creation of the *Bundesliga* in the 1960s marked the beginning of a journey through the wilderness for the Hamburg team, which meandered through the lower divisions of German football. This changed in the 1970s when a handful of dedicated players took FC St. Pauli to the first division for the first time in its history. Unfortunately, that milestone coincided with the golden age of HSV, St. Pauli's greatest rival.

Everything changed in the 1980s thanks to a group of young people from the autonomous, punk and squatting movements who began turning St. Pauli into the cult club it is today. Since then, the club has rebuilt its identity around a totally different set of parameters. Aside from being a symbol for millions of football fans, FC St. Pauli became an attractive brand. A quick glance at the official FC St. Pauli store at the Millerntor suffices to show that the club has become a consumer good. Fans and tourists queue up to pay for clothing, T-shirts, tracksuits and any other merchandising that they cannot wait to get their hands on. 'St. Pauli is a powerful brand, even though many people prefer not to see it that way', says a club employee in the documentary *FC St. Pauli: Between Myth and Reality*. For years, however, the club earned very little from the sale of merchandising because of a contract drawn up by executives when it was in a critical financial situation. It was an agreement negotiated under pressure, as financial imperatives took precedence over contractual considerations. Predictably the club's marketing strategy has been subject to criticism. Some fans that are against the undermining of the club's values do not take kindly to the skull and crossbones becoming an object of mass consumption, or being a fad. This is the view of some older fans, annoyed by the increasingly large numbers and constant presence of foreign fans who treat the Millerntor as yet another tourist attraction.

All these changes have taken place alongside the unstoppable gentrification of the St. Pauli district. Although the Social Democrats have ruled Hamburg since 2011, the local government continues to implement urban planning policies that encourage speculation and reclassification of land. These practices have led to an increase in rents and house prices, which in turn negatively affects students and migrants.[1] Both the autonomous movements and parties such as Die Linke have been highly critical of the actions of the local authorities. While the SPD refused to recognise the existence of problems with the right to housing in the city, various groups and organisations drew attention to the seriousness of the situation. Ignoring their demands, the municipal authorities continued to approve the construction of new buildings, even though the city has 2,000 empty apartments and a million square metres of unused floor space. Naturally, this has encouraged widespread squatting but – unlike what occurred in the past – this it is being cut short by a rapid police response and fast-track evictions.

---

1. In the 1980s, low-income public housing stock consisted of 400,000 dwellings. Two decades later, it had dropped to a quarter, of which 6,000 are sold annually to SAGA and private buyers at market prizes.

As a result of the changes that have turned an area that once drew criminals, prostitutes, alcoholics and sailors into a 'cool' part of Hamburg peopled by students and liberal professionals, St. Pauli has lost its working-class character. These changes can also be seen in the Millerntor stands. In this sense, FC St. Pauli reflects the gentrification of the district. Once again, football is a powerful social metaphor.

Meanwhile, FC St. Pauli executives continue to look for ways to increase the club's income without betraying its intrinsic values. This has been (and still is) one of the of the club's greatest challenges: the constant battle to strike a balance between the 'legend' and the dictates of modern (commercial) football. At St. Pauli, football is not just a form of entertainment, it is a way of life. Of course, as one fan says, the 'St. Pauli legend' is known outside of Germany, 'but in St. Pauli, it is a reality'. It is the result of an accumulation of circumstances that converged at a certain moment in time and, in the late 1980s, began flowering. Origins like this would probably be impossible to replicate today: squatting, relegations to lower divisions, demonstrations, repression and memorable goals coming together to create a unique, authentic and genuine story. A story that has made the club like no other, and helped forge the St. Pauli legend.

Despite having once been a conservative bourgeois club that had never stood up for anything, its imaginary changed radically in the 1980s. It was then that its antagonistic identity took shape and breathed new life into a team that lacked both a soul and fan base. Those years, which are often idealised, laid the foundations for the club's resurgence. In the eyes of many fans, this hard-won uniqueness was threatened when the club, with Corny Littmann at the helm, prioritised sporting success and income from sponsors over its community dimension. These fans believed that the explosion in support resulting from FC St. Pauli's worldwide popularity as an alternative club ultimately distorted its socio-political essence. 'Wearing a T-shirt with the skull and crossbones fifteen years ago meant identifying with a particular political faction. Now it seems

more like a fad for tourists', said a disgruntled fan in favour of pre-
serving the club's extra-sporting spirit. No doubt he would want
to prevent – if it's not already too late – St. Pauli's Jolly Roger from
ending up like the face of Che Guevara or Marilyn Monroe, or the
Ramones logo, reproduced on thousands of items and co-opted as
a simple fashion or consumer object.

According to various sources, the 'romantic' faction that wants
to preserve the club's rebellious history accounts for about 20 per
cent of its supporters. The other 80 per cent are fans who want to
see their team win on the pitch and are less concerned about its
extra-sporting values: those who want FC St. Pauli to play in the
Bundesliga because that results in greater advertising revenue, and
thus the chance of securing more expensive signings – an attitude
that is by no means unusual given the way football has changed
around the world. As one St. Pauli fan said:

> FC St. Pauli is certainly better known now, but most of its sup-
> porters are more bourgeois than those of the 1980s, when local
> blue-collar workers, artists, punks, and activists were in the
> stands. This is also due to gentrification and the way the St. Pauli
> district has changed [...] The 'business' seats in the stadium, the
> stands full of young yuppies, are signs of cultural change. The
> stadium itself has changed a lot, I honestly preferred the old one
> because it was more simple and human.

Fortunately for this minority of nostalgic fans, they are the most
active faction of St. Pauli supporters, and at the same time the most
actively involved and connected with the club's professional structure. They are responsible for empowering supporters and forging
ties with the community, elements that have guaranteed partici-
patory democracy in the decision-making process. This strong
presence can have a mirage-like effect, however, making it seem
larger than it is. In fact, its impact on the club's leadership is less
than it appears, even though there is more synergy with the current
president than there has been with predecessors. All the same,

these St. Pauli fans have shown that it is possible to self-organise to try to influence the club and regain a share of control. This is the only way to withstand attempts at commercialisation and to establish an alternative management model that takes fans into account. It is the one way to give football back to the people.

The tendency of some fans to move away from defending the identity forged in the 1980s has been mirrored on pitch. Gone are the times when first-team players interacted with the community and actively participated in the political and social initiatives of fans, residents' associations and squatter movements. Ippig, Stanislawski, Gronau – St. Pauli players who mixed with fans to share their enthusiasm and anxieties, smiles and tears, victories and defeats (well, mainly defeats). All of this is lost, and it will never fully return. In this sense, St. Pauli is a club like any other, with players who are increasingly disconnected from their environment, from the everyday life of their fans. They are what is misnamed 'good professionals': young players who only live for football. There is still a spark of hope because, despite the growing gulf with fans, some St. Pauli players have also become involved in social causes and humanitarian actions. In any case, whether they win or lose the Millerntor is always full. The scoreboard does not change anything; support from St. Pauli's fans is unconditional. Whether the team plays in the first, second or third division, St. Pauli is much more than a result. It is more than a match or a tournament. It is a love affair that goes beyond success.

Obviously, St. Pauli fans are not a uniform mass, but mixed. Indeed, there is no shortage of critical voices. FC St. Pauli's president since 2014, Oke Göttlich, said that it was necessary to satisfy everyone, that is, the two main groups of fans: the fundamentalists and the pragmatics. Coming from the working-class terraces, he has no doubts about priorities: 'What matters is doing things because they feel real and, at the end of the day, being able to look people in the eye and say, 'Dear fans, this club means something. It is just unfortunate that we have to be professionals.'

The most cherished wish of St. Pauli's top chief is to maintain the social aspect of the club, to avoid undermining its identity and the social and ethical values it is associated with. 'We will always stand against racism and homophobia. We will always look out for the weak and poor because it is important to us. It's in our blood […] but we want to see the same passion and effort on the football field', Göttlich said in an interview.

And this is where they find themselves. Trying to reconcile, if it is possible, a strongly alternative identity and having a greater sporting impact. The club itself can grow without sacrificing its uniqueness. This is the underlying issue that St. Pauli fans are discussing in the midst of the commercialisation process that has consumed football. A tug-of-war between those who want to enjoy the football played by their team at any cost, and those who fear this means abandoning the club's inherent values. 'I would come to the stadium even if we played in the Third Division', says a fan who would like the club to place more importance on defending the identity it has forged since the 1980s. Some even see the advantages of perpetuating St. Pauli as a 'loser' club. As one supporter says, 'There would be less tourists at the stadium.² It would obviously be better for us.' Their philosophy goes beyond victory and results. These fans would rather the club remain true to the alternative identity of the past. More accustomed to defeats than to victories, these supporters downplay the fact that St. Pauli is already undoubtedly a losing team. Their experience of football does not depend on success or titles. 'If St. Pauli wins, we go to the bar, drink beer, and celebrate. If we lose, we go to the bar, drink beer, and forget about it.' This sums up their attitude.

---

2. This St. Pauli fan was referring to the crowds who visit the Millerntor attracted by 'the St. Pauli legend'. These fans are disparagingly referred to as the 'tifo tourists' or 'stadium tourists'. As a member of Skinheads St. Pauli says, 'There are a lot of people in Germany who own at least one item of St. Pauli merchandise. We don't know whether they are really fans of the club, or they came to Hamburg on holidays.' To avoid being associated with these football 'tourists', in April 2016 members of the *Fanclub Catalunya* made shirts with their logo printed on the front, and on the back the words '*Wir sind keine Touristen. Wir sind der Fanclub Catalunya*' ('We're not tourists. We're *Fanclub Catalunya*').

In the midst of this heated, critical debate, the club's management is trying to keep everyone happy, seeking bright ideas to fill budgetary shortfalls without turning to companies or interests that would corrupt their essence. This is a struggle that makes St. Pauli unique: a *rara avis* in the world of football today. As we have seen, since the 1990s football has gone through a process of transformation, prioritising business aspects over the sport and its supporters. Without a doubt, against this backdrop St. Pauli is an exception in professional football, not only in Germany but worldwide. Perhaps the club is an aberration? Be that as it may, the Pirate club is atypical because of its idiosyncrasy. This probably explains why it has eleven million fans and almost 300 fan clubs around the world. These are crazy figures for a club without any aura of success and which has often played in the lower divisions of German football. In this regard, it is also symptomatic that despite being born as a male-only club, it is currently the German team with the highest percentage of female fans.

Apart from attracting this worldwide legion of disenfranchised fans that are fed up with the consumerist turn that has football in its grip, the club's singularity has also sparked antagonism from rival fans. Right-wing football fans have directed their hate at St. Pauli for obvious reasons.[3] Ideological hostility aside, St. Pauli also has other detractors, critics who see the club's popularity as a (passing?) fad, or who denounce the contradictions of the club's values in the context of professional football. Today, Pirates' fans have the power to veto team sponsors thanks to the club's management model – a bonus that sets St. Pauli apart from other teams, and that its fans hope to maintain.

St. Pauli is, in short, proof that another way of understanding the world and football is possible. It is pure romanticism. It is the

---

3. In addition to the aforementioned attacks that St. Pauli fans often suffer at the hands of far-right radicals when they travel to other stadiums, there are also anti-Pauli scarves and stickers made by rival *ultras*. So slogans like *'Scheiß St. Pauli'* ('Fuck St. Pauli'), *'Anti St. Pauli'*, *'FCK STP'*, *'Anti St. Pauli Scheiß Zecken'*, *'Vorsicht Zecken'* ('Beware parasites') and *'Kein Ort für Pauli fans'* ('No place for St. Pauli fans') can often be seen in the parts of Hamburg controlled by HSV *ultras* and in stadiums elsewhere.

closest thing to neighbourhood football, to the popular football that our great-grandparents watched from the stands a hundred years ago. Maybe it is not quite the same, but it is the closest thing to it. What is certain is that once you know its history, past and present, it is difficult not to love St. Pauli.

Epilogue
Against Modern Football

The birth of many football fan groups or crews, and even the very emergence of St. Pauli as a cult club, cannot be understood without reference to the motto 'Against Modern Football' and its popularity in European football stadiums. Sport, and by extension football, has become a vital part of the lives of individuals and societies. Since the Roman poet Juvenal wrote the phrase '*mens sana in corpore sano*' ('a healthy mind in a healthy body') in his first-century satires, sport has been an integral element of society and culture. It is a way of interacting and cooperating that creates and strengthens community ties between the people who practise and follow it. As a sport and as a symbol, football has been part of the evolution of culture and societies, particularly in the last hundred years. Accordingly it has suffered from the effects of capitalism – from its industrial and 'productivist' beginnings to its financialised version narrated as post-industrialism. This has led to a gradual distortion of soccer's essence, something that has intensified in the last four decades.

Any attempt to define what we call 'the modern idea of football' inevitably leads us to the irrational process of capitalist accumulation. The need for the productivist model to find a destination for the surplus produce created, to preserve wealth and profits, was the first argument behind creating a new, parallel, complementary status for workers: that of *consumers*. This new category did not just make it possible to maintain mass-production levels. It also became a crucial – as well as alienating – element in constructing collective identities that could replace the traditional ones of class and community. In this sense, the creation of the concept of 'modern football' is embedded in the historical process of global capitalist expansion, which has been imposed on the world of sports as on other areas of social life.

Within the framework of this alienating logic of material appropriation, we are presented with an 'absolute'-type definition of football – the game and its supporters. A kind of all-encompassing idea that, as Herbert Marcuse theorised, takes us into a self-contained world lacking any ideal beyond itself that would make it possible to step away and criticise it. In other words, we have a single, unambiguous concept of football as a competitive leisure activity, a show for the masses detached from any political universe. In this framework, the term 'modern football' does not refer to the aesthetic elements of the game, to new tactics or the introduction of innovative ways of playing. Rather, it refers to an intrinsic ideological intention hidden behind the veil of spectacle and spread by the mass media. It is not argument between *catenaccio*[1] or 'total football'.[2] It is the marketisation of a human activity that was based on mutual support, and had helped to shape class-consciousness. It is also a distortion of popular culture, commercialised and reduced to a means to do business. And lastly, it is the ideological use of sport, concealed behind the idea that 'sports and politics must be kept separate'. This is promoted by nationalistic governments and pro-system parties that, in fact, make political use of football when their squads play international matches. 'Modern football' thus imposes absolute acceptance of a concept of sport embedded within neoliberal thought and characterised by all of capitalist globalisation's characteristics. In short, the term is inescapably linked to the Marxist concept of *alienation*, applied to football as a mass phenomenon.

In line with Argentinean journalist Dante Panzeri and his idea of an industrial revolution in football (similar to what we call modern

---

1.   [Translator's note]: a footballing tactic using a moving 'chain' of players for defending.
2.   [Translator's note]: a system in which outfield players change positions and that employs versatility and creativity.

football), we find it has the following most relevant features: the huge amount of money at stake, the dehumanisation of the players along with the sport, the replacement of improvisation with productive obedience, the rise of the selfish player and the gradual extinction of altruistic players, the shift from natural to advertising role models and the dehumanisation of football itself – given that players are viewed as marketable assets from their youth.[3] These characteristics are simply the effects of the capitalist system on any social activity. The development of industrial capitalism, which has paved the way for the emergence and expansion of financial capitalism, requires (to survive and as a prerequisite for being able to operate) the generalisation of a specific scheme of thought that extends to all areas of life. This system, violently imposed by political and economic elites and burned into the collective imaginary through an expanded mass media, rests on the basic pillars generated by what has been termed 'one-dimensional thought'. In other words, exacerbated individualism, a fictitious need and desire for irrational consumption of perishable goods to achieve immediate satisfaction, the gradual material and ideological impoverishment of the population, the disintegration of the working classes through heterogeneity and fragmentation, and the belief that it is impossible to create plausible social and economic alternatives (or that capitalism is the only system that works).

Herein lies what we could call the alienation in or alienating component of football today (the *alma mater* of modern football, in its individual or personal sense), which is defined by and framed within a series of identity-related parameters. There is the central discourse of football being cross-class (the idea that among the supporters of a particular club, everybody follows the same team, disregarding differences in political standpoints or social backgrounds); the defence of football as being exogenous to politics ('football is not political' is a claim repeated by precisely those who use sport ideologically); and the use of football, in the words of the

---

3.   D. Panzeri, *Fútbol: Dinámica de lo impensado* (Madrid: Capitán Swing, 2012), p. 60.

German philosopher Jürgen Habermas, as a refeudalisation of the public sphere, as a scene merely to distract.

This perspective gave rise to the traditional opposition to football by some left-wing intellectual groups who saw how sport was used by dictatorial and totalitarian regimes. This certainly was the case at the 1934 FIFA World Cup held in Italy when the Mussolini's National Fascist Party was in power.[4] And also at the Berlin Olympic Games organised by the Third Reich in 1936.[5] These Games were, incidentally, boycotted by the Spanish Republic, whose 'Popular Front' government decided not to participate in protest against the racial and religious discrimination imposed by the Nazis. At the same time, a People's Olympics was organised in Barcelona, as an initiative of the Catalan Committee for People's Sports. These alternative Games, based on working-class antifascist values, were to be held in the Catalan capital from 19 to 26 July 1936. In the end the event was cancelled because a faction of the Spanish army launched a coup attempt. The People's Olympics was to include the participation of exiled Jews and delegations from Catalonia, the Basque

---

4. Italy organised the second edition of the World Cup in the spring of that year. The fascist Italian government used the tournament as propaganda for national extremism and to demonstrate the existence of the 'new man' capable of displaying the strengths needed to organise a warlike competition and win it. In order to achieve victory and boast of its power, Italy nationalised Argentinian players – including Luis Monti and Raimundo Orsi. In the quarter-finals, the *squadra azzura* (blue squad) faced the team from Republican Spain, a bitter foe of *Il Duce*. A draw led to a tiebreaker match, which ended in victory for the Italians thanks to controversial refereeing that was, according to some sources, influenced by Mussolini. Finally, with the benefit of various refereeing mistakes, the team led by coach Vittorio Pozzo won the cup after defeating Czechoslovakia in the final 2–1, with an Angelo Schiavo goal in extra time.

5. In the summer of 1936, with Nazism in full swing, Berlin hosted the Olympic Games. The National Socialist leaders aimed to show the world the supposed superiority of the Aryan race. One of the most notable episodes of the games involved athlete Jesse Owens, the African American from Alabama, who managed to humiliate the regime by winning gold in the 100 and 200 metre sprints, long jump and 4 × 100 metre relay race. A feat that, according to several eyewitness accounts, provoked an angry response from Hitler, who refused to congratulate the winner. For more on the Berlin Olympics, see C. Hilton, *Hitler's Olympics: The 1936 Berlin Olympic Games* (Stroud: Sutton Publishing) and González Aja, *Sport y autoritarismos*, pp. 49–77.

country, Galicia and Alsace. There were also German and Italian delegations, made up of exiled athletes belonging to trade union or left-wing party clubs.

Another example of the instrumentalisation of sport is the 1978 FIFA World Cup held in Argentina under General Jorge Rafael Videla's military regime (euphemistically called the National Reorganisation Process). Here we find different responses (by Argentinean dissidents) regarding how to politically oppose a sporting competition used by the dictatorial regime as a form of propaganda and whitewashing. While the Mothers of the Plaza de Mayo[6] carried out demonstrations parallel to the games, the armed resistance called a truce to avoid increasing support for the government.[7]

Opposition to football from certain left-wing sectors was summed up in the article 'Football: A Dear Friend to Capitalism', published after the 2010 World Cup in South Africa by Terry Eagleton, Lancaster University's professor of philosophy. It can be countered by emphasising certain rebellious aspects that are linked to elements of working-class culture. Football is not just the opium of the people or a distraction from political and social problems. Rather, as various authors have pointed out, it has also been a means to forge group pride and class-consciousness through bonds of solidarity between groups and supporters.

In line with this argument, if we try to explain or further explore the different parameters that define modern football (which arise from the consequences imposed by capitalism), we find that individualism and the fragmentation of the working class are key. It bears repeating, as our basic premise, that football has traditionally been a sport linked to the working class. All that is required to play

6. [Translator's note]: movement of mothers of people 'disappeared' by the right-wing military in those years.
7. César Luis Menotti, the Argentinean national team coach known for his left-wing politics, stated that the team did not play for Videla's dictatorship but for the people. He even refused to shake hands with the dictator after winning the final against the Netherlands. The Dutch team did not include its star player Johan Cruyff, who had refused to participate in the World Cup.

is a ball and a few people, unlike other team sports that require a significant degree of specifically equipped facilities. Everybody will have a mental image of children in all parts of the world playing in a field, street or square, in some village or city, with just a ball and a couple of items of clothing marking out the goal. No other equipment is necessary, just the desire to play. And this is largely why football is and has been the sport with the greatest number of followers among the working classes.

Football is essentially a working-class sport, and that solidarity is inherent to it as a team game. All the same, it is clear that the individualism, fragmentation and alienation produced by capitalism have affected the game. The contemporary system breaks down social ties in villages, neighbourhoods, factories and even families (through forced migration). At the same time, it promotes the creation of artificial communities: exemplified in rural desertion and new urban architecture, residential areas built away from densely populated urban areas are fed by an irrational fear of the poor. People's sense of identity and shared existence are no longer the result of everyday interactions based on social-structural elements (class and neighbourhoods that, as groups of dwellings, reproduce class differences). Instead, communities break down in the face of the supremacy of the individual (a situation that is made worse by the prevailing desire for immediacy, that is, the need for instant gratifications with use-by dates). Thus, globalisation values change through experience. The knowledge that comes with experience is not important. What matters is the capacity to constantly adapt to modifications, a capacity wrongly described as 'flexibility' (a term used to disguise policies that cut back social rights and increase the precariousness of working conditions, among other things). As a result, it becomes impossible to aspire to historical continuity, to attain security, to develop character through lived experience. This state of affairs also directly affects some football clubs. For example, those that completely forget their history in the midst of the euphoria of their name and merchandising sold globally. They forget their past trials and tribulations, the events that shaped their identity, their links to the towns or cities they are part of, their stand against authoritarian or totalitarian regimes and the attacks they suffered as a result, and their sympathy for certain ideological positions. This leads them to lose their roots, and to become an object of global consumption. Then they stop associating with their neighbourhoods, towns or cities, and become a kind of centre of international attention detached from their surroundings. They lose the roots they developed from. This can be seen in the symptomatic image of football stadiums as tourist attractions, with ticket prices that are beyond the reach of the locals, and without the passion and solidarity of fans.

As social movement theories also applicable to football clubs point out, the flexibility imposed by the system does not do away with the need to forge social ties and develop identities. As an underlying premise, we should be aware that the compulsive need to produce meaning and identity (my community, my neighbourhood, my scene, my team) is one of the characteristics of our time. This is by no means a negative impulse, given that identity shapes personalities and behaviours, both individual and collective. Football and football clubs have been spheres linked to identity throughout their history. The connection with a particular city or town, having fans and supporters from the local area and rivalry with teams from other cities or neighbourhoods – some of which have opposing worldviews – have been indicators of identity construction. As is also the case with social movements, the success of individuals coming together to form an organised fan base does not just depend on their ability to organise the resources available to them and to maintain their collective activity (support for a club) over time. To a large extent, it also depends on their ability to generate a 'we' and to create an identity from a set of defining characteristics that provide a sense of belonging that allows the group's activities to continue. A group's collective identity, or the capacity of a group to define itself, is, as Alberto Melucci writes, 'an interactive and shared definition produced by different interacting individuals and that concerns the orientation of their action and the field of opportunities and constraints in which the action takes place'.

The importance of this identity-building process – which leads us to Antonio Gramsci and his concept of cultural hegemony – is due to the fact that as the sense of belonging and the interaction among individuals increases, so does social cohesion and possibilities for mobilisation. However, this idea of coming together is circumvented by modern football. It is therefore necessary to draw a distinction between *identity* and *identification*: a shared and mutually supportive social construction, on the one hand, is not the same as today's identification by large numbers of fans with certain clubs under the hold of the elites and emphasising – often anonymously – the importance of players (individuals) over the club (the group, the community). Modern football subverts the framing and promotes the latter: identification with a club based on individuals and success. These days, enthusiasm for a team is determined by its performance on the pitch and the players it has. A club increases its fan base in line with how many minutes of news coverage it gets, and fans come together exclusively or fundamentally through buying club merchandise (an idea we will return to below). This leads us back to capitalism, to weak and changeable identification with teams, often making it impossible to achieve supporter continuity.

Essentially, football has always been a place of convergence, discussion and belonging. As such, it acts as a parameter around which to construct identities (with 'identity' obviously interpreted in a very different way from the identitarian approaches of the new radical-right parties in Europe, who see identity as focusing on birth and origin rather than sharing and community). However, football is an activity with a mass following precisely because it tries to shift conflict from the political arena to that of spectacle (as happened with the Roman circus). This, together with football's potentially enormous reach and business potential (as a natural consequence of globalisation and of treating the individual as consumer), means that it is dominated by the same political and economic elites as the centres of power. The boards of directors of most football clubs are made up of the same people who control the boards of multinational corporations, and have a direct and self-interested relationship with the political class. The reality described becomes even clearer if we consider the fact that clubs in many countries are forced to become public limited companies once they reach a certain division. We are talking about the same elites that try to conceal any type of rebellious endeavour or expression of ideological propensity that does not conform to what is 'politically acceptable'. The ones that treat football as an alienating object of consumption and project an image of it that is structurally alien from any political movement. Despite everything, the conception we have tried to describe and that attempts to instil in us an idea of football as a mere spectacle for the masses, or alienating distraction for people, is in itself a stance that reveals an ideological will. In other words, it is an aspiration embedded in the ideologising desire of the elites.

The other key characteristic of what we call modern football has to do with the commercialisation of playing and following sport as a human activity. Football is currently dominated by advertising and consumerism. It is a giant business that has to be taken care of. The human character of football has been replaced by the (once again unequivocal) idea of the sport as an element of financial exchange, something to be bought. Its humanness and relational aspects have been destroyed, turning it into a mere means of doing business. Thus, football and its participants are used as an incentive to unlimited consumption within the capitalist logic of production and consumption of obsolete goods. This takes place in a simple context of material appropriation that omits all cultural references and rejects any alternative to the current standardising cultural model. As such, the distortion of society thereby brings with it the distortion of football and its clubs, which end up exemplifying the imposition of the 'single thought' that has been widespread since the fall of the Berlin Wall and the collapse of the USSR.

This overall context tends to encourage simple identification (rather than belonging) through the purchase and ownership of merchandising. Supposed identities are artificially built on obsolete elements. Thus, in the modern world, football has become part of a purely capitalist logic of production and consumption. It is objectified, distorted and commodified. This reinforces the one-dimensional concepts transmitted by the elites, which perfectly define what modern football is all about: football is merely entertainment and business, and fans are simply a mass of consumers. This also takes us to the idea of football as an element of social control, through the elimination of solidarity and active participation and its substitution by passive spectatorship. Participants cease to be active supporters, and become simple recipients of sensations without any kind of influence over decisions regarding the direction their club will take.

In short, modern football is merely the transposition to the football field of the general changes brought about by capitalist globalisation. It entails a break with the traditions, experience and past history of clubs and teams, which were created by players and fans. It entails the commercialisation and distortion of a human activity that is essentially based on solidarity, but now becomes a consumer object. It transforms fans from active agents into a mere mass of consumers. As such, modern football exemplifies the process of alienation and depoliticisation and is the opium of the people. It takes the form of a simple, universal spectacle for the masses, like a new Roman circus, and becomes disconnected from its geographical roots. Modern football is an entertainment industry and a moneymaking business for the economic elites who control the system. At the same time, by distracting people from politics it is an ideologising force. In other words, modern football is a tool through which neoliberal thought is channelled (follow the winning team, not the local club; success lies in having the best players; the market is the correct means by which to distribute the financial resources of football clubs; clubs need to become public liability companies in order to ensure free competition within the football business). It is also radically conservative (there are no class distinctions within teams because sport must remain separate from politics; it is thus necessary to forget the history of clubs, because things were totally different in the past) and it serves the interests of state nationalisms (as one must extol national unity in international competitions).

In view of all this, we believe in the need to defend a new concept of football. It is time to recover football as a human activity that is part of society, not outside of it – to reclaim soccer from the inside, from the stands, through collective self-management, so that it also becomes a tool for empowerment, solidarity and community building. There is an urgent need to decommercialise football, to humanise it and to eliminate the dire consequences of reducing it to being a means of capitalist business (e.g. doping, bribes and gambling). In committing to this change there are some clear examples we can look to. Clubs that are expressions of ideas that are the opposite of modern football, and that are influenced by landmarks such as Corinthians Democracy.

In the early 1980s, at the height of the military dictatorship in Brazil, the Corinthians Paulista football club was in serious social and sporting crisis. The executives and players of the club, led by Sócrates and Wladimir, decided to make radical changes, adopting a team management model based on bottom-up self-management.[8]

---

8. This experiment, in which club players and employees decided the future of the club, shared revenue equally among them and even democratically elected the coach (in 1982 they chose Zé Maria, pro-democracy activist and former member of Brazil's 1970 world champion team), became a symbol of opposition to the dictatorial regime. The team had a mission ('At the start, we wanted to change our working conditions; then sports policy in our country; and finally, politics as such') and wore shirts with explicit messages. For example, to encourage people to vote in the first elections to elect the governor of São Paulo on 15 March 1983, the team wore a kit with the words 'Dia 15 Vote' ('Vote on the 15th'). On other occasions they displayed the motto 'Ganhar ou perder, mas sempre com democracia' ('Win or lose, but always in democracy'). The Corinthians Democracy experiment ended in 1985 with the arrival of democracy in Brazil, when Sócrates moved to Italy to play for Fiorentina and the former directors of the São Paulo club regained control. Sócrates (full name Sócrates Brasileiro Sampaio de Souza Vieria de Oliveria) was the main figurehead of the Corinthians, a qualified doctor and true alma mater of the experiment. 'The Doctor', as he was popularly known, was a member of the Democratic Labour Party and used to run on to the pitch with his fist raised. Sócrates died on 4 December

Following this example, several other clubs also adopted direct, democratic and cooperative management. These include community share clubs such as AFC Liverpool, Unione Venezia, Ciudad de Murcia, Atlético Club de Socios, UC Ceares, FC Tarraco, CD Badajoz 1905, CPF Orihuela Deportiva, Avilés Stadium, Union Deportiva Ourense, Xerez DFC, Palencia and CF Aliança Internacionalista Popular, to name just a few. All of them are non-profit clubs based on the principle of 'one person, one share', and thus one vote in the assembly. They are clubs that develop ties with their local communities and have a policy of affordable ticket prices. These kinds of clubs are directly influenced by the cooperative movement and inspired by the story of FC United of Manchester. In 2005, when Manchester United was bought by the American billionaire Malcolm Glazer (who also owned the Florida-based American football team the Tampa Bay Buccaneers), the team's most active fans (as well as popularising the chant 'Hate Glazer, Love United') decided to create a new team that would faithfully represent the foundational spirit of 'The Red Devils'.

The promoters of FC United drew inspiration from AFC Wimbledon, a pioneer in the empowerment of English football fans, which was founded in 2002 by fans of Wimbledon FC after the latter club relocated to Milton Keynes. Following in the Londoners' footsteps, on 14 July 2005 a group of fans dissatisfied with the sale of Manchester United to the American tycoon founded FC United. More than 4,000 people pledged financial support. The club is structured as a non-profit democratic organisation owned by its fans. After starting in the tenth tier of English football and earning three successive promotions, the team settled in the seventh division, with an average attendance of more than 2,500 fans. FC United, known as 'The Red Rebels' because of the political connotation and the colour of their shirts, are a kind of return to the roots of football – to its proletarian origins. The club also demonstrated

---

2011, the day the Corinthians played a match that made them Brazilian champions. Thus, a wish he made in 1983 became a prophecy: 'I want to die on a Sunday, with Corinthians as champions.'

the viability of trying to stop the commercialisation of football. Its creation was not without controversy, however, as not everybody shared the same views. An example is Sir Alex Ferguson, Manchester United coach from 1986 to 2013, who criticised the founders of the FC United for being more concerned with their new club than with the future of United. On the other hand, former players of the Old Trafford team publically positioned themselves in favour of the new club, including French striker Eric Cantona – a true icon of Manchester United.

As well as these cases in which democratic organisation and social engagement have emerged from the club itself (in other words where management and fans have taken a different path to 'business football'), at FC St. Pauli the push for democratisation and empowerment came from the stands. In their case, this other form of democratisation, of placing decision-making power back in the hands of fans, and reconnecting with the community and the local area, emerged spontaneously. As such, St. Pauli has become a unique model of grassroots democratisation that is still going strong after three decades.

Bibliography

Ackermann, R. (2012). *Warum die NPD keinen Erfolg haben kann: Organisation, Programm und Kommunikation einer rechsextremen Partei* (Berlin: Budrich Unipress Ltd).

Backes, G. (2010). *'Mit deutschem Sportgruss, Heil Hitler!' Der FC St. Pauli im Nationalsozialismus* (Hamburg: Hoffmann & Campe).

Bajohr, F. (2002). *Aryanisation in Hamburg: The Economic Exclusion of Jews and the Confiscation of Their Property in Nazi Germany* (New York: Berghahn Books).

Bauman, Z. (2007). *Tiempos líquidos: Vivir una época de incertidumbre* (Barcelona: Tusquets).

Becher, P., Begass, Ch. and Kraft, J. (2015). *Der Aufstand des Abdenlandes. AFT, Pegida & Co.: Von Salon auf die Straße* (Cologne: ParyRossa).

Biermann, A. (2011). *Rote Karte Depression* (Munich: Gütersloher Verlagshaus).

Blaschke, R. (2011). *Angriff von Rechstaußen: Wie Neonazis den Fußball missbrauchen* (Göttingen: Die Werskstatt).

Bohé, D. (2009). *FC St Pauli zur Zeit der NS-Diktatur: Eine Kritische Auseinandersetzung mit den Personalien Wilhelm Koch und Otto Wolff* (Norderstedt: GRIN).

Boll, F. and Kaminsky, A. (1999). *Gedenkstättenarbeit und Oral History: Lebensgeschichtliche Beiträge zur Verfolgung in zwei Diktaturen* (Berlin: Arno Spitz).

Breverton, T. (2004). *The Pirate Dictionary* (Gretna: Pelican Publishing).

Casassas, J. (ed.) (2005). *La construcción del presente: El mundo desde 1948 hasta nuestros días* (Barcelona: Ariel).

Castells, M. (1998). *La era de la información: El poder de la identidad* (Madrid: Alianza).

Cazzullo, A. (1998). *I ragazzi che volevano faré la Rivoluzione 1968–1978: Storia de Lotta Continua* (Milan: Mondadori).

Comfort, R.A. (1965). *Revolutionary Hamburg Labor Politics in the Early Weimar Republic* (Stanford: Stanford University Press).

Cowan, A. (2010). *Hanseatic League: Oxford Research Guide* (Oxford: Oxford University Press).

Davidson, N. (2014). *Pirates, Punks and Politics. FC St. Pauli: Falling in Love with a Radical Football Club* (York: Sportsbooks).

Eisenberg, C. (1999). *English Sports und deutscher Bürger: Eine Gesellschaftgeschichte 1800–1939* (Paderborn: Schöningh).

Evans, R.J. (1987). *Death in Hamburg* (London: Penguin Books).

Evans, R.J. (2006). *La nascita del Terzo Reich* (Milan: Mondadori).

Friedrich, S. (2015). *Der Aufstieg der AFD: Neokonservative Mobilmachung in Deutschland* (Berlin: Bertz und Fischer).

Fulbrook, M. (2014). *A History of Germany 1918–2014: The Divided Nation* (Oxford: Blackwell).

Galczinski, R. and Carstensen, B. (2009). *FC St. Pauli Vereinsenzyklopädie* (Göttingen: Die Werkstatt).

Geiges, L., Marg, S. and Walter, F. (2015). *Pegida: Die schmutzige Seite der Zivilgesellschaft?* (Bielefeld: Transcript).

Geronimo (2011). *Fire and Flames: A History of the German Autonomist Movement* (Oakland: PM Press).

Gilbert, A. and Vitagliano, M. (1998). *El terror y la gloria: La vida, el fútbol y la política en la Argentina del Mundial 78* (Buenos Aires: Grupo Editorial Norma).

Giuntini, S. (2014). *Calcio e dittature: Una storia sudamericana* (Mergozzo: Sedizioni).

Goch, S. and Silberbach, N. (2005). *Zwischen Blau und Weiß liegt Grau: Der FC Schalke 04 in der Zeit des Nationalsozialismus* (Essen: Klartext).

González Aja, T. (ed.) (2002). *Sport y autoritarismos: La utilización del deporte por el comunismo y el fascismo* (Madrid: Alianza Editorial).

Gordon, A. (2007). *The Lisbon Lions: The Real Inside Story of Celtic European Cup Triumph* (Edinburgh: Black & White Publishing).

Gotta, R. (2008). *Fuimos campeones: La dictadura, el Mundial 78 y el misterio del 6 a 0 a Perú* (Buenos Aires: Edhasa).

Grandi, A. (2003). *La generazione degli anni perduti: Storie di Potere Operaio* (Turin: Einaudi).

Grenville, J. A. S. (2012). *The Jews and Germans of Hamburg: The Destruction of a Civilization 1790–1945* (Abingdon: Routledge).

Harris, V. (2010). *Selling Sex in the Reich: Prostitutes in German Society, 1914–1945* (New York: Oxford University Press).

Havemann, N. (2005). *Fußball unterm Hakenkreuz: Der DFB zwischen Sport, Politik und Kommerz* (Frankfurt: Campus Verlag).

Herzog, M. (2008). *Fußball zur Zeit des Nationalsozialismus: Alltag-Medien-Künste-Stars (Irseer Dialoge. Kultur Und Wissenschaft Interdisziplinar)* (Stuttgart: Kohlhammer).

Hesse-Lichtenberger, U. (2002). *Tor! The Story of German Football* (London: WSC Books Ltd.).

Hilton, C. (2006). *Hitler's Olympics: The 1936 Berlin Olympic Games* (Stroud: Sutton Publishing).

Katsifiakas, G.N. (2006). *The Subversion of Politics: European Autonomous Social Movements and the Decolonization of Everyday Life* (Oakland: AK Press).

Koonz, C. (2003). *The Nazi Conscience* (Cambridge: Belknap Press).

Kuhn, G. (2011). *Soccer vs. the State: Tackling Football and Radical Politics* (Oakland: PM Press).

Krüger, A. and Riordan, J. (eds) (1996). *The Story of Worker Sport* (Champaign: Human Kinetics).

Kruke, A. (2012), *Arbeiter-Turn-und Sportbund (1893–2009)* (Bonn: Archiv der sozialen Demokratie der Friedrich-Ebert- Stiftung).

Langmaak, W. and Schulte, H. (2013). *Drei St. Pauli Leben* (Göttingen: Verlag die Werkstatt).

Leiva, J. (2012). *Fútbol y Dictaduras: Resistencia vs. propaganda* (Simat de la Valldigna: La Xara Edicions).

Lemmons, R. (2013). *Hitler's Rival: Ernst Thälmann in Myth and Memory* (Lexington: University Press of Kentucky).

Lowe, K. (2007). *Inferno: The Devastation of Hamburg 1943* (London: Penguin Books).

Maertens, R. (2010). *Wunder gibt es immer wieder: Die Geschicte des FC St. Pauli* (Göttingen: Verlag die Werkstatt).

Marchi, V. (1994). *Ultrà: Le sottoculture giovanili negli stadi d'Europa* (Rome: Koinè).

Marcuse, H. (2010). *El hombre unidimensional* (Barcelona: Ariel).

Martin, S. (2004). *Football and Fascism: The National Game under Mussolini* (Oxford: Berg).

Martínez López, M. (2002). *Okupaciones de viviendas y de centros sociales: Autogestión, contracultura y conflictos urbanos* (Barcelona: Virus).

Melucci, A. (1989). *Sistema politico, partiti e movimenti sociali* (Milan: Feltrinelli).

Metelmann, T. and Vinke, H. (2009). *Kiez-Klub FC St. Pauli: Ein Kultverein und sein Stadtteil* (Bremen: Edition Temmen).

Molthagen, D., Melzer, R., Zick, A. and Küpper, B. (2015). *Wut, Verachtung, Abwertung: Rechtspopulismus in Deutschland* (Bonn: Dietz).

Nagel, C. and Pahl, M. (2009). *FC St Pauli. Das Buch: Der Verein und sein Viertel* (Hamburg: Hoffmann & Campe).

O'Kane, J. (2006). *Celtic Soccer Crew: What the Hell Do We Care?* (London: Pennant Books).

Oberschelp, M. (2010). *Der Fußball-Lehrer: Wie Konrad Koch im Kaiserreich den Ball ins Spiel brachte* (Göttingen: Die Werkstatt).

Observatorio Metropolitano de Madrid (2015). *El Mercado contra la Ciudad: Globalización, gentrificación y políticas urbanas* (Madrid: Traficantes de sueños).

Panzeri, D. (2012). *Fútbol: Dinámica de lo impensado* (Madrid: Capitán Swing).

Peiffer, L. and Schulze-Marmeling, D. (2008). *Hakenkreuz und rundes Leder: Fußball im Nationalsozialismus* (Göttingen: Die Werkstatt).

Peinado, E. (2013). *Futbolistas de izquierdas* (Madrid: Léeme Libros).

Perryman, M. (2001). *Hooligans War: Causes and Effects of Football Violence* (Edinburgh: Mainstream Publishing).

Petroni, M. (2015). *St. Pauli siamo noi: Piratti, punk e autonomi allò stadio e nelle strade di Amburgo* (Rome: DeriveApprodi).

Puls, U. (1959). *Die Bästlein-Jacob-Abshagen-Gruppe: Bericht über den antifaschistischen Widerstandskampf in Hamburg und an der Waterkante während des zweiten Weltkrieges* (Berlin: Dietz Verlang).

Purden, R. (2011) *We Are Celtic Supporters* (London: Hachette Scotland).

Reng, R. (2015). *Matchdays: The Hidden Story of the Bundesliga* (London: Simon & Schuster).

Richard, A.I. (2016). *Pegida under Closer Scrutiny: How a Regional Protest Movement Evolved Into a Pan-European Movement* (unpublished doctoral thesis, Leiden University).

Rondinelli, N. (2015). *Ribelli, Sociali e Romantici! FC Sankt Pauli tra calcio e resistenza* (Lecce: Bepress Edizioni).

Röpke, A. and Speit, A. (2008). *Neonazis in Nadelstreifen: Die NPD auf dem Weg in die Mitte der Gesellschaft* (Berlin: Christoph Links).

Ryser, D. (2013). *Slime: Deutschland muss sterben* (Munich: Wilhelm Heyne Verlang).

Sanderson, C. (2009). *'Nie Wieder Faschismus, Nie Wieder Krieg, Nie Wieder 3. Liga!' A Social History of FC St. Pauli, 1986–1991* (Coventry: Warwick University).

Santacana, C. and Pujadas, X. (1990). *L'altra Olimpíada: Barcelona '36* (Barcelona: Llibres de l'Índex).

Savage, J. (2007). *Teenage: The Creation of Youth 1875–1945* (London: Chatto & Windus).

Schildhauer, J. (1988). *The Hansa: History and Culture* (New York: Dorset Press).

Schlüter, B. (2013). *Die Fans vom Hamburger SV und des FC St. Pauli Im Vergleich: Eine sozialisationstheoretische Analyse* (Hamburg: Diplomica Verlag).

Schmidt-Lauber, B. (2005). *FC St Pauli: Zur Ethnographie eines Vereins* (Berlin: Lit Verlag).

Schulze, H. (2001). *Breve historia de Alemania* (Madrid: Alianza editorial).

Sennett, R. (2006). *La corrosión del character* (Barcelona: Anagrama).

Suso, R. (2016). *La claveguera marró: L'NSU i el terror neonazi a Alemanya* (Manresa: Tigre de Paper).

Tate, T. (2013). *Girls with Balls: The Secret History of Women's Football* (London: John Blake Publishing).

Tomlinson, A. and Young, C. (2006). *German Football: History, Culture, Society* (London: WSC Books Ltd).

Totten, M. (2012). *Fan Power: Calling the Shots. Lessons from the Iconic Fans of Cult Club Sankt Pauli FC* (Leeds: Leeds Metropolitan University).

Usall, R. (2011). *Futbol per la llibertat* (Lleida: Pagès editors).

Villani, P. (1997). *La edad contemporánea 1800–1914* (Barcelona: Ariel).

Von Mering, S. and Wyman McCarty, T. (eds) (2013). *Right-Wing Radicalism Today: Perspectives from Europe and the US* (New York: Routledge).

Vörlander, H., Herold, M. and Schäller, S. (2016). *Pegida: Entwicklung, Zusammensetzung und Deutung einer Empörungsbewegung* (Wiesbaden: Springer).
Williams, J. (2003). *A Game for Rough Girls? A History of Women's Football in Britain* (London: Routledge).
Zint, G. (1980). *Republik Freies Wendland* (Frankfurt: Zweitausendeins).
Zwerin, M. (2016). *Swing frente al nazi* (Madrid: Es Pop Ediciones).

FILMOGRAPHY

Ehlail, T. (2011). *Gegengerade.*
Schadewald, B. (1993). *Schicksalsspiel.*

DOCUMENTARIES

Gerlach, R. (2013). *Lampedusa auf St. Pauli.*
Grimm, F. (2011). *Das ganze Stadion.*
Millerntor Roar! (1991). *Und ich weiß warum ich hier stehe.*
Montague, J. (2010). *Punks, Prostitutes and St. Pauli: Inside Soccer's Coolest Club.* CNN.
Shoo TV, (2011). *Paulinen Platz.* Sport Economy.
Theroux, M. (2011). *FC St. Pauli: A Socialist Football club in Hamburg's Red Light District.*
Vice Sports, (2015). *FC St. Pauli: Between Myth and Reality.*

ARTICLES IN SPECIALISED JOURNALS

Amenda, L. (2005). 'Chinesenaktion: Zur Rassenpolitik und Verfolgung im nationalsozialistischen Hamburg', *Zeitschrift des Vereins für Hamburgische Geschichte*, no. 91, pp. 103–32.
Daniel, P. and Kassimeris, C. (2013). 'The Politics and Culture of FC St. Pauli: From Leftism, through Anti-Establishment, to Commercialization', *Soccer & Society*, no. 2, vol. 14, pp. 167–82.
Griggs, G. (2012). '"Carlsberg Don't Make Football Teams … But if They Did": The Utopian Reporting of FC St. Pauli in the British Media', *Soccer & Society*, no. 1, vol. 13, pp. 73–82.
McDougall, W. (2013). 'Kicking from the Left: The Friendship of Celtic and FC St. Pauli supporters', *Soccer & Society*, no. 2, vol. 14, pp. 230–45.
McElligott, A. (1983). 'Street Politics in Hamburg, 1922–32', *History Workshop Journal*, no. 16, pp. 83–90.
Merkel, U. (2012). 'Football Fans and Clubs in Germany: Conflicts, Crises and Compromises', *Soccer & Society*, no. 3, vol. 13, pp. 359–76.
Totten, M. (2015). 'Sport Activism and Political Praxis within the FC Sankt Pauli Fan Subculture', *Soccer & Society*, no. 4, vol. 16, pp. 453–68.

MEDIA CONSULTED

11 Freunde Ara
As
BBC
Clarín
Crític
Der Spiegel
Der Tagesspiegel
Deutsche Welle Diagonal
Die Welt
El Gráfico
El Mundo
El País
Fusion
Hamburger Abendblatt
Huffington Post
Kaiser Magazine
Kölner Stadt Anzeiger
La Jornada
Les Inrocks
Marca
MOPO
Mundo Deportivo
Página 12
Panenka
Süddeutsche Zeitung
The Guardian
The Independent
The Telegraph
Time
World Soccer
Zeit
Zeitschrift des Vereins für Hamburgische Geschichte

Index

AfD *Alternative für Deutschland*
(Alternative for Germany), 173,
175
AFM *Abteilung Fördernde Mitglieder*
(Active Support Members'
Department), 130, 132–5, 183,
184, 186n17
Africa, 14, 68, 151n18, 187, 200, 212,
213, 214, 215
South Africa, 233
AGIM *Arbeitsgemeinschaft Inter-
essierter Mitglieder* (Interested
Members' Group), 108, 130
AIDS, 59, 73, 100, 112n6
Altona, 11, 30n8, 38n7, 40, 42, 51, 86,
92, 93, 108, 113, 115n14, 145n3,
148n9, 149n13, 157n2, 161, 167,
182
Altona FC, 18n21, 63
Hamburg-Altona Football Associa-
tion, 17, 18, 19
SAGA *Siedlungs-Aktiengesellschaft
Altona* (construction company),
78, 80, 82, 221n2
Americas
Central America, 94n32
Latin America, 105n47, 128n7,
151n18
North America, 25
South America, 37n6
United States of America, 17n19,
53, 58, 206n5, 209n7
ANS/NA *Aktionsfront Nationaler
Sozialisten/Nationale Aktivisten*
(Action Front of National Social-
ists/National Activists), 110n1,
111, 112, 114n11
antifascism, 71, 77, 81, 90, 98, 101n42,
114, 118, 120n23, 129, 138n3, 139,
146n5, 163n15, 165, 176, 177,
178–87

anti-Nazis, 42, 42n13, 42–3n14,
43n14, 121n24, 184
antiracism, 97n34, 102, 103, 113n9,
118n18, 120, 122n25, 125, 127,
128, 129, 134, 138n3, 139, 140,
146n4, 149, 158n5, 159, 163n15,
166n18, 171, 176, 179, 183, 193,
205, 207, 208, 225. *See also* racist
chants
anti-Semitism, 31, 81n14, 111, 117n17
Argentina, 17n19, 105n47, 119, 143n1,
233
ATSB *Arbeiter-Turn- und Sportbund*
(Workers' Gymnastics and Sport
Association), 7–8n9, 26, 27n1
Auerstedt, 2, 10
Austria, 3, 19, 40, 55, 142, 145, 172n25
Austro-Hungarian Empire, 7n8, 19

Baden, 4
Baden-Württemberg, 84n17, 109
BAFF *Bündnis Aktiver Fußball-Fans*
(Active Football Supporters' Asso-
ciation), 128, 129n8
Bayer Leverkusen, 97, 126, 131n14
Berlin, 4, 5, 6, 14n13, 29, 43, 46, 56,
57, 70, 77, 78–9, 80, 88n21, 89,
99n37, 100n39, 111, 112, 113,
117n17, 120, 145n3, 152, 156n1,
172n25, 216
Berlin FC, 118n18
East Berlin, 117n17, 205
Hertha Berlin, 119, 163
Kreuzberg, 70n1, 76n7, 92, 101n42,
119, 121n24
Olympiastadion, 101
Soviet blockade of, 49
Tennis Borussia Berlin, 170
Union Berlin FC, 162, 184, 185, 200
West Berlin, 99n37
Berlin Olympic Games (1936), 36,
39, 232

Berlin Wall, 98, 125, 237
Beust, Ole von, 145, 148n9
Bielefeld, 29n6, 156n1
   Arminia Bielefeld, 63, 170
Blankenese, 22, 27
Brazil, 51, 128n7, 173, 239, 229–40n8
Bremen, 5, 41n13, 99n36, 100n39,
   121n24
   Radio Bremen, 95
   Werder Bremen, 57, 64, 69, 98, 113,
   152, 218
Britain, 5, 6, 20n25, 21n28, 24n31,
   29n6, 42, 13, 43, 46, 448, 9, 50,
   73n2, 80, 89n23, 98n35, 110, 115,
   118, 121, 141, 178n1, 191–5, 198,
   206
Brux, Sven, 113n9, 126, 127, 137n2
Bundesliga, 33, 57, 63–6, 68–9, 72,
   74, 77n6, 88, 94, 95, 100, 101n42,
   102, 106, 107, 132, 142, 143, 144,
   146, 153, 154, 156, 157, 158, 165,
   175n30, 192, 206n2, 219, 220, 223
Bundesliga 2, 63, 68, 69, 77n6, 102,
   107, 143, 153

CDU Christlich Demokratische Union
   Deutschlands (Christian Demo-
   cratic Union of Germany), 58, 68,
   76, 81n13, 81n14, 145, 173n27,
   173n28
Celtic FC, 93, 137–41, 154, 195, 216
Chinese community, 45, 212
Cold War, 56, 98
Cologne, 78n7, 126n1, 137n2, 172n26,
   176n34, 203
   Cologne FC, 57, 68, 143, 169n22
concentration camps, 111
   Ahlem-Hannover, 29n6
   Auschwitz, 39n8, 102n44, 121, 183,
   183n10
   Buchenwald, 24n32, 39n8
   Moringen, 39n8
   Neuengamme, 29n6, 39n8, 41,
   41–2n13, 91n27, 129, 140, 184n12
   Sachsenhausen, 42n14, 129, 184n12
   Theresienstadt, 37, 37n6
   Uckermark, 39n8
Corinthians Democracy, 239,
   239–40n8

Cuba, 149n10, 150, 151, 152n21,
   205n1
Czechoslovakia, 41, 232n4

Demuth, Dietmar, 64, 109, 142
Denmark, 11, 12, 71, 90n25, 115n16,
   172n25, 209n7
DFB Deutscher Fußball-Bund
   (German Football Association),
   7, 7n9, 8, 22, 26, 31, 35, 37n5, 50,
   55, 56, 57, 66, 68, 74, 96, 98, 108,
   117, 121, 122, 129, 130n11, 131,
   134n18, 145, 146, 147, 152, 158,
   162n14, 163, 164, 183, 184, 185,
   187n17, 198, 199, 203
DFL Deutsche Fußball Liga (German
   Football League), 129, 131, 132,
   133, 163, 175, 176, 184
Dortmund, 55, 57, 88n21, 95, 111,
   112, 114, 115n12, 174, 175n30,
   175n31
Dresden, 4n3, 117n17, 172n25
Dresden English Football Club, 4, 5,
   6n6
Dresdner SC (Dresdner Sport-Club),
   5, 44n15, 45, 49, 50
Duisburg, 57, 144
DVU Deutsche Volksunion (German
   People's Union), 81n14, 99,
   150n14
Dynamo Dresden, 5, 118n18

Ebbers, Marius, 154, 162, 165
Elbe, River, 9, 10, 11, 15, 18, 27n4,
   36, 77, 90, 91, 161, 194. See also
   pirates
Eimsbütteler Turnverein, 9, 18, 29
Eintracht Braunschweig, 6, 57,
   118n18, 144, 165
England. See Britain
Europe, 3, 83, 129, 138, 140, 171, 192,
   196, 214, 218, 236

Fanladen, 102n43, 106, 107, 113n9,
   119, 125 30, 134, 135, 138, 140,
   142, 149, 159n10, 171, 175, 178n1,
   180, 183, 184, 186n17, 206, 210

FAP *Freiheitliche Deutsche Arbeiter-partei* (Free German Workers' Party), 99–100, 111n4, 112n6
FARE (Football Against Racism in Europe), 134, 149
FIFA, 152n22, 212, 232, 233
First World War, 19, 20, 22, 24, 41n13
FPÖ *Freiheitliche Partei Österreichs* (Freedom Party of Austria), 82n14, 145
France, 3, 4, 10, 12, 19, 43, 55, 56, 92, 122, 178n1
Frankfurt, 6, 66, 70, 76n7, 79, 81–2, 88n21, 101n42, 113n7, 114, 120, 172n25
  Eintracht Frankfurt, 37, 57, 111
  Football Club Germania, 6
  Kickers Frankfurt, 6
  Victoria Frankfurt, 6
FRG Federal Republic of Germany (West Germany), 50, 51, 56, 98, 110
Frosch, Walter, 63, 64

Galatasaray, 102n44, 103, 120
Gauligas, 32, 41, 55, 56
GDR German Democratic Republic (East Germany), 57, 98, 99, 105, 117n17, 205n1
German Empire, 4, 21, 112
German Gymnastics Association, 8n6, 26
Gestapo, 24n32, 27n1, 38n7, 39n8, 43n14, 45, 184
Glazer, Malcolm, 154, 240. See also Manchester United

Hafenstraße, 36, 70, 71, 74, 77, 80–84, 86, 88–94, 100–101, 103, 104, 113n9, 114, 115n12, 115n14, 116, 118, 119, 126, 130, 137, 150, 160, 163n15, 164, 178, 198
Hamburg, 5, 9–25, 27–32, 35–46, 47, 48, 49, 50, 51, 52, 53, 57
  Germania Hamburg, 7n7, 18n21
  Hafenstraße (port area), 36, 70, 71, 74, 77, 78, 80–83, 84, 86, 88, 89, 90, 91, 92, 93, 94, 100, 103, 104,
    114n9, 114, 115n12, 115n14, 116, 118, 119, 126, 130, 137, 150, 160, 163n15, 164, 178, 198
  Hamburger Berg, 10
  Hamburger FC, 9, 21, 63–109
  Hamburg-St. Pauli Turnverein, 9, 10, 16, 17, 18, 19, 26, 41n13
  Hamburg Senate, 10, 12, 13, 36, 80, 83, 95, 104, 166
  Hamburg Uprising (1923), 23, 24n32
Hammonia, 21, 200
Hannover FC, 66, 131n15, 142, 155
Hansa SC, 23
Hansa Rostock, 106, 118n18, 120, 121, 153n24, 154, 169n22, 181, 182, 183, 185–6, 217
Hanseatic League, 13n9, 21, 85, 90
Harder, Otto 'Tull', 29n6, 42
Heiligengeistfeld, 17, 20, 22, 23n30, 43, 44, 52, 77n6, 84n17, 142
Herberger, Sepp, 44n15, 57
Hindenburg, 24n32, 35
Hitler, Adolf, 21n28, 24n32, 25n34, 31n9, 35, 36, 46, 118n18, 121, 172n25, 184, 232n5
Hitler Youth, 38n7, 39n10, 40
Holocaust, 86n20, 129, 176
Hooliganism, 101n42, 102n44, 110–22, 139, 156n1, 172n17, 181n6, 184, 187
HSV *Hamburger Sport-Verein* (SV Hamburg, football club), 21, 28, 29n6, 40, 42, 44, 64, 65, 69, 72, 85, 86, 88, 91n27, 95n32, 96, 101n42, 110, 113–19, 122, 125, 131n13, 133, 138, 139, 143, 148, 156–7, 164, 172n26, 179, 183, 191, 203, 220, 226n3

interwar period, 25, 27, 41, 92
Ippig, Volker, 92, 94, 102, 116, 139n6, 154, 216, 224
Iran, 58, 79, 140n8
Iraq, 171, 214n10
Ireland, 138n5, 191–5
Islamophobia, 81n14, 172n26
Italy, 79, 118, 141, 167, 179, 215, 232
  Lampedusa, 167, 187, 214
  Lampedusa FC, 215, 216

Jena, 4, 10
Jews, 4, 29n6, 31n9, 37–8, 116, 143, 183n10, 232
Jolly Roger (symbol), 92, 143n1, 159, 160, 163, 165, 168, 217, 223
Jolly Roger (bar), 118, 139, 153, 156n1, 171, 179, 183, 187n18, 194, 215
Jordan, Ernst, 8, 27
Jürs, Peter Julius, 41, 42

Kaiserslautern FC, 57, 63, 88n21, 102n43, 111, 131n13
Karlsruher FV, 23
Karlsruher SC, 57, 96, 109, 167, 170
Kaufmann, Karl, 29n6, 36n3, 38n7, 46
Kenya, 68, 197n2, 200
Kiel, 20, 29n6
Holstein Kiel FC, 6, 28, 41, 67, 148
THW Kiel, 203
Klasnić, Ivan, 109, 142, 154
Koch, Reenald, 144, 148
Koch, Wilhelm, 29, 31, 44, 48, 58
Koehler, Walter, 31, 38
Kohl, Helmut, 68, 85n17, 98–9
KPD Kommunistische Partei Deutschlands (Communist Party of Germany), 8n9, 23, 24, 27n1, 35, 184, 205n1

Lampedusa, 167, 187, 214
Lampedusa FC, 215, 216
Leipzig, 5, 7, 8, 14n13, 27n1, 105, 120, 172n25
Leipzig Declaration against discrimination, 135n19
Lokomotive Leipzig FC, 118n18, 165
Red Bull Leipzig, 169, 176
VFB Leipzig, 17n21, 18
Littmann, Cornelius 'Corny', 146, 148, 149, 159n7, 181, 222
Liverpool FC, 93, 110, 240
Lorkowski, Michael, 63n1, 68, 69, 94n32

Mabuse, Doc, 89, 91–3
Machate, Fritz, 49, 50

Magdeburg FC, 117n17, 118n18, 153, 203
Manchester United, 110, 154, 240–41. See also United of Manchester
Mannheim, 7, 49, 142, 144
Mannschaft, 8, 66–7, 119, 121, 197n1
March Revolution (1848), 3, 4n3, 10
Maslo, Uli, 106, 107, 108
Mediterranean, 3, 214
Merkel, Angela, 171, 176n34
Miller, Karl, 44, 44–5n15, 45, 50
Millerntor stadium, 9n2, 11, 12n7, 14, 37n6, 39n8, 40, 43, 44, 52–4, 64, 71, 74, 77n6, 86, 87, 89, 92, 93, 95, 96, 97, 98, 101n41, 106, 108, 109, 112, 114, 115, 116, 118n19, 119, 120n22, 121, 126, 128n6, 132, 133n17, 135, 137, 140, 141, 143, 144, 145n3, 149n12, 149n13, 151, 152, 154, 155, 156, 161, 163n15, 164, 165n17, 167, 170, 174, 176, 177, 178n1, 181, 182, 186, 187n18, 192, 194–5, 196, 198, 201, 203, 205, 206, 207, 212, 215, 219, 220–22, 224, 225n2
Millerntor Roar! (MR!) (fanzine), 97–8n35, 100, 101n42, 102, 103n45, 116, 119, 120n22, 121n25, 126n1, 126n3, 138
Munich, 77, 78n7, 99n36, 99n37, 111, 184n13, 139n6
1860 Munich, 4, 6, 57, 106, 135
Bayern Munich, 95, 97, 102, 118, 137n1, 141, 143, 147, 148n8, 152
Munich 1893, 5
Münster, 57, 66
music, 39, 48, 103, 104n46, 115, 117, 118n19, 122n25, 140, 148, 150, 155, 169n23, 179n3, 180n5, 186n17, 191, 204–19
punk, 70n1, 71, 72, 72–3n2, 75, 78, 79, 80n11, 82n15, 83, 85n19, 86, 89, 90, 90–91n27, 92, 93, 94, 97n35, 103, 107, 110–11n1, 113n7, 115, 117, 121, 126n1, 140n3, 155, 186n17, 191, 205, 206, 207, 220, 223

Naki, Deniz, 181, 185, 217–18

Napoleon, 4, 5n4, 10, 12
NATO (North Atlantic Treaty Organization), 51, 68, 110, 215
Nazi Party, 12n7, 25n34, 29n6, 31, 38, 99n37, 120n23, 150n14
Nazis, 27n1, 30, 31, 32n11, 35, 36, 38, 39n8, 40, 41, 45–6, 55, 102n44, 103, 109, 110–22, 150, 232
Nazism, 31, 46, 79, 100n38, 220, 232n5
neo-Nazis, 85, 103, 114, 115n12, 116, 117n17, 118, 125, 176n34, 180, 203
NFV *Norddeutscher Fußball-Verband* (Northern German Football Association), 18, 20
Nicaragua, 94, 151, 200, 216
Nordkurve, 93, 126, 160, 170, 177, 200
North Rhine-Westphalia, 58, 126, 166, 172n26
Norway, 17n19, 21n18, 29n6, 36
NPD *Nationaldemokratische Partei Deutschlands* (National Democratic Party of Germany), 81, 82n14, 99, 100n38, 111n4, 112n6, 113n7, 114n10, 150n14, 172
NSDAP *Nationalsozialistische Deutsche Arbeiterpartei* (National Socialist German Workers' Party), 25, 29n6, 30, 31, 35, 36, 40, 41, 58, 220
Nuremberg, 56, 111, 113n7, 114, 116, 131n13, 142
Nürnberg FC, 23, 37, 49, 57, 119, 142, 147n8

Oberliga Nord, 31, 49, 50, 57, 66, 68, 69, 74, 88

Panzeri, Dante, 230–31
Paulick, Otto, 94, 97, 144n2
Pegida *Patriotische Europäer gegen die Islamisierung des Abendlandes* (Patriotic Europeans against the Islamisation of the West), 172, 173n27, 176n34
pirates, 11, 90, 91, 159n7, 160. *See also* Elbe, River
flag, 87, 88, 89, 91

Jolly Roger (symbol), 92, 143n1, 159, 160, 163, 165, 168, 217, 223
Störtebeker, Klaus, 90–91, 159n7
Pirates (club), 57, 65n2, 71, 91, 101n42, 102n43, 105n47, 106, 109, 125, 139, 143n1, 148n9, 157, 165n17, 166, 174, 175, 179, 186, 193, 204, 207, 216, 218, 226
Poland, 17n19, 42, 163n15
Prague, 7n8
Deutscher FC Prag (DFC Prague), 7, 17
Slavia Prague, 42
Prussia, 3, 4, 5n4, 7, 11n4, 17n21, 20
punk, 70n1, 71, 72, 72–3n2, 75, 78, 79, 80n11, 82n15, 83, 85n19, 86, 89, 90, 90–91n27, 92, 93, 94, 97n35, 103, 107, 110–11n1, 113n7, 115, 117, 121, 126n1, 140n3, 155, 186n17, 191, 205, 206, 207, 220, 223

racist chants, 111, 112, 116, 117, 119, 120, 139n5. *See also* antiracism
RAF *Rote Armee Fraktion* (Red Army Fraction), 58, 81n12
Reeperbahn, 11, 13n10, 14, 39n8, 45, 47–8, 53, 64, 74, 115n15, 119, 139, 167, 204, 211
refugees, 86n20, 100n38, 100n39, 117n17, 120n23, 135, 140n8, 152, 167, 171, 172n25, 173–5, 177, 183n11, 186, 187n18, 194, 195, 205, 213–16
Rehder, Henry, 17, 26, 29
resistance, anti-Nazi, 42, 42n13, 42–3n14, 43n14, 121n24, 184
Rote Flora, 104, 104–5n46, 167, 168
RTL TV network, 72, 95, 96

SA *Sturmabteilung* (Stormtroopers, Brownshirts), 27n1, 30–31, 30n8, 38, 91n27, 112n6, 113n7
SAGA *Siedlungs-Aktiengesellschaft Altona* (construction company), 78, 80, 82, 221n2
Saxony, 5, 19, 22n29, 44n15, 76n5, 90n24, 99n36, 100n39, 102n44, 150n14, 172n25

Schalke, 31, 44n15, 49, 57, 102, 111,
    131n13
Schreiner, Berni, 27, 28
Scotland, 137–40, 154, 191–5
Second World War, 29n6, 30, 31,
    32n11, 36, 38n7, 42, 44, 44n15, 56,
    78n7, 89n23, 166n19, 213
SED *Sozialistische Einheitspartei*
    Deutschlands (East German Com-
    munist Party), 98
Social Democrats. *See* SPD
    Sozialdemokratische Partei
    Deutschlands (Social Democratic
    Party of Germany)
Social Romantics (*Sozialromantiker*),
    156–77, 196
Soviet Union, 27n1, 37n6, 43, 45n15,
    46, 49, 56, 85n17, 237
Spain,
    Barcelona, 202n11, 207n6, 232
    Basque Country, 141, 232–3
    Catalonia, 172n25, 193, 197,
        202n11, 207n6, 232
    Republic of, 138n1, 232
SPD *Sozialdemokratische Partei*
    Deutschlands (Social Democratic
    Party of Germany), 14n14, 15–16,
    20n26, 21, 22n29, 23, 24n31,
    25n34, 27n1, 30, 35, 36, 47, 58,
    76, 80, 81n14, 83, 109, 143, 145,
    173n28, 221
Sport-Dome, 95–7
SS *Schutzstaffel* (Protection Squadron,
    Nazi paramilitary organisation),
    29n6, 37n6, 38, 40n11, 42, 89n23,
    91n27, 99n37, 111, 184n12
Stanislawski, Holger, 142, 153n23,
    154, 157n2
Stuttgart, 56, 77, 88n21, 111, 122,
    131n13
    Stuttgart Fußball Verein 1893, 5
    Stuttgarter Kickers, 6, 94, 102, 109,
        122, 142
    VfB Stuttgart, 95, 122
Sump, Richard, 21, 27
swastikas, 102n44, 111, 127

Sweden, 31n9, 51, 172n25
Switzerland, 8, 55, 172n25

Thälmann, Ernst, 22n29, 24n32, 25
Third Reich, 10n3, 13n10, 29n6,
    36–41, 46, 47, 100n39, 112n5,
    220, 232
    Nazification process, 37, 38
Turkey, 173n28, 214n10, 217

UEFA, 115, 117, 138, 174, 179, 212
Ulm 1846, 4, 74
ultras, 92, 148, 149, 166n18, 226n3
USP, 178–87
United of Manchester, 154, 195, 240,
    241. *See also* Manchester United
USSR. *See* Soviet Union

Versailles Treaty (1919), 25, 40
Victoria, 5, 6,
    Victoria SC, 22, 35, 41, 86
    Victoria SV, 28, 53
Vierth, Amandus, 17, 26
Volksparkstadion, 64, 65, 86, 87,
    91n27, 113n7, 116, 121, 138, 139,
    148, 156, 179
    Gegengerade, 87, 91, 92, 93, 102n42,
        130, 135, 160, 163n15, 164,
        176n35, 177, 178n1, 179, 180,
        187n18, 215

Weimar Republic, 21, 22, 24, 35
Weisener, Heinz, 95, 108, 144n2
Wilhelm Koch Stadion, 86, 109
Wolff, Otto, 29, 31
Wolfsburg VfL, 53, 95n32, 122,
    131n14
women's football, 155, 194, 196–203
World Cup, 55, 56–7, 118, 119, 122,
    128n7, 152n22, 173, 212, 232, 233

xenophobia, 88, 99, 103, 111, 117n17,
    118n18, 129n8, 173n27, 175,
    183n11

Yugoslavia, 57, 122, 178n1